RISE UP

A New Guide to
Public Speaking

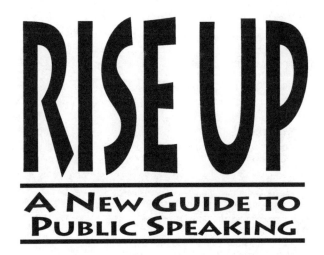

RISE UP

A New Guide to
Public Speaking

SANDIE BARNARD

PRENTICE HALL CANADA, INC.,
SCARBOROUGH, ONTARIO

Canadian Cataloguing in Publication Data

Barnard, Sandie, 1946-
   Rise up: a new guide to public speaking

ISBN 0-13-564634-0

1. Public speaking. 2. Oratory. I. Title.

PN4121.B37 1993   808.5'1   C93-094448-8

Prentice-Hall, Inc., *Englewood Cliffs, New Jersey*
Prentice-Hall International, Inc., *London*
Prentice-Hall of Australia, Pty., Ltd., *Sydney*
Prentice-Hall of India, Pvt., Ltd., *New Delhi*
Prentice-Hall of Japan, Inc., *Tokyo*
Prentice-Hall of Southeast Asia (Pte.) Ltd., *Singapore*
Editora Prentice-Hall do Brasil Ltda., *Rio de Janeiro*
Prentice-Hall Hispanoamericana, S.A., *Mexico*

Interior and Cover Design: Alex Li
Composition: Heidy Lawrance Associates
Manufacturing Buyer: Anita Boyle

ISBN: 0-13-564634-0

1 2 3 4 5 WL 97 96 95 94 93

Printed and bound in Canada.

CONTENTS

ACKNOWLEDGEMENTS

The people I wish to acknowledge first are the people in my work-shops who rose to give their first speeches. I always knew speaking was important but their eloquence and courage taught me how much we need to share the skills. To the members of the FWTAO, especially the Dufferin and Sault Ste. Marie Associations, thank you. I am also grateful to Heather Bishop, Roberta Bondar, June Callwood, Edward L. Greenspan, Q.C., Rick Hansen, Kahn-Tineta Horn, Waneek Horn-Miller, Peter Jaffe, David Nichol, Gloria Steinem, David Suzuki and Linda Tillery. Their voices enrich this book. Rose Anne Hart, Thomas Coon, David Kent and Deborah Murray graciously allowed their speeches to be included. Sarah MacLachlan kept her word and Cristina Page and Diana James helped with long distance details.

Tanya Long, my editor at Prentice Hall Canada, is perceptive, persistent and thorough. Working with her has been a pleasure. The spirit of this book also owes much to Lynne Fernie and Lorraine Segato of Parachute Club. The lyrics to "Rise Up," the vision and joy in those lines, inspired me many times.

To my friends Sheila Goulet and Jack David, who advised, questioned and praised unstintingly—thank you. Kate Scott and the Tri-Town BPW provided evenings of friendship and debate, and Sue Cavanagh, my wedding expert, supplied anecdotes, warnings and riotous fun. Deborah Murray, my neighbour, is courageous to let her progress as a speaker appear in this book. She paid me the greatest of compliments—she willingly took my advice. And Joan Jamieson read every 10 pages and liked every chapter best. She is an intelligent and indefatigable sounding board.

The person who helped me with the secret parts of speaking, who shared her zeal for audiences, for getting things done, and who provided comfort when it was time to pack for yet another trip is Nellie McClung. Her forthrightness, her courage and her empathy fill her books. After all these years, thank you Nellie.

Last of all my thanks to Wilf and Kodiak, Foofur, Shag and Terror; they brought contentment and adventure to every working day.

To Joan and Val
—for all the happy days at the South Mag

FOREWORD

I like speakers. I like going into a crowded hall, feeling the buzz of anticipation. And I like the surprises. Watching the platform party, I try to guess who will be unexpectedly witty, perceptive or direct. Often the keynote speaker is every bit as interesting as predicted. Sometimes, however, the shorter speeches—those of welcome or thanks—are the highlights. Good speeches have vitality and grace; they make connection. There is a current of understanding between the speaker and the audience.

Often very simple speeches are moving. Years ago I heard a tribute to a community worker given by a friend and colleague; it sparkled with stories, admiration and humour. It was speaking at its best.

. Speaking has changed radically in the last 15 years. Previously it was the domain of the inner circle, the powerful, the scholarly, the rich. Now we are widening the circle, having conversations with each other. The old way of speaking was more concerned with making an impression than with making connection. In the early '70s I attended a university convocation held outdoors. The professor delivering the address was learned—and boring. He rambled through sheaves of paper, never looking up, not knowing if what he said made sense to us. Indeed, during part of his speech a train rumbled across the track behind him drowning out every word. When we could hear him again, it was as if there had been no interruption. It made no difference.

The new way of speaking *does* make a difference; it's speaking directly about the things you believe in. Its aim is to convince, not dazzle; to talk with passion and courage, not overwhelm your listeners with a spiel. There comes a time when each of us must speak up—and when that time comes for you this book has what you need: concrete examples, outlines and insider advice.

I designed this book for people who speak to make a difference in their organization, jobs or communities. It has sections for people with little experience and other parts for competent speakers who want to get better. If you want to be a good speaker, this book will help. But it can't do everything. Speakers work hard: they consider their audiences; plan carefully; rehearse; pay attention to detail; and speak brilliantly. That work is up to you—use this book as a guide and go for it!

The first four chapters cover the basics of speaking: getting ready, analyzing your audience, finding out what you want to say, putting your speech together, rehearsing, and speaking as well as you possibly can. The next five chapters are resources for particular situations. If you need to speak on hard issues, go to Chapter 5; if you want the inside story on the challenges women face when they speak, check Chapter 6. Chapter 7 is a complete and practical guide to speeches for special occasions. Chapter 8 covers thinking on your feet: the impromptu speech, interviews, panels and presentations. Chapter 9 has two sections: a sampling of the questions people ask me most often about speaking, and checklists for every occasion.

Why take my advice? Because I've been there. I know the magic that happens during a good speech, the point at which speaker and audience unite and ignite. I love the shared energy, the insights that develop, the rapport, the laughter and the excitement. I've also lost my notes, suffered killer introductions and had my microphone go dead. I've given hundreds of speeches and interviewed other good speakers about their work. During the 15 years I taught public speaking at a community college I was impressed with the compassion and directness of my students. It's the same in workshops; people want to give voice to their concerns.

It's hard to find out about the nuts and bolts of giving a speech: how much do you look at the audience? do you use notes? do you get nervous? what happens when they get your name wrong? The fun of writing this book has been asking other speakers those very questions. I went to individuals who are noted for the speaking they do as part of their work—for business or for social action. The interviews, found at the conclusion of every chapter, form a complete insider's guide to speaking. None of these people had ever been asked about speaking and their responses are generous and informative.

Call it nervousness, anticipation, excitement—everyone gets keyed up before a speech. Good speakers welcome that extra surge of energy; they use it to their advantage. That's important for you to know. When my friend Roberta Bondar strapped herself into her seat on the space shuttle Discovery, she was nervous as well as excited. The fear didn't stop her—it was part of the process and she used it.

When you RISE UP to speak, think of the worlds of possibility that exist. Your speech can provide the information, the reassurance, the spark that someone needs that very moment. The very act of speaking teaches you more about yourself and your work. Use the gift of voice to make a difference in the world. Know that we are listening. Everyone's time has come.

CHAPTER
1

SHARING THE POWER:
EVERYONE'S TIME HAS COME

Rise Up, Rise Up
  Rise and share your power
Rise Up, Rise Up
  We're dancing to the sun
Rise Up, Rise Up
  The spirit's time has come
  Women's time has come
  Everybody's time has come.

— **Lorraine Segato & Parachute Club**

▲▲▲▲▲▲▲▲▲▲▲

SHARING THE POWER:
NEW WAYS OF SPEAKING

Two speeches I heard last year best illustrate how much speaking has changed in the last two decades. Both were good. One speaker was a woman, an elementary school teacher, who told me she didn't think she was very good at public speaking. The other was a humorous and passionate man, much in demand as a speaker.

The woman began her speech by saying, "When I was a child my favourite story was Cinderella. Not because I wanted to marry a prince but because I wanted to be a fairy godmother and grant wishes." The gift she wanted to give the schoolchildren of her region was a host of women principals. To finish, she declared she would give the gift as fairy godmothers do, not in five years' time but—with a snap of her fingers—instantly.

The man, Peter Jaffe, was a member of the Canadian Panel on Violence Against Women and a psychologist with the London Family Court. To start his presentation on violence he showed a slide of his 10-year-old son and spoke of how hard it was to raise a child, especially a boy, to be non-violent. He told story after story, each one illustrating one of his major points, each one memorable. It was a conversation with his audience.

Both these speakers were exciting, intent on sharing their ideas and conviction. They wanted to reach, rather than impress, their audiences and they spoke with rather than at their listeners. Furthermore, they talked in their own voices; they sounded like themselves rather than some echo of an old-fashioned orator.

All of us can RISE UP and speak with reason, wit and conviction. We can share the excitement, the passion, the possibility of reaching out and connecting! The new way of speaking is committed to sharing power. Yes, you want to get your point across but you also acknowledge that your audience exists. They hear and respond to you. They have ideas and worth.

Speaking has changed radically in the last 15 years. Previously it was a power activity based on status, bombast and statistics; now the focus is on talking to other people, explaining, persuading, building rapport. What I call the old way of speaking is predominantly male, white and power-based. It reinforces the idea that you are either one up or one down—speakers are out to be undeniably one up. The new way of speaking widens the circle; it welcomes and respects the voices of all people.

The difference between the old and new ways of speaking is best illustrated by what is commonly called a podium, that solid wooden coffin-like structure turned on end that effectively cuts the speaker off from the audience. Tall men fare best behind the barricade, the speaking equivalent of a fortress-desk. They are protected from the audience, their body language is impossible to detect, and messages flow only one way. Shorter people, women among them, are lost behind the coffin, seemingly overcome by the situation, and cut off completely from their best source of support—the audience.

The speakers who rise to speak in the new way are like fire and yeast—familiar yet powerful. Impelled by conviction and determined to take their fair place in our world, they are irresistible. Fire is light and warmth, energy and possibility. Rocket fire brings new worlds within our reach; yet there is also the possibility of disaster. But fear is the price we pay; it doesn't stop us. Roberta Bondar, Canada's first woman astronaut, hurtled to space in 1991 atop tons of burning fuel. I once asked her if she was afraid. "Of course," she said. "Only a fool wouldn't be afraid. I don't want to come back stardust."

Anyone who bakes bread knows the power of yeast—irrepressible like our laughter, our courage and our conviction. Like yeast, speakers who feel strongly will not be pushed down. Everyone's time has come.

NEVER THROW AWAY AN OPPORTUNITY TO SPEAK

When you talk to people, you can affect their lives. You may not think you're doing it, but a brief remark can give someone a new idea, advice they need that very day, the courage to go on. Speaking is extraordinarily important. It is also unbelievably exhilarating. To speak your ideas aloud, to share the excitement, to feel a spark ignite between you and the audience is very liberating. What compels ordinary people to speak out? A former student of mine who lives in a small town is trying hard to fight a proposed chemical dump. Outside of school she had never spoken publicly; however, she decided it was time: "I knew that if I didn't speak up for our town, something I loved very much would be lost. I think the need gave me courage."

The next time you need courage to speak out, remember that others have found the courage. As David Suzuki says, "Why else do we live if we don't struggle for things that matter to us?"

THE NEW BASICS

Where did most people learn about speaking? Teachers and family are the most common sources. Where did they learn it from? Unless we were lucky enough to live close to a great story-teller or political organizer, we picked up some very old-fashioned ideas: write your speech; memorize it completely; read from a huge wad of paper or deliver it from memory—never just talk.

Here are new basics; all the plans and examples in this book depend on them. Some you have heard before but ignored when you were nervous; others you don't believe because that's not how other people do it. How many speeches by other people do you remember? Most people persist in using ineffective, outmoded methods because that's what they were taught. Give these basics a chance and give yourself the opportunity to make great speeches.

SPEAKING IS <u>NOT</u> READING

Nothing turns people off more than having someone read to them. And yet the urge to read is very strong. Remember this—speaking is not reading and speaking to people is not reading to them. Most people read speeches because they wrote them in the first place. They don't say, "I have to make up a speech" or "put together a speech." They say, "I have to write a speech." As soon as you start to write, you use your writing vocabulary and your writing sentence structure. If you try to deliver what you've written, it sounds stilted; on top of that, you can't make eye contact or you'll lose your place. And you wonder why people aren't attentive! *You're reading to them.* And you're reading stuff you wrote to be read, not spoken.

What do you do if you don't write speeches? That's for Chapter 2.

GET YOUR PURPOSE CLEAR

Why are you speaking—to relay a string of statistics accurately or to explain and/or persuade? If your purpose is to reach people, then concentrate on talking to them. Do not immerse yourself in sheets of statistics. An HIV/AIDS educator explained his temptation to read: "I have to read right from the paper because I might miss something or get some figures wrong." What is his major purpose—to get the statistics absolutely correct or to convince his audience of the importance of his topic? Most audience members will forget the numbers as soon as they walk out of the room, but they will remember stories and a speaker's conviction.

If you need the assurance of accuracy, put the data on overheads and use them as notes. Hand out a fact sheet. Do whatever makes you feel confident about your job—to talk to people.

PRACTISE OUT LOUD

In this book you'll find one-week and 24-hour countdowns. I use them myself whenever I'm nervous about a speech and can't remember what to do next. The major reason for the countdown sheets is to outline the timing for your preparation. Everyone has her own priorities when she's making up a speech: I get excited about what I have to say and about new, exciting ways of framing my examples. Then I plan my outfit—some things never change.

That leaves practice. What do you usually do? Many people tell me they read their speech over—but that's reading. You have no idea how it sounds or how the sound of your own words makes you feel. How many times have you written something that had a totally unexpected effect on you when you spoke it aloud? Besides that, you've already got the points for reading—this is speaking.

Once your speech is almost together, practise it at home. I talk to my cats to start; they usually clean themselves with one hind leg straight up in the air. After that, I call in my partner and my neighbour. I've coached them before so they know how nervous I am and they listen to the whole thing, even if it's rough. Then they tell me what works for them. Their comments are often a revelation. As I was writing this book, I had a major speech to do for an audience of 400. When I had the home practice, my friends' faces didn't register much at some of my material and I thought it was corny or maybe not on topic. When I finished, the very parts I doubted were their favourites; they said they were absolutely caught up in the material. What I had read as disinterest was actually absorption. And they were right—those were the parts people commented on when I made my speech.

You need to practise out loud for three reasons:

- To get used to how your speech sounds, how it flows, when you need your notes.

- To use a supportive practice audience to give you feedback, advice and praise!

- To listen to yourself. It's important that you sound like yourself.

LIKE WHAT YOU'RE SAYING

My next-door neighbour was running for elected office in a professional association. She came to me for advice but my questions surprised her: "Do you like what you are saying? Do you like the way you sound? Do you sound like yourself?" She didn't know that she should *like* her own speech, the ideas she had gathered, the arguments and proofs. No matter how contentious the subject, you must like what you have to say about it. If you can't hear yourself or your speech is too stilted, there are several possibilities:

- You wrote it out and it sounds unnatural when it's spoken.

- You tried to be all-wise and sound so theoretical and removed that you can't convince anyone, let alone yourself.

- You're too nervous to practise. This is too true! People get so anxious that they research, write and organize notes to occupy time. They have no feeling for or connection with their research and don't sound like themselves.

If any of these happen to you—STOP! Go deep within yourself to discover what you really want to say. Then follow the outlines in Chapters 2 and 3.

SPEAKING FROM THE HEART

"Stop trying to sound like the speakers you admire. Sound like yourself —your voice has never been heard before." Vicki P. McConnell, Los Angeles mystery writer

CONVICTION

The first rule of public speaking is to have something to say. Believe in what you're saying—speak from the heart. If your commitment to a subject is strong, that energy and enthusiasm will show in your delivery. Even nervous speakers can move their listeners when it is apparent that the importance of their topic has given them the courage to speak. Carole Edwards is a free-lance Wellness Education Consultant who knows that speaking from the heart works. She says, "If you're passionate about something, whether it's an issue, a piece of information or a story, your talk should demonstrate your commitment, should show it's something you truly believe. If you are that convinced yourself, then chances are your audience are going to take it as credible, they are going to feel it as well as hear it, and it means more."

LANGUAGE

Have you heard the story about two students talking about a visiting lecturer?

"Wow! That was an incredible speech!"
"Yeah, it was so significant."
"What statistics! What proofs!"
"Yeah—did you understand it?"
"No—did you?"

David Suzuki says, "Anyone who can't speak in very simple language is trying to cover something up." Find your own words, your own examples. Avoid glib generalities and find specifics that interest and excite you. If you are going to discuss the benefits and costs of medical plans, use real examples and stories; they mean a lot more than vague statements. When you practise, listen for your own voice, your own words.

VOICE

Put your hand over your heart. Can you get your voice to come from that spot in your body? If you do the breathing exercises in Chapter 5, and you consciously try to get your voice to come from your heart, you will sound warm, convincing and in control.

Basically your voice is the barometer of your self-confidence. If the sound is coming from high inside your head, you sound (and probably are) nervous. You've stopped breathing.

If the sound is coming from your chest, near your heart, you are breathing well. You are in control and sound confident. Your voice will encourage trust. In most situations, speak from the heart.

In times of stress, if you need to sound very calm, breathe even deeper and get the air to come from your diaphragm (if you were wearing a cinch belt from the 1950s, that's the area of the diaphragm.) The resulting tone creates a mood of evenness.

NERVOUS ENERGY

"I fall to pieces." Patsy Cline worried about falling to pieces—but she didn't. Neither will you. Most beginners are afraid of the big three; they are sure they will panic, puke or perspire. Some people blush; the rosy colour starts at neck level and rises steadily, like a gas gauge. Once before a speech my stomach knotted into balls of fire and I had to lie down in an empty cloakroom, praying the pain would go away in time for me to make the after-dinner speech. A famous publisher is convinced that his throat is dry whenever he has to speak because all the water in his body has gone to his hands and armpits.

Nervous energy is normal; what's more it's useful. Actors call it getting up for a performance; athletes need to be on the edge for a big meet. Speakers need that same high, the rush of adrenalin that gives them extra drive. What you need to do is channel the nervous energy and make it work *for* you.

Consider these insider tips about jitters.

- Your audience is there to see you succeed, not fail; they're pulling for you.

- Prepare carefully; knowing your material well reduces anxiety.

- You look more confident than you feel. Most of the shaking is going on inside you. Remember, we only see the confident outside of people.

- The more experience you have, the easier it will get. You should still be nervous but you'll know how to channel the energy.

- Find an outlet for the nervousness. One woman I know aims to have a moment near the beginning of her speech when she doesn't have to talk. She asks the audience to look at an overhead, ask their neighbours a question related to the topic, get out a pen—anything to give her a free moment to breathe.

What are you most afraid of when someone asks you to do an introduction or give a workshop? People who talk every day as part of their job turn to jelly when it becomes a public thing. Look at this list of common fears:

"blanking out"
"making a fool of myself in front of others"
"being too emotional"

"not knowing enough"
"shaking and turning red in the face"
"my voice shaking and stopping"
"being too intimidated"
"forgetting what to say"

Most people share some of the same fears; let's deal with them immediately.

- You will *not* blank out because your notes will keep you on track and you're going to start with short, specific tasks.

- You will *not* make a fool of yourself. You are going to look like someone who is trying very hard and everyone's sympathy will be with you. This is not a game of one-up or one-down, with the audience trying to catch you making a mistake.

- How emotional is too emotional? If you care deeply and your voice shakes, let it. Showing emotion is not allowed in the old way of speaking. It's just fine in the new way. Slow down and breathe to get control of your voice.

- Do we need to know everything before we speak? No, speak from what you know and discuss what is important to you.

- If you blush, everyone's sympathy will be with you and they'll be pulling for you.

- If you shake, no one will notice unless you try to turn over a piece of paper. Use note cards, made out of good heavy paper.

- If you're intimidated, have faith in yourself. What you have to say is important. Take a friend to look at; he or she will praise you extravagantly afterwards.

- You won't forget what to say IF you follow the lessons of this book and *plan, make notes, consult your notes and practise!*

ARE WOMEN MORE NERVOUS THAN MEN?

We certainly are—and with good reason! Women who speak up in their communities or offices are challenging the status quo. Our traditional role, whether we like it or not, has been to listen and keep quiet. Whenever we take our speech from the kitchen to the community, it rattles the status quo and people often get hostile.

Whenever we speak up, two things are certain. One, the world will be a better place, more human and humane, more feminine and feminist. Two, someone will attack us. The remarks vary: you or your group will be punished; you sounded strident; you looked foolish; you overreacted. There are very good reasons to be nervous. However, since there is no right way to speak—the act of speaking itself is what rattles folks—go right ahead. As Nellie McClung, a Canadian pioneer of women's rights and a very fine speaker, said, "Never retreat, never explain, never apologize—get the thing done and let them howl."

Susan Faludi, the author of *Backlash: The Undeclared War Against American Women*, admits to an unnerving fear of public speaking. Faced with an audience, she would rather retreat like "a Victorian lady with the vapours." She writes, "While both sexes fear public speaking, women—especially those challenging the status quo— seem to me more afraid and with good reason. We do have more at stake. Men risk a loss of face; women a loss of femininity. Men are chagrined if they blunder at the podium; women face humiliation either way. If we come across as commanding, our womanhood is called into question. If we reveal emotion, we are too hormonally driven to be taken seriously."

Faludi goes on to say that speaking has a "transformative effect … on the speaker herself…. Women need to be heard—not just to change the world, but to change themselves."

Here's a checklist to help keep you from falling to pieces.

TAMING THE JITTERS

Channel your nervous energy by:

1. Knowing your material well.

2. Practising at home—out loud.

3. Having a friend in the audience for support and praise.

4. Speaking on something you know well.

5. Pampering yourself. Will a new shirt or hair cut make you feel better? How about some juice or coffee?

6. Following this pattern when you start to speak:
   pause
   count to three

make eye contact
breathe (in 2-3-4, out 2-3-4)
relax

7. Putting your notes on the podium. Avoid holding them in your hand; the shaking will give you away.

8. Holding onto something—the edge of the podium, a lucky stone, etc.

9. Knowing that your nervousness is not only normal, it's an ally.

10. Having something important to say and concentrating on getting it across.

THIS IS NOT A RECORDING: WORKING WITH YOUR AUDIENCE

Why don't people look at you, nod or smile when you're speaking? One woman told me, "The very worst thing is there's no feedback; it's like talking to a bunch of cabbages out there. They isolate themselves from me." Why do people act like that? Even worse, why do they cross their arms and sneer? Do people mean to be cabbage heads? I don't think they realize their reactions matter. They are so used to being ignored at work, in overcrowded classrooms, in busy stores and in video bars that they have no idea you can see them!

Speakers and listeners share energy; the vibrations go back and forth. The same woman who bemoaned cabbage heads told me she actually asks her audiences for help. "Look at me" is how she starts.

We need to train ourselves, as listeners, to avoid isolating the speaker. Instead, we can look attentive, make real eye contact (not the fake glaze we use when we're making our list of errands for later), and smile, murmur, laugh, make noise to let him or her know real people are listening! This is the mistake I make most often—I forget to ask the audience to respond and schooled as they are in the old way of speaking, where they don't matter, they give nothing to me. But I need response—all speakers do.

Two basic things help promote interaction: the set-up of the room and the design of your speech.

SET-UP OF THE ROOM

If you want people to respond to what you're saying, make sure you connect with them. In other words, go for rapport. Ask for the room to be set up so that you can see most of the audience. If possible, group the chairs so they are not in rows and there is no vast space between you and your listeners. If there is a platform, move the microphone to the front of it. Look at the lectern. Does it hide your body? Ask for a lectern with a pedestal base and a slightly tilted top that comes to mid-chest. This allows you to place your notes conveniently—and see everyone. In return, the audience gets your full message, verbal and non-verbal.

BEGINNING, MIDDLE, AND END: THE WELL-DESIGNED SPEECH

People listen and respond to clearly organized speeches. They also remember them! The old formula for a speech holds true:

- Tell them what you are going to say.

- Say it.

- Tell them what you've said.

Generally, this follows the plan you've learned elsewhere as introduction, body and conclusion. A detailed discussion on the organization of a speech follows in Chapter 2.

Some people use elaborate outlines with heads and subheadings. Others prefer to work with scraps of paper and old envelopes. Organization does not need to be elaborate but it must be there. The introduction needs a grabber that seizes the audience's attention and leads them to your thesis—the main argument or point of your speech. It includes an overview of your three to five main supporting statements. This flows to the body of your speech in which you give the main arguments in the order you listed them. Then, in the conclusion, you clearly summarize your points and drive them home with a zinger, which leaves your audience convinced of your argument and admiring your technique. The plan looks like this.

I Introduction (Beginning)

a. Grabber: a hook to seize audience attention
b. Thesis: a precise statement of your main idea or argument

c. Overview: an outline of your main supporting points

II Body (Middle)
Main Point One
plus supporting statements
Main Point Two
plus supporting statements
Main Point Three
plus supporting statements

III Conclusion (End)
a. Reference to Thesis
b. Review of Main Points (if necessary)
c. Zinger—A Strong Finish

TALK TO YOURSELF: ONE-MINUTE MINI-SPEECHES

Good speakers are like good skiers: they make it look so easy. They also know about the hours of practice, the rush of excitement, and the need for good coaching. Coaching for speakers? Of course. Whenever I ski down a hill, I can hear my instructor's voice: "Crouch, relax." It took me years to get it right.

How can you coach yourself in speaking? Some people talk to themselves before they start. Others write cues on their note cards: pause here, look up, slow down, smile.

To achieve the technique and maintain it, you need to practise. Designing a good speech is half your job; delivering it well is the other. Talk yourself through the preparation of your speech so that you will have time to practise. Then, as you rehearse, *listen to yourself.* Your aim is to like your speech and the way you sound.

Are you ready for some practice? Here are some good starting topics. Plan a one-minute mini-speech and deliver it to yourself. When you're confident, try it out on a friend or colleague.

a. Truth or Not

In as convincing a manner as possible, tell the group two truths and one lie about yourself. You can talk about travel adventures, skills, family, anything. The group's job is to guess which of the three details is not the truth.

b. The Perfect Gift

If you could give your business, your community or your organization a gift, what would it be? Discuss the gift and the reasons for your choice.

or

Decide on the item you would present to your boss or a political leader that would make your concerns obvious. Outline what message it sends.

DELIVERY TECHNIQUES TO REMEMBER

1. When you reach the lectern, pause and count to three mentally.

2. Make eye contact. At the very least, look once to the left, once to the right, and once to the centre back.

3. Pause at the end before you leave the lectern.

These techniques should help you to relax and project an image of assurance.

OUTLINE OF A SPEECH

Name: _____

Date of Speech: _____

Purpose Statement: _____

INTRODUCTION
Grabber:

Thesis:

Overview:

BODY
Supporting Argument #1

Supporting Argument #2

Supporting Argument #3

CONCLUSION
Reference to purpose (thesis):

Summary of main steps:

Zinger:

SELF-EVALUATION FORM

This form is to help you evaluate your own speech.

Type of Speech: _____

Title: _____

Date: _____

DELIVERY
Physical Presence
Did I make eye contact with others?
Was my posture natural and appropriate?
Was I aware of my facial expressions and hand gestures?
Were there any distracting mannerisms that I was aware of?
Did I feel good?
Could I feel an energy exchange with my audience?

VOCAL DELIVERY
Was my voice under control?
Did I sound confident?
Was I aware of breathing calmly?
How was my enunciation?
Did I manage to avoid um's and ah's?
Did I sound interested/excited/committed?
How did my voice sound to me?

DESIGN AND CONTENT
How well did the introduction and conclusion work?
Did the framework unify my speech?
Was there a natural progression from point to point?
Did my notes keep me on track? Did I use them?
Did the audience seem to understand the organization of my speech?
Was the information clear?
What was the energy level of the conclusion?
What would I change the next time?
What worked very well?

OVERALL EFFECTIVENESS
Did I connect with this audience?
Did I achieve my purpose?
What do I remember most about making the speech?
What unexpected or unforeseen things happened?
What am I most pleased about?

OTHER COMMENTS

EXPERT ADVICE: THE REAL STUFF

Whom would you ask for advice on speaking? Speakers, of course. To prepare this book, I questioned outstanding speakers from all areas of work; in the interviews that conclude each chapter, people such as June Callwood, David Suzuki and Gloria Steinem share their strategies for preparation and delivery.

"A good speech must entertain. It is pointless to make an important point in a boring fashion because it may be lost. It has to be made in an entertaining and dramatic way." Eddie Greenspan, lawyer

"People should be nervous; if you're not scared to death before you give that speech, chances are it's going to be a bomb. Don't be afraid of the fear. Use it to your advantage. All of that fear gets the adrenalin going and you use it." David Nichol, President, Loblaw International Merchants

"Don't adjust your underwear in public." Gail Heaslip, communications consultant

"They [academics] tend to talk down to people and use jargon to cover up their inadequacies. That's total crap. Anybody who can't speak in very simple language is trying to cover something up." David Suzuki, scientist, broadcaster, environmentalist

"Be well prepared. Rehearse your speech out loud to yourself or a spouse or a colleague a few times before you deliver it. Try as much as possible to be yourself at the podium. You are usually your own worst critic so don't let every little slip throw you. Just relax and enjoy your audience." Jeanne Sauvé, Governor-General of Canada: 1984-1989

"Don't read to people! Don't stand up in front of four people or 400 and read to them. It's insulting. Have notes—don't get lost but whatever you do—don't read to me." John de Shano, President, Levi Strauss, Canada

"If you fail to use any part of yourself out of shame or fear, then the theft of self-esteem has begun. You have suffered the suppression of part of yourself. So, if you don't speak your thoughts, if you don't use your voice, your self-esteem is affected." Gloria Steinem, writer, founder of Ms. magazine

"Keep the level of enthusiasm up throughout the whole speech—there's somebody out there who is as interested in minute fifteen of your speech as in minute one." Roberta Bondar, astronaut, physician

*"People don't want to see you fail; nobody enjoys a speaker's pain....
They don't want to watch you make a mess of it. They yearn for you to
do well... there's very positive energy going for you."* June Callwood,
journalist, broadcaster, community activist

RULES FOR GOOD SPEECHES

VALUE IT!

1. Never miss an opportunity.

2. Explore the topic as if it were a gold mine: sift through all the possibilities until you find a rich vein.

3. Know your audience. What do you have to offer them?

4. Research. Research. Research. Know the topic well and get excited about it.

PLAN IT!

5. Stop researching. Think. Relax. Go inside yourself to find the important thing you want to say.

6. Get your thesis down to one simple, clear-cut statement. Apply the One-Sentence Shower Test described in Chapter 2.

7. Hammer out an overview—a three-part proof that makes the direction of your speech clear to you and your audience.

8. Test the thesis and overview. Can you state them clearly? If you are still wallowing in generalities, go back to Step 2 and get a new angle.

9. Add colour—stories and examples that speak to the heart *and* mind.

10. Make clear *notes* in point form.

DO IT!

11. Practise, by yourself at first. Then persuade your friends and family to listen. Experiment with tone and gesture. Know your speech well.

12. Listen to yourself. Do you like your speech?

13. Get psyched up. A healthy amount of nervousness gets the adrenalin flowing.

14. Arrive on time, take some private time to calm yourself, mingle with the audience to get a feel for the group and the occasion.

15. Pause—

16. Make eye contact—and

17. RISE UP! Go for it—connect with your audience. Give it everything you've got.

DAVID SUZUKI

Dr. David Takayoshi Suzuki is a world renowned geneticist, a television and radio show host, and a university professor. He speaks unceasingly for the things in which he believes, and the combination of his integrity, scientific ability and personal warmth makes him a popular speaker worldwide.

SB: How do you make a speech interesting for such diverse audiences?

DS: *I think of an audience in terms of my father. He was a labourer and I pitch my speeches to him. When I taught I found I had a talent for translating esoteric material into terms that everyone could understand and get excited about.*

   One of the problems we have today is that people think if you don't have an education, you can't understand what's being discussed. In my shows, we assume that the audience, anybody, can understand the material.

SB: Do we use jargon too much?

DS: *Academics tend to talk down to people and use jargon to cover up their inadequacies. That's total crap. Anybody who can't speak in very simple language is trying to cover something up.*

SB: Have you heard a good speech lately?

DS: *The greatest speaker I've heard recently is George Wald at Harvard. He gave a lecture on the Origin of Life and it was so wonderful that I could have wept with enjoyment. It's a great subject and he used good visual images. He shared his personal philosophy and made it seem he was talking to you personally.*

SB: What speech are you proudest of?

DS: *In a subtle way my speeches evolve and change from week to week; they are constantly undergoing a process of growth. Really, I'm fondest of the latest one.*

SB: As Canadians, how could we improve our skills as speakers?

DS: *Discourse is not part of our culture; we have no love of give and take, of really debating. When I was young, I used to go to dinner at my girlfriend's house, and her father loved to debate and argue. I enjoyed it and got right into it.*

    I also think that television is an alienating medium in terms of conversation. There's an emotional response to pictures but very little thinking involved.

SB: You give generously of yourself to so many issues. Why do you take the time to speak about difficult issues?

DS: *Why take the trouble to speak up? Because you care, because it matters to you as a human being. You have to stand up and fight for the things you believe in. Why else do we live if we don't struggle for things that matter to us?*

CHAPTER 2

GET THE THING DONE:
THE THREE-PART PLAN THAT WORKS

Why take the trouble to speak up? Because you care, because it matters to you as a human being. You have to stand up and fight for the things you believe in.

— **David Suzuki**

As soon as someone asks me to make a speech, my brain goes into high gear and I think of all the ideas I have on the subject, how I can fit my ideas to the theme I've been asked to deal with, the stories and examples that I could use. In short, I get excited about the prospect. I think and plan—mentally. I talk to myself, jot phrases down on a pad of paper. Most of my speeches get started this way. Sometime later, days or perhaps weeks, I take out my rough notes and follow Nellie McClung's advice; I "get the thing done."

This chapter has two functions:

- to present a clear, workable design for *any* speech;

- to show you how to apply that design to your speeches.

As always, the overall purpose is to help you create and deliver great speeches—speeches your audience can follow and remember. Speeches *you* like.

THE PLAN THAT WORKS

Why do you need a plan? You've just spent a summer living with bats in your attic. You've researched the problem by visiting the Ministry of Natural Resources, the library, the museum and the local pest-control office. You know everything about bats: how to remove them from old buildings, plans for bat houses, their environmental value, the mythology of bats, their reproductive cycle, the use of bat droppings for fertilizer. You are brimming with bat lore and bat stories.

Indeed, you know so much about bats that you could talk for hours, *and that's where the danger lies.* What do you hope to accomplish? Will people be able to follow you? How should you organize the material?

ORGANIZE IN THREES

A speech MUST be clearly planned. You already know the basic outline—it's repeated here because too many speakers make a shopping list of ideas and amble through them. Organize yourself! You'll understand how your speech works and so will your audience!

Introduction: Grab the audience's attention and tell them what you're going to tell them.

Body: Tell them.

Conclusion: Tell them what you've told them and leave them with a powerful finish.

Not only does your speech have three major components, but you should also arrange your main arguments, reasons, steps or challenges in three clear sections. Why three? The human brain cannot absorb and remember more: the audience does not have written backup. Although your speech is well researched, dynamic and logical, the audience is listening, not reading. They need very precise statements of your argument, your reasons and your summary.

If you prepare a speech on how to catch and release a bat without harming it in 13 easy steps, no one will be able to remember more than 4. By the time you get to the crucial step ten, no one will have retained the information.

Organize in threes: stoplights have three colours; baseball has three outs. Three is a magic number—use it as an organizing principle.

In an expanded form, the plan looks like this.

THE THREE-PART PLAN THAT ALWAYS WORKS

I. Introduction

The introduction itself has three parts.

1. Grabber: Why should anyone listen to you? The grabber answers that question. It captures the attention of the audience and makes them *want* to listen to you.

2. Thesis: Why are you speaking? The thesis is a clear and precise statement of the point you wish to make, the explanation you have to offer, the argument you are presenting.

3. Overview: Where is the speech going? The overview is a preview of the main points you will use to support the thesis.

II. Body

Present the main supporting arguments outlined in the overview *in the order you gave them*. Remember, pare your reasons down to three strong points. Throw out your weak ideas.

- Supporting Argument 1: plus back-up and examples

- Supporting Argument 2: plus back-up and examples

- Supporting Argument 3: plus back-up and examples

III. Conclusion

The conclusion also has three main functions.

1. It rounds out the speech and adds a sense of completion.

2. It reinforces the thesis and reviews main arguments, if necessary.

3. It delivers a strong, final statement. If appropriate, it urges the audience to action. Everyone should remember it.

The following outline of a simple demonstration speech shows how to apply the three-part plan.

SAMPLE SPEECH: THE SOUTH MAGNETAWAN BAT BRIGADE

Purpose: After hearing my speech, the audience will know how to remove a bat from a house without injuring it.

I. Introduction

1. *Grabber:* A personal story: "Imagine waking up at night to the flutter of a bat's wings as it swoops just above your face."

2. *Thesis:* How to remove the bat from the room without hurting it or frightening yourself.

3. *Overview:* Three main sections:
equipment
capture
release

II. Body

Equipment

- bat hat with wide brim for protection
- bright flashlight
- sieve and sturdy cardboard

Capture

- forcing yourself to get up off the floor
- finding the bat
- putting the sieve over the bat and slipping the cardboard behind to make a cage

Release

- carrying the sieve cage gently to a door
- releasing the bat with a gentle swooping motion in order to avoid hurting its wings
- shutting the door quickly to prevent the bat from re-entering.

III. Conclusion

- Refer to purpose and the main steps—equipment, capture and release.

- Clincher: "This humane way of getting rid of bats really works. The only problem is that bats have excellent memories and may live for 20 years. Sooner or later, they'll remember the entrance and visit you again."

This, then, is the framework of a speech. By using this simple and dependable outline, you will be able to build your argument, no matter how complex, and know that the structure is sound. You will not get bogged down in detail and your audience will be able to understand and follow you.

The next step is to get *your* speech organized.

THOUGHT CIRCLES: AN ALTERNATE DESIGN

I speak a lot about speaking. And I can predict what most groups will want to know: what to do if they blank out; how to hold the audience's interest; how to deal with nerves; how to sound convincing; and what to do about putdowns. My central theme never varies: we are all good speakers, and if we stretch ourselves to make a connection with our audience, we can be convincing.

Sometimes I use the thought circle technique: I put my theme in the middle of the page and draw a circle around it. Then I draw arrows to other smaller circles, each one representing a main idea: be interesting, be organized, speak from the heart, use notes—don't read, use nervous energy well, listen to your voice, and hold the line on putdowns.

This way I can order my speech in whatever way suits the audience. They may want certain questions answered immediately and I'm ready. After I introduce my topic, usually with stories, and state my basic thesis, I'm ready to look at my thought circles and pick the one for the moment. This technique also adds to the spontaneity: I can ask groups to suggest their most pressing needs. Bear in mind that I am certain of my main idea and each one of the smaller circles is a component of my speech with which I am very familiar.

Presenters who speak often on a topic, and whose main purpose is to share information, enjoy this method. It keeps them fresh and promotes audience interaction.

HOW DO YOU START?

Start by thinking. By letting your mind wander. Think of everything you know about the topic. The first stage of making a speech is extremely important and it is also the one where most people panic. They either sit down to write the whole thing out from word one or they gather all the print resources they can and make pages of notes.

The impulse to write is a panic response. You do not make a speech by writing—you make it by thinking, by talking to yourself. Put on relaxing music, take a bath, go for a walk. Go inside yourself for what *you* know. This is your speech; put *your* ideas and opinions first. Jot down brief notes and figure out what is important, what you know and what you need to find out.

So many times, I've been asked to help people make a speech. My first question is, "What do you want to say?" Often, they sort through a pile of notes tossing off numbers and ideas. I interrupt and say, "What do *you want* to say?" They pause; perhaps they have discovered their own ideas, often not. *This is your speech. Figure out what you have to say.* Research comes later.

This is not easy. You have to spend a long time thinking, talking to yourself and going inside your head to find your ideas. After that, you need to consider your audience. Who are they? And what can you offer them?

The process looks like this:

- Getting the Idea
- Analyzing the Audience
- Hammering Out a Thesis
- Finding the Way In

GETTING THE IDEA

There are three scenarios in arriving at a general topic:

1. The occasion—or your job—requires you to make a speech on a specific thing.

2. You are asked to make a speech—the topic is wide open. Your choice.

3. The double flip: start with a given topic and, using your own

inventiveness, arrive at a slightly different but workable and interesting topic.

Scenario One: The Occasion Determines the Topic

Your manager asks you to outline the new medical/dental benefits package under consideration. What is your reaction? Do you like the package? Is this speech going to be greeted with enthusiasm or do you have to sell the proposal? You need to clear up with your manager exactly what the purpose of the presentation is. Should you compare other packages with the one under consideration? This is the point at which you need to get basic questions answered.

Scenario Two: The Wide-Open Topic

Make a fifteen-minute speech "on anything that you find interesting or significant." This type of wide-open invitation looks easy— your local chamber of commerce has faith in your speaking ability. But how can you be sure the audience will appreciate your choice? First of all you have to consider all the possible topics that suit your audience and the occasion.

If you get a wide-open invitation, STOP and remember what I am going to say.

Do not try to find your FINAL topic immediately. People either worry too much because the perfect topic does not spring complete into their minds or they spend too little time experimenting—they go directly to old reliable material and present it in the old reliable way.

BRAINSTORMING

Experienced speakers brainstorm all the time to find an idea or fresh approach that they like and that the audience will enjoy. It works like this:

- write down a list of topics: driving schools, banks, video shops, food banks, whale-watching, economic sanctions, literacy, fast foods, generic drugs, etc.

- choose one of these topics and, for the next two minutes, write down as many things associated with that topic as you can.

In brainstorming, there are only three rules:

1. Don't stop writing things down.

2. Don't think.

3. Don't evaluate.

If brainstorming is new to you, you will need practice to develop speed. Take another word and repeat the process. Do not ignore this step! In order to get truly involved in your speech, you need to have a handle on it, an approach that you're comfortable with and that excites you. Whether it's a passionate argument why adopted children should be helped to find birth parents or a methodical outline of how to set up a wheeltrans bus system, make sure you know the topic and have the interest, energy and conviction to follow it through. A former student of mine summed it up: "I think that's the whole secret. If you are going to be bored, your audience is going to be bored. The secret is finding a topic that interests you."

Here are the criteria of a good topic:

1. It meets the requirements of the occasion.

2. It interests you.

3. It interests the audience.

4. You know, or can find, sufficient back-up material.

5. You can develop and organize it within the time available.

Scenario Three: The Double Flip
Let's say you're asked to speak on management strategies. When you try to brainstorm, you can only think of managers: personnel, interviews, motivation, unemployment, three-piece suits, teams, beast, promote, dismiss. It's a good list, and the concept that appeals to you most is the boss as a beast because you have a particular person in mind. Now you need to relax. Daydream at the bus stop. Lie down on the couch and tell your family you're thinking.

Eureka! You've got it. The boss as an animal: the dinosaur, out-of-date; the weasel, cut-throat; or the wolf, loyal pack leader. You've narrowed it down and you have examples. If this speech matches the above criteria, it will work.

You do not have to worry about always staying exactly within the topic as it is first suggested. Think of offbeat ideas. If you have any doubts, check it out with your colleagues and think of your audience.

CRISIS CONTROL

Priming the Pump. What happens if you brainstorm and still can't find a thing to talk about? What else can you do? You have around you all the resources you need: your friends and family, the radio, television, news and issue programs, newspapers and magazines. Search for a topic that you can develop.

What if THEY Won't Like It? Who are they? The community group you're speaking to, your boss, the board of education whose ruling you oppose, your peers? Speakers worry about being liked, and with good reason. So much of our being is at stake when we speak. If you are speaking to a friendly group and you follow the advice in this book, your speech will be interesting, you will be convincing and THEY will like you.

If, however, you are expressing concerns to people who do not like any opposition, you're right. They won't like you. If you want to be liked stay home—there is no right way to speak so that THEY will like what you have to say. On the other hand, if you speak out on behalf of a principle that you and others value, you will have acted with integrity, you'll feel empowered, and changes may occur. Your friends, if you tell them that you need support, will praise you for what you said and how you said it!

MATCHING YOUR SPEECH AND YOUR LISTENERS: AUDIENCE ANALYSIS

Knowing your audience is essential every time you speak! It is your responsibility as a speaker to be as aware of each audience as possible. The more complete the analysis, the more prepared you will be on the occasion. Take Rick Hansen as an example. Hansen is a wheelchair athlete, writer and speaker. His Man in Motion tour around the world in a wheelchair from 1985 to 1987 lasted 792 days. He wheeled 24,901 miles (40,073 kilometres) through 34 countries. And as he wheeled he spoke to hundreds of groups of people. I asked him how he made each speech special. He replied: "There were times when I came in from the road and I was just fried.... Then I had to turn around and go out into a town hall where there were 300 people waiting, and they'd been there for hours.... You have to dig down very deep within you, to the essence of what drives you and come up... with the image of somebody who is positive, who has a wonderful message that's important for people to listen to. You want to make those people feel they're important; they're the most important people in your day, in your life, at that time."

Consider these situations:

1. You've prepared a speech on the superiority of country inns and why they are better than large hotel chains. Your audience turns out to be a group of managers from several chains. Wouldn't it be better to speak on the fine qualities of small inns that are found in larger hotels?

2. You're a social service worker dealing with street kids. You're going to municipal council to ask for funds for shelters. Will they be more convinced by a discussion of the needs of your clients or proof of the financial savings if they care for them before they get into trouble?

DOING THE ANALYSIS

Do an informal analysis with the person who asked you to speak. If necessary, ask questions and have the contact person get back to you. I've listed a number of possible questions below and in the checklist in Chapter 9. You can also rely on yourself as a guide to the needs and interests of a group with whom you are familiar.

For example, I was involved in a referendum debate regarding a change to the Canadian Constitution. I figured that the audience would be people concerned enough to come out on the night of a final World Series game but not completely familiar with the text of the material under debate. Whenever I mentioned a point, I gave them the page and paragraph number so they could look for themselves at the contentious wording. They were more convinced by that than by the vague references other panelists made to the document, or their "trust me, I've read the whole thing" remarks.

One speaker I know relies on a gut reaction to each audience: "Every group has different individuals in it with different life experiences, some good, some bad. The important thing is to assess the group, to use as many people in the group as you can—they usually have something good to say that's useful for others to hear. I trust my reading of the group."

Often, you do not have to change your speech so much as your examples. Last week, I heard two chiropractors talking about good back care; they used many examples of people bending over to pick up small children. Their presentation, which was generally very effective, would have been better with a little audience analysis—everyone present had grown children.

ANALYSIS CHECKLIST

Here are some of the items to check so you can get a clearer picture of the group and the situation. You'll notice that I've not given any indication of general characteristics for each heading; it is dangerous to make such generalizations. Guard against unfair assumptions while at the same time determining how many factors might affect the way you approach that audience. If you're speaking about the use of crack in high schools, to which groups would you have to explain what crack is? In my region, understanding of the word is more determined by a person's age, whether they live in town or on a farm, and the ages of their children, than by their level of education or race.

1. What does the audience already know about the subject of your speech?
2. What do they need or want to know?
3. What are the occupations of your listeners?
4. Is there an internal political situation you should know about?
5. What is the level of disposable income of the group?
6. What is the educational background of your listeners. In what areas?
7. What is the community like? What different kinds of families are there?
8. What are their interests and hobbies?
9. Are you being invited to speak by an organization? What are its aims and objectives?
10. How many people will be in the audience?
11. What is their racial or cultural background?
12. Are your listeners parents or non-parents?
13. Why are they asking YOU!

CRISIS CONTROL

Derogatory remarks, even those disguised as jokes, about race, religion, gender, disability, size, class or sexual orientation are unacceptable anywhere! What some speakers defend as jokes are unacceptable slurs. They undermine your credibility and insult your listeners by assuming they would accept such remarks.

ANALYZING THE OCCASION

A friend of mine was asked to make a speech to a conference of youth leaders on the need for HIV/AIDS education. This was her specialty and she was pleased to be invited. She also knew the group well and thought they would be receptive. But things broke down. The audience had no idea that their luncheon address was going to be on HIV/AIDS and my friend didn't realize the group was not prepared for the topic. Both audience and speaker were taken aback. Although the event co-ordinator should have told my friend about the state of things, every speaker knows it's her job to find out all the details.

Ask yourself if your speech matches:

- the audience

- the occasion

- the time allotted.

These insider tips will help you analyze the occasion.

1. Why are you speaking? What is the occasion? Is this a formal dinner or an informal gathering? Do you need to persuade your listeners, entertain them, or inform them? Were you chosen because of your reputation for dealing with the subject clearly? Beware of the internal politics of a group. For example, a performance review indicates a division wastes time and you've been brought in to help improve efficiency. Your reception will vary depending on whether you've been billed as a helpful consultant or their punishment.

2. Where will you be speaking? With even a cursory knowledge of basic human needs, you'll be able to make sure your listeners'

needs are met. They must feel worthwhile and respected in order to get the most out of your speech. You should also pay attention to the speaking environment.

- Is there enough air in the room?

- Is it too hot or too cold?

- Can everyone see and hear? Are there appropriate arrangements for translation and/or signers for the hearing impaired?

- Did someone arrange for coffee, tea and juice?

3. When will you speak? If you speak first, make sure latecomers feel comfortable entering the room. If you speak last, you may face a tired or hungry group. After a meal, you'll need a high-energy approach to revitalize a mellow audience. If you're scheduled to speak after a discussion you know will take forever and arouse strong feelings, negotiate for another time.

4. Who else is speaking? If you are going to be one of several speakers, find out their approaches to the subject in advance. You can then plan a complementary or contrasting position, rather than repeating what has already been said. Enrich your listeners rather than bore them.

   I remember speaking to a national teachers' conference in Newfoundland. A cabinet minister had just taken his "message of welcome" time to score political points in a particularly nasty debate. Immediately after his verbal slams I was introduced. How could I hope that such a tense and angry crowd would be able to listen to me? After I thanked them for inviting me to the conference, I said that my topic was "Rising Up to Speak" not "Firing Up the Crowd" as the former speaker had done. The ironic laughter which followed helped to smooth over an unpredictable situation.

5. What format suits the group? Depending on the occasion, the size of the group, their level of knowledge of the topic and their reasons for coming to hear you, consider these types of presentation. Your own speaking skills and comfort with the subject will also influence your choice.

   - a straightforward presentation

   - speech and question period

- short introduction to a full question-and-answer period.

For handy reference on this area of preparation consult the first four checklists in Chapter 9.

THE THESIS—THE HEART OF THE PLAN

This is it—the critical part of speech design. You know the plan of a good speech, how to find a topic and determine who your audience will be. Now, what are you going to say?

The thesis is the central statement of your speech; if you're discussing the best holiday spot on the west coast, holistic medicine, or the political realignment of eastern Europe, the rule is the same. Review all your ideas and arguments and come up with one key statement. Imagine people leaving the room after your speech. They're talking about your presentation and reminding each other of your examples. One says to the other, "But exactly what was he/ she trying to prove?" The answer is your thesis. It is the *one* line everyone should remember.

Hammering out your thesis takes effort; it's like taking the unshaped metal and forging a workable concept. All the time and intensity of thought will pay off later. This is where you sweat it.

Do you remember the topic "manager as animal"? How about a thesis like this: "Tyrant or team leader? Managers are like animals: dinosaurs, weasels and wolves. The successful ones are team leaders and, like wolves, their loyalty is to the pack." Great thesis but does it have to be so long? No, it can be very short. Here's one on hamburger places: "The things I look for in a burger restaurant are friendliness, atmosphere, and hot peppers." A nurse giving a workshop on palliative care had this thesis: "Palliative care attempts to reassure the patient, ease his or her suffering, and help the patient face approaching death."

MAPPING YOUR SUCCESS: MORE ON THE THESIS AND OVERVIEW

The perfect plan is like a road map; the *thesis*, or main idea, is your destination; the supporting ideas outlined in the overview are the details of your route. Look at the examples just given. Can you identify the main supporting points in each case?

The preview makes it clear where your speech is going. Have you ever tried to drive someone home and been forced to follow terse commands: "Turn right here! Now left! Quick, left again! Okay, stop!" Isn't it easier to have someone say, "Go along Burrard Street, and turn right on Pender. Stay on Pender and merge with Georgia at the intersection. Then continue west on Georgia and you'll run right into Stanley Park."

That is what the overview does: It lets the audience know the main turns the speech will take as you drive home your thesis. They can anticipate your reasons and work with you instead of wondering where you're heading. To continue the analogy of a journey, a speech with a definite thesis and precise overview enables the audience to recognize the landmarks and appreciate the route.

The overview also makes things clear for *you*, the speaker. Once you have worked hard on the thesis and organized your ideas in three or four main sections, your speech is basically made. You need to fill in the examples and proofs, but the design is clear. That gives you the freedom to devote your efforts to talking directly to people.

PUTTING IT ALL TOGETHER

Imagine you are asked to do a speech on what to consider when first renting an apartment in a highrise. Your brainstorming might produce this list:

neighbours	sauna and weight rooms
cost	heat control
condominiums	play areas for children
subsidized housing	security
no yard work	noise
rent review boards	fire safety
slow elevators	pool
great view	location
party rooms	crime

You decide on security because your friend had some recent problems with it and can provide excellent background material. Once you research further, you realize that security is itself a general heading and you have to brainstorm again. You produce a second list that reflects a more detailed analysis:

need for better peepholes in doors	parking garages
cheap locks	poor lighting
keys kept by former tenants	theft
elevators	loud fights
criminal activity	mailbox theft
balconies on lower levels risky	main door too accessible to strangers

Considering this list, you have two possible routes: "Why are there so many security problems?" or "What are the major danger areas?" You might be able to cover both these topics, but the person who made this speech decided he had only enough time to cover one. These are the thesis statements he considered; remember, they were prefaced by the grabbers.

a. "Security problems in high-rise apartments are the result of shortsighted or selfish attitudes on the part of architects, owners, and tenants."

This thesis statement almost has the overview in place. The following statement is even more specific. It classifies the danger areas.

b. "The areas of greatest risk in highrise apartments are the foyer, the elevator and the parking garages."

In each case the thesis and the overview give the audience an exact outline of the purpose of the speech and the major points. The audience knows where the speech is going and how it will get there.

THE ONE-SENTENCE SHOWER TEST

How do you know if your thesis is clear? Take the one-sentence shower test. You've worked hard on your speech and you're in the shower. Go ahead! Talk about all the proofs you worked so hard to develop. Now, challenge yourself: *"Can I state in one sentence what my whole speech is supposed to prove?"*

Pass this test and you have a thesis on which to build a clear speech. Ramble until the water runs cold and you had better start narrowing things down and concentrating on one precise idea.

ROUNDING OUT YOUR PLAN

Once you have your thesis and overview—a persuasive, brilliant plan—you are ready to flesh out your speech. The three-part plan is a base for your speech; it anchors you, provides instant cues as you speak. But you need more: details to fill in the outline.

Each of your three main points needs its own subsection and yes, you can deviate from the rule of three. Two to five—but no more—examples or illustrations will do for each. Now is the time for research and creativity; organize the subsections any way you want, as long as you can get enthusiastic and your audience can understand.

The next chapter details two things you need to round out your plan—interesting examples and irresistible introductions and conclusions. But first, how are you going to reach your audience? What do you have in common? Where is the key to reaching them?

FINDING THE WAY IN: THE KEY TO AUDIENCE INTEREST

Marc Benoit spent the first half of his working life as an underground miner. He decided he wanted to explain to his present colleagues, who were addiction counsellors, the pressures that miners face. He had years of experience to draw on, stories of hardship and union efforts to get safety regulations observed, technically accurate examples of machinery breakdown and dangerous working conditions. How could he reach his audience, most of whom had never been near a mine? Should he start with statistics, accurate and technical descriptions of equipment, a thorough outline of labour statutes? Where did *his* circle of involvement, passion and knowledge intersect with the *audience's* circle of interest and awareness? He started like this: "It's dark, absolutely dark. If you turn off your helmet light you cannot see anything, not even the outline of your hands. It's noisy—machinery deafens you all day long. And it's sharp and hard. If your hands brush the walls, or if by chance you fall, the jagged rock will cut you, maybe to the bone. This is a mine."

Marc decided that his audience had to experience the mine, know the feeling of mining before they could ever understand the pressures of that kind of labour. Within one minute, his audience was completely absorbed. When he went on to outline the pressure of the work—physical danger, unsafe conditions and unenforced labour regulations—his audience knew inside themselves a little of what he meant.

This is what I call finding the way in. Picture your audience—how much do they know of your subject, how interested are they? Often, even the words we use don't match; that is, if I'm talking to a group about language, the etymology of words and how the roots of words carry bias, I get quite worked up about the whole issue. But our interest levels, our understanding of the subject, even our vocabularies may be nowhere near a common point.

How do I bridge the difference; what's the key to finding my way in? I think: What do we have in common? Where do the two circles, one representing the world of the speaker and the other the world of the audience, intersect? When I made this speech last year to teachers, I thought of children and how they are influenced or hurt by the undercurrents in our words. When I gave the same speech to a business group, I thought of employees and customers, how they react to words we use unconsciously but which carry a ton of baggage.

Think of your audience! Who are they, what do they know of your topic? Then listen to yourself. Do you sound like you are speaking to the audience you pictured or to a group of insiders as involved in your subject as you are? Brainstorm to discover the key, a way of reaching your audience, finding your way in to an area of mutual interest and concern.

DO YOU LIKE YOUR SPEECH?

Deborah Murray is my neighbour. An elementary school teacher and director of her teachers' association, she's also the person I have coached the longest. We became friends when I heard moaning behind the cedar hedge that separates our yards. "What's the matter," I asked. "My speech," she said, "it sucks." Obviously, she is a woman who knows when she's in trouble; I went over and asked for details.

It was her second time to run for the position as director in her organization, her second time of making up her election speech.

I listened to it. For ten torturous minutes, I heard the history of the organization, the professional history of my neighbour, an outline of the legal challenges the group was facing, and the work it did for its members. The speech was politically correct and exhaustive in detail. As Deb says, "It was intelligent and said all the right things. But it made me feel stiff and tense. I knew in my head and my heart what I wanted to say but it was so formal." She was right; the structure was so formal that she had to concentrate on the format, the words themselves rather than on her feelings and the audience.

When I asked her about the speech in the year previous, when she had been unsuccessful, she said, "It was the same—knowledgeable and sophisticated in concept. But it pushed people away—there was no human touch."

"What do you want to say?" I asked.

"Pick me."

That was it! Where have you had the same feeling? Pick me. Pick me. On teams in the schoolyard, lined up waiting to be chosen for a ball team.

Deb loves baseball; even as she spoke, her expression changed. The earnest frown of concentration she had worn to give her first address changed to a gentle, humorous expression as she talked about sandlot games in her hometown. She had her speech. She organized it along the theme of being chosen to be on the executive, a bigger team playing in a much larger league.

Can you make a serious speech using such homely examples? Won't you be called naive? In Chapter 5 Peter Jaffe talks about addressing professional audiences: "The more professional the audience, the more down-to-earth the story has to be.... That's what people can relate to, even very sophisticated and academic audiences."

Deb Murray waffled; her political advisors said her speech wasn't "serious" enough. She debated; her friends told her she sounded like herself when she talked about baseball. She liked the baseball speech. She used it. She won.

USING NOTES: THE ONLY SECRET

There is a secret to delivering a good speech. USE NOTES. Every one of us gives better speeches, sounds more relaxed, more confident and more sincere when we use notes. It takes practice to do it well, and courage. But it is ultimately much more convincing.

There are two vital reasons why you should not read from a written script:

- It's boring. Written language sounds different. The audience knows you're reading and they drift off. They want people to talk to them.

- It's isolating. Your only relationship is with the page; your interest in the material is secondary to getting the words out in the order you wrote them. Your first-hand experience, your involvement, your humour, your emotions are all dulled by the reading. And you can't look up. If you do, you'll lose your place. Eye contact is impossible; how do you know the audience is still there? As David Nichol, President of Loblaw International Merchants, says in the interview in Chapter 8, "They hang on to that script, they read it—I mean, they shouldn't have chairs, they should have beds for the audience!"

If speaking from notes is so much more effective, why don't people do it? These are some of the responses I got from a recent workshop:

"I thought business people always read stuff out to sound impressive."
"I read because I'm too nervous to look at the audience."
"What if I make a mistake? At least if I read, I won't forget anything."

What is more important to you? Getting every last statistic correct or convincing your audience that your suggestion has merit? If you want to convince people, talk to them! They'll believe you more readily if you make eye contact, or move, or even make a mistake. You'll be human. People have been misled for too long by glib presenters reading their material; they want to know if the person making the proposal actually believes in it. They want to hear you talk to them. If it helps, put the essentials on overhead transparencies; then you can focus on the group.

And that's the crux of the matter—focusing. It is hard to look at the audience before you. Quite honestly, I'm often too nervous to make eye contact for the first few minutes of my speech—it takes a while before I can look directly at the group—and then I'm so heartened by what I see. They're looking back—interested, vital human beings. I'm not alone.

You have to make a choice. Do you want to be a good speaker or not? If you do, practise using notes. Use your nervousness as a catalyst to get you to rehearse. You don't really need to read the details of where you live and how you got your first job—you know those things! Make clear notes and remember to use them. Pause in your speech, take a breath, look down and concentrate on where you are.

Do good speakers need notes? Yes, we do. Sometimes, we give speeches so often, we shift into automatic and rattle off the anecdotes and arguments that have worked well in the past. It's a trap I have fallen into. The result is a speech that isn't tailored to the group; there isn't the same rapport. Every speech needs to be fresh and every speaker needs some notes—even five or six words on a card— to keep on track. I *always* take the time to make a set of notes; who knows what disasters lie between my last rehearsal and the speech itself? The notes are my insurance.

How do the experts do it?

"I work only from notes. I write in note form, sometimes full sentences, on folded pieces of white paper. Never any longer than five sides of notes. Just one word will sometimes remind me of a story. I take care with the opening and the end." —June Callwood

"Yes, I always use notes rather than writing out a speech word for word.... To write it out word for word, you might as well send a letter. There are things you think of or ways you express yourself while you're standing there. The atmosphere and the circumstances change what you say." —Gloria Steinem

MAKING CLEAR SPEECH NOTES

- These are notes, not novels: have a maximum of five to seven cards.

- Put the notes on heavy paper or cards so that no one can tell if your hands are shaking.

- The size is up to you—larger cards cut down on the number required.

- Writing must be large—visible from at least 15 inches (40 cm) away.

- Use point form.

- Number your arguments. Use coloured pens to highlight key points.

- You may wish to write essential lines out in full. (I like to write out my conclusion and any line I consider essential—two or three per speech maximum. When I reach these lines, I *don't* read them. I pause, review the phrasing, look directly at the audience, and give it my best.)

- Include statistics or names you might forget.
- Write out punchlines to jokes.
- Number your speech cards.
- Use one side only—under pressure, it's hard to sort double-sided notes.
- Don't have too many cards and avoid a constant turning of notes. Your eyes should be on the audience.
- Keep an extra set handy.
- Give yourself delivery cues at the sides in bold letters:

  pause   relax
  smile   slow down
  breathe!   eye contact

- Practise your speech with the notes you will use. Improvise a lectern at home to see if the notes work.

PATTERN OF A SPEECH— WITH VARIATIONS

What does a speech outline look like once it's assembled? You know the plan, you've got an idea of how to start, you can hammer out a thesis and you're focused on your audience. Here are two speech plans for you to examine. What, you want the whole text? Sorry, speeches are made, planned, *designed*. There are no full texts of these ones. But the notes are clear enough for you to follow and the introductions are complete. These people got the job done—and their speeches were great.

DEBORAH MURRAY'S 1991 CAMPAIGN SPEECH—PICK ME

I   Introduction

Grabber: "Today's selection process takes me back to Spruce Street

North in Timmins. There were fields and immense willows, an open creek. We played sandlot baseball and I can still call up the memories of standing there in line with my friends as the captains studied us—and in my heart I was saying 'pick me—pick me'."

Thesis: Nothing so marks our lives in these days as change. It impacts incredibly on us as teachers. And I'm excited by our potential as members of our organization and the change we will help to effect.

Overview: — the contributions our Federation has made

— the challenges we face with the learners of today and tomorrow

— the effect working in this organization has had on me

II Body

1. contributions we have made:

   — report on technological education

   — curriculum outlines

   — story of my trip to the most northern region

2. challenges of today and tomorrow:

   — the warmth and concern shown during the legal efforts to maintain our present membership as a women's organization

   — review the major points of the argument and talk about the cheering

   — learners are different—"we can't strike out with today's students"

   — story of classroom discussion of sexuality

   — challenges around equity, poverty and violence

3. changes in me:

   — stories of evenings spent with various associations

   — playing in the big league

   — committees I'm on

   — lessons learned

III Conclusion

Review thesis: — "Having known you I have learned much and I have changed."

Zinger: "I'm a little bit older and a little bit wiser than those sandlot days. We can do much with shared work and the instruments of co-operation: listening, understanding and accommodation. I ask for the opportunity to work on your behalf in implementing our vision. Pick me."

TED MOREAU'S INFORMATIVE SPEECH— MIDNIGHT HEROES: THE INDEPENDENT TRUCKER

Ted Moreau was asked to speak on an aspect of contemporary work. His aim was to show how the independent trucker used to be a folk hero like the cowboy. However, technology and societal changes have altered the job.

I   Introduction

Grabber: "It was 4:30 in the morning. The dimly lit yard was mystical with all the sleeping steel horses lined up in a row. Dad parked the pick-up and slowly we walked toward his rig. The smell of diesel fuel floated up and into me from the oil-soaked gravel lot. Dad opened my door and lifted me high onto the seat. The soft smell of leather, the view and all the knobs and gadgets enchanted me. This was it! The experience of a lifetime."

Thesis: The independent trucker, like the cowboy, was a folk hero. Now, three things have altered this image:

Overview: — mobility

        — gender roles

        — independent status

II   Body

1. mobility:

     — influenced by changes in technology

     — remote area access

— cost of maintaining remote area access

2. gender roles:

— society has been major influence

— changes in trucks make strength less of a factor

— equal rights

3. independent status:

— primarily influenced by the economy

— larger companies

— have to work for others, megacompanies

— secondarily influenced by technology

— electronic gadgets

III Conclusion

Review: the plight of the trucker today

Zinger: "The independent trucker used to be like the cowboy. He travelled over good roads and bad, in all types of weather, and had the strength to handle the iron horse beneath him. While sitting in a roadside truckstop, drinking strong black coffee and smoking endless cigarettes, he was the essence of the modern hero. My dad, the epitome of the oldtime trucker, has retired now and I regret the passing of the trucker hero."

THE SOUTH MAGNETAWAN BAT BRIGADE— THE DEMONSTRATION SPEECH

The speech that started this chapter—on the capture and release of a bat—is an example of a fairly common type of speech, the demonstration. We often make this kind of speech as part of our job: a health care worker demonstrates how to give insulin; an environmental technician shows how to release a fish without harming it; a chef helps her assistants make a creole sauce.

The purpose of the speech is not to talk about a subject, *but to explain it so clearly as you demonstrate that the audience learns the procedure and remembers it.* After your presentation, the audience should remember the main steps and be able to work on their own.

There are two basic pointers:

1. Make the topic specific. Limit the demo to one procedure such as spiking your hair or using a microphone. Someone who tries to demonstrate how to take a good picture can't hope to cover such a vast topic; limit it to framing your subject or choosing background.

2. Use a three-part plan. Imagine a before-and-after situation: before your speech, the audience knows little about throwing a cream pie; after you're finished, they'll know how to throw the pie and escape. What if there are 12 steps in making a Caesar salad dressing? Organize them into three sections: ingredients, mixing, presentation. Take the eight steps in doing a running pry, a fancy canoe stroke, and present them in three major groups: position, stroke and follow-through. Remember, *you* already know the technique; the audience has to remember!

I've seen people do the following demonstrations: How to cut glass, pour beer, make paper, diaper a baby, give an intramuscular injection, clean a chimney, tie-dye material, prepare squid for cooking, make a gumbo base, pan for gold, make a simple table, a duck decoy, espresso, popcorn, Caesar salad, Irish cream liqueur.

A *modified demonstration* can be useful if you don't have time to bake cookies or wait until glue dries. If you need to bake, bring in the ingredients *and* samples of the finished product. The components of a birdhouse can be assembled up to the stage of glueing, the next example can be worked until it is time to paint, and then the third and complete model is shown. Don't bore your audience! Use a modified demonstration for any process that involves a series of repetitive actions.

Rehearse with your props! Rehearsal is essential to a smooth performance. Your credibility will be enhanced if you know your subject well and handle your materials confidently.

1. Rehearse with the materials until you are familiar with them. You can then concentrate on eye contact with your audience.

2. Have interesting props. If you have a collection of materials— ingredients for a recipe or pots of nails—put them in separate containers with large, colourful labels.

3. Check your sightlines. Set up the demonstration at home exactly as you will do it. Then, walk from your position as speaker to

where the audience will be. Is anything blocking the view? Make sure the audience's view is unobstructed.

4. Can your notecards be seen at a distance? Many things require your attention. Practise handling the materials, connecting with the audience, and checking notes all at once.

5. Practise your movements often. Can you pour liquids, fold paper, join pieces of wood or slice mushrooms without your hands trembling?

6. Repeat key ideas and include a summary.

7. Use the audience, involve them, appeal to them. Make sure they understand.

Warning: If you demonstrate a procedure involving health or safety —boosting a car battery or helping a choking victim—you must be properly trained. Incorrect instructions can result in accidents. A responsible speaker does not alarm or frighten the audience. I've seen a starter's pistol, produced unexpectedly, terrify a group and a carelessly handled fondue pot go up in flames. In both cases, the audience was so unnerved they couldn't concentrate.

DELIVERY TECHNIQUES TO REMEMBER

For your first speech you were asked to:

- Pause at the lectern and count to three.
- Make eye contact.
- Pause when you finish.

Now, add the following:

1. Assume a confident posture.

2. Breathe before you start. You will have better voice control.

3. Make eye contact and consult your notes!

RICK HANSEN

Rick Hansen is a wheelchair athlete, writer and speaker. Inspired by the example of his friend Terry Fox, Hansen embarked on the Man in Motion tour around the world in a wheelchair.

In 1983, he shared athlete of the year honours with Wayne Gretzky and in 1987 he became a Companion of the Order of Canada. He is now married to Amanda Reid and the father of two daughters, Emma and Alana. He heads his own motivational speaking company; is the National Fellow at the University of British Columbia where he also acts as consultant on disabilities to the president; and serves on various boards.

SB: During the Man in Motion tour, you spoke many times each day, and yet you made each group and each speech special. How did you do it?

RH: *When I am speaking to the public, whether it's one person or 100,000 people, I want them to perceive me as I am feeling. I try to wipe the slate clean of the last speech because every speech is different—different environment, different people. What you have to do is come from the heart, speak from the heart in a way that allows people to gain a sense of what you feel, as well as what you think. They must know that you care about them, that you think they are important.*

These days, so many people are getting into public speaking, and becoming proficient at it, even slick. They get mechanical and monotonous or repetitive, sometimes losing the life, and the feeling and the essence of what speaking is all about. It's story-telling, and communicating, and educating. I think that part of public speaking has got to be preserved.

SB: Even when you were exhausted, you made that kind of an effort?

RH: *No doubt about it. There were times when I came in from the road and I was just fried. I'd wheeled 70 miles that day, dealing*

*with headwinds and shoulder injuries, and perhaps be cold and
wet. We'd also have to deal with logistical matters and crew
problems. Then, I had to turn around, and go out into a town
hall where there were 300 people waiting, and they'd been there
for four hours. The last thing you feel like doing is trying to
overcome what you're feeling—which is a lot of depression,
anguish and pain.*

*You have to dig down very deep within you, to the essence of
what drives you, and come up with not the image of somebody
who's hurting, but the image of somebody who is positive, who
has a wonderful message that's important for people to listen to.
You want to make those people feel important; they're the most
important people in your day, in your life, at that time.*

*When you're tired and at the edge, and you don't think you
have any more to give, sometimes that's when you come up with
your best performances.*

SB: How did people respond?

RH: *That was the magic of the tour. People could relate to it in normal life; it leapt the bounds of disability. Anyone who is setting
goals, chasing dreams, dealing with adversity and setbacks along
the way, could relate to the message. They realized the value of
teamwork, of co-operative endeavour, of the results possible when
they challenge themselves.*

SB: When you spoke at the Bowden Correctional Centre in
Alberta, you started your speech with the line, "We are all
imprisoned in different ways." That was a great way to establish a bond. How do you do that?

RH: *I treat each crowd differently. I never say the same thing. My
words reflect a lot of the crowd I'm with. At Bowden, I wanted to
say something those guys could relate to. It was important to
find an analogy. They have their own personal battles to deal
with, and I wanted them to be able to relate to the message, and
perhaps, in turn, find inspiration for their own lives.*

SB: How long did it take to find that opening?

RH: *It was spontaneous. I don't like to come into a place with set
lines because so much depends on the crowd and the atmosphere.
You have to be organized, don't get me wrong, but you also have
to leave room to react spontaneously.*

SB: What was your message? What were you out there to tell us?

RH: *What inspired me on my journey was not trying to raise funds for spinal cord injury research, but the inherent message Terry Fox delivered. Terry was a good friend of mine and although he was trying to raise money for cancer research, he created so much awareness of the potential of disabled persons. He brought the country together; he made people feel a way they had perhaps never felt before.*

    That message of awareness of disabled persons was so important. I thought if I could challenge myself to fulfil an old dream of physically wheeling around the world, and bring that message with me, that I could be a catalyst. I could be a messenger for a better understanding of disabled persons.

SB: What challenges did you issue?

RH: *I wanted to challenge people in their communities to see how they could remove the many barriers that still remain in the way of disabled persons achieving their potential. Outdated attitudes and physical obstacles have to be removed. We need to instil the idea that it's a community effort. Sometimes people want to slough it off; it's not their responsibility. But it's only a split second away from happening to any one of us.*

SB: Do you get nervous when you speak?

RH: *I get nervous when I have to be organized for an extended speech. I don't get nervous when I speak from the heart, but I'm also trying to learn to be organized for a longer presentation. The combination of being organized and maintaining sincerity means so much to me that I get nervous.*

    I'm new to a more formal speaking style. The message or vision is always clear, but I'm always tired and in a hurry. I want to have enough control so that I can get off a plane and know I can always come through. I don't want to rely on having a good day, but be sure I can do it.

SB: What advice do you have for people who want to speak well?

RH: *Organize yourselves. Speak from the heart. Be sincere. Give the audience everything that's in you, just like it's your first speech. Have a feeling for the audience and a sense of being with them. If you're speaking to kids, don't revert to old ideas of "adults and kids." Just talk to them so they understand you, and so that you have a feeling for them and what they face.*

CHAPTER
3

POSITIVE VIBRATION:
GETTING YOUR SPEECH TOGETHER

Years of actually getting up in front of audiences have taught me only three lessons:
1. *You don't die.*
2. *There's no right way to speak, only your way.*
3. *It's worth it.*

— **Gloria Steinem**

▲▲▲▲▲▲▲▲▲▲▲▲

ake it interesting.

ake it organized.

ake it from the heart.

Whenever I tell people their speeches should be interesting—exciting, fun, suspenseful, moving—they get nervous. Do adults like interesting things as well as children? Aren't we supposed to be concerned with ponderous proofs, significant statistics and erudite experts? Of course. We would also like to be entertained—it's not enough to make things exciting for children and serve up bland, boring material to each other. This is a big difference between the old way of speaking and the new; previously, speakers concentrated on impressing their listeners, not reaching them. Now, the focus is on connecting, getting the audience engrossed and your message across.

Sometimes it's easier to be boring than it is to risk new ways of reaching out. Don't forget, we're fighting that old internal movie of the venerable scion of industry reading significant truths from a thick stack of paper. When I interviewed Eddie Greenspan, outstanding criminal lawyer, it surprised me that a person involved in law, a field I perceive to be full of tedious references to subsections of the subsection, said emphatically: "It is pointless to make an important point in a boring fashion because it may be lost. It has to be made in an entertaining and dramatic way." If Greenspan can make judicial complexities intriguing, there's hope.

Dare to be interesting. Have faith in your audience and risk presenting your material in a way you enjoy! Start with the introduction.

GETTING IN: GREAT INTRODUCTIONS

Seize the audience's attention. Once they are listening attentively, deliver your thesis and overview. Good speakers experiment with openings that intrigue listeners. These openings are called grabbers; they have two main functions: to seize the attention of the audience and make them want to listen; and to give both speaker and listeners a chance to locate each other. It takes a few minutes for people to get attuned to your voice, observe your body language, focus on you. If you're in a good room, you will have a chance to gauge the audience, sense their mood and their responsiveness. Grabbers are worth the time you spend designing them—they set the mood of your whole speech. When you're planning the grabber, remember these pointers:

- Your Audience: Who is out there? Why have they come to hear you speak? Where do your areas of concern overlap? How can you reach them? You don't have much time. Kate Scott is a lawyer who specializes in family law; she came to me for advice during a custody case she wanted very much to win. Her dilemma? "I know the technical part but how do you get the darn judge interested? They pretend to be listening but they are gone! Their minds are out there on the golf course."

- Yourself: Like your own speech. Believe in yourself and what you have to say. Find a grabber you feel good about.

- Frame Your Speech: Think of a picture frame with the main body of your speech inside it as the canvas. The frame itself consists of the grabber and your conclusion; if you link the grabber to the conclusion, you achieve a sense of wholeness. The audience thinks, "Hey, that final example relates back to the story in the introduction." They enjoy the sense of completeness.

- Be Entertaining: Every year I do a public speaking clinic with the Civil Engineering Department at the University of Toronto. These students will soon have to make oral presentations to municipal councils, environmental assessment boards, community interest groups—something engineers never had to do in the past. Although technically competent, they need to learn to make their reports interesting; if not, their listeners' attention will wander and decisions may go against them.

How do you make the proposal for an industrial park lively? Why not take in three briefcases: a traditional attaché case, a bright green case (mine is a child's play suitcase on loan from my nephew Aidan) and a backpack. Each bag relates to a part of the presentation: the attaché case holds the technical outline and financial overview; the green case has the environmental background of the project; and the backpack has the section of the report that details community benefits. I even suggest they put the appropriate overheads inside each bag. As well as providing colour and suspense, this simple technique also gives the audience a memory aid—they associate the arguments with the appropriate bag. (If you think this might be "gimmicky," try the word "interesting" instead. Remember when newscasts had to be boring to be credible?)

CHOOSING YOUR GRABBER

Getting in as a speaker is like getting in as a swimmer; depending on your style, and the climate of the group, you can ease in slowly, dive in gracefully or jump in feet first. Here's a list of common grabbers; all are effective in the right circumstances.

- Stories and examples
- Real stuff

- Direct approach
- Unusual or startling statement
- Quotations
- Humour
- Music
- Historical references
- Special occasions
- Gloria Steinem's specialty—community discussion

STORIES AND EXAMPLES

Stories touch people. No matter how sophisticated your audience or your topic, telling a story intrigues your listeners.

Have you ever dreamt of inventing, developing and marketing a product that absolutely sweeps the market? The passion, the dedication, the sheer gall of what it takes was summed up by Ron Foxcroft, inventor of the Fox 40 whistle, the unbelievably loud, "pea-less" whistle, marketed as the ultimate referee's whistle and the loudest street-safety signal. Foxcroft started his presentation by describing the fear he felt for his life at a pre-Olympic basketball game in Brazil. He had blown a conventional whistle to declare the ball out of play but the ball or pea in the whistle jammed. When the fans found out that their team's basket did not count and play had to go back to the point where he had made his ruling, they rioted onto the court. Foxcroft vowed that if he got out alive, he would invent a never-fail whistle.

I love this story. I remember it years after I first heard it and I remember almost all of the presentation. Desperation drove him to his most daring marketing move. He went to the Pan-American Games with two prototypes of the whistle in his pocket; it had cost him $150,000 to get that far and if he didn't get orders he was doomed. In the middle of the night, he blew the Fox 40 in the hallway of the coaches' dorm. They all responded to the noise and immediately placed orders for the incredible whistle. Fox 40 was a hit!

What happens to people when they tell a story? If they've chosen wisely, they relax and get involved in the telling. What happens to the audience? They get interested, eager to hear more. Audiences are tired of fancy bar graphs and reams of stats; they're either inundated with expert opinions or don't believe them. Stories work.

Diane Francis, business commentator and analyst, uses anecdotes to explain financial matters. "Business is as interesting as watching paint dry. It's full of details and numbers. But it's the people who do business that are interesting.... Business is like sport—it involves people and action."

Where do you find stories? All around you. Remember the things you see that you consider significant or touching. Jot down examples that you read or hear on the radio or television. Ask your friends and colleagues. And remember, use stories that mean something to you; you'll be able to tell them better than anecdotes you plucked at random from a reference book.

REAL STUFF

This is my own term for three-dimensional objects that you place in front of your audience as you speak. These things embody each of your main points and they provide visual appeal as you speak. (They are too simple, too homey to be called audio-visual aids. For the most part, they are "found" objects, discovered in the back of my cupboard, garage sales, offbeat stores.) How do they work? Last year I gave a speech to educators on the "elements" of elementary school. As I discussed the traditional elements—earth, air, fire and water—and related them to values, creativity, passion and life force—I unrolled coloured banners. The technique added suspense: what did each colour represent? The banner also provided a great conclusion; when I finished, I had the basis of a rainbow and children are the rainbow, the promise of our world. Is this corny? If you mean sincere, emotional, apt, yes it is. But it is also a genuinely satisfying way to conclude a speech.

More real stuff. I'm doing a workshop with workers in a women's shelter. The title is "Being There When Things Are Tough" and my props fit in my bag: a statue of a robin hunched down in its feathers, a lucky rock and my coffee mug. The robin reminds me to listen bravely, hunkered down in the storm. The rock is for staying grounded, being there, listening. The mug is for making tea, the simplest way I know to care for someone. Each prop introduces one of the speaking strategies we'll work on; people remember real stuff and the concepts it embodies.

Why use this technique? It's fun. It's a change. I sometimes get frustrated when speakers won't use the simple examples all around them; they go for complicated abstractions and everyone gets lost. It works well if you are the after-dinner entertainment or if you are presenting to a group that is workshop weary.

Real Stuff I've used or seen others use recently:

- a top that plays tunes used to show that traditional toys can have a new "spin,"

- an onion used to show that people may pretend to be dry and crusty on the surface. Inside, they are tender and they weep.

- a new version of stacking dolls, a cob of corn that opens down the back—inside are smaller cobs of corn; they too open to reveal mini-cobs.

DIRECT APPROACH

Faith Popcorn is a dynamic speaker who has predicted the major trends of the 80s and 90s. *The Popcorn Report* starts with the sentence "These are bizarre times." The next few sentences outline the socioquake that will change mainstream consumer America. This is an example of the direct approach. If your topic is so dramatic or your commitment so intense, the sincere or direct approach is often the best.

Do not use this type of grabber lightly; it only works if the topic is serious and your commitment to it obvious.

UNUSUAL OR STARTLING STATEMENT

Sheri Alexander, a travel counsellor, surprised her audience to attention with this grabber: "If malaria, yellow fever and hepatitis don't mean anything to you, maybe the words 'lawsuit,' 'reputation' and 'unemployment' do. It is your legal responsibility as travel agents to make sure that the health requirements of your clients have been outlined before their departure."

Questions can be used to intrigue your listeners. "What word are government officials forbidden to say?" (The answer is recession.)

On a more serious note, last month I heard a man from Northern Ontario begin his talk with the stark statement: "A better air ambulance system would have saved my son's life."

Statistics have to be brief and breathtaking to work as a grabber. In Faith Popcorn's discussion of "Down-Aging," she says that in the 1989 New York Marathon more than 10,000 runners or an incredible 42 percent were over 40! The numbers amazed me as much as the feat.

CRISIS CONTROL

Your statement may be unusual or challenging but it cannot be insulting or your listeners will retaliate by closing their minds. Telling a group that they are the most poorly motivated, coffee-swilling underachievers you've ever encountered is a turnoff, not a grabber.

QUOTATIONS

What quotations work? How do you fit them in? After years of hearing speeches I have one plea: do not use encyclopedias of quotations simply for the sake of getting a remark that relates, however obscurely, to your topic. I am tired of speeches about light rapid transit that begin with the phrase: "As Descartes so aptly put it." Or discussions of marketing strategies that refer to Cicero, Masefield or Hegel. Where are the people we recognize and value—Alice Walker, Nelson Mandela, Martina Navratilova, Gandhi, Michele Landsberg, Martin Luther King Jr., Elijah Harper, Stephen Lewis, Rosemary Brown, Lily Tomlin, Arthur Ashe?

Use quotations that have internal resonance for you and your audience. And once you've used them, refer to them later in your speech to make it clear why they were chosen.

Build your own reference file; when you listen to the radio or scan the paper, copy down quotations or lyrics that impress you. Several of my favorites are:

"Early to bed, early to rise, never get tight and advertise."—Timothy Eaton, founder of Eaton's Department Stores

"We don't kill people who talk about self-esteem by beating them to death like they did to Steve Biko. We kill them with ridicule."—Gloria Steinem

"Free your mind and the rest will follow."—k.d. lang

"You don't miss the water 'til your well runs dry."—Sufi saying

"For the first time I knew I had the power of speech. I saw faces brighten, eyes glisten, and felt the atmosphere crackle with a new power."—Nellie McClung

"I am convinced that intelligence, patience, and eloquence can, sooner or later, lead the human race out of its self-imposed tortures provided it does not exterminate itself in the meantime."—Bertrand Russell

HUMOUR

Why is humour so far down the list? Because it is such a dicey subject. I use humour often in the form of stories or shared experiences that everyone in the group can laugh at. But for too many people, humour means jokes; indeed books for the old way of speaking recommend starting your speech with a few jokes. And the examples they give are often racist or sexist or homophobic. How many times have you heard generally decent people start their speech at the company dinner or church supper with a string of one-liners that fall flat. They do not intend to be offensive; they are unconsciously repeating old and hurtful patterns.

Humour involves stories which build a feeling of recognition, a sort of "thank god, I'm not the only one; it's happened to you too" feeling. Imagine a circle, everyone is in it, laughing together—rather than insiders laughing at outsiders.

I often quote Susan Faludi, author of *Backlash*, who was so afraid of public speaking that she once stood "knock-kneed and green-gilled before 300 people. Was it too late to plead a severe case of laryngitis? I am Woman, Hear Me Whisper."

Or consider Anne Wilson Schaef, author of *Meditations for Women Who Do Too Much*. She was the guest speaker at a luncheon for one of the Fortune 500 Corporations. "I went to the bathroom to 'pee my anxieties down the toilet' as we say in clinical circles.... Just as I reached the door to the auditorium, I was aware of a breeze and realized that my skirt was caught up in my panty hose... of course it made a great opener for my speech."

MUSIC

Books are not your only source of quotations: "Give Peace a Chance" and "We Shall Overcome" are familiar to all of us. From Rita MacNeil to k.d. lang, from Woody Guthrie to Sweet Honey in the Rock, from Judy Garland to Barenaked Ladies, music can enliven a speech and provide just the right words. Quote the lyrics or put the song on a tape and watch the looks of delight and surprise on the faces of your listeners. Be sure to clarify how the words and music relate to your topic.

HISTORICAL REFERENCES

Events in the lives of great people such as Martin Luther King Jr. or Amelia Earhart can provide a good starting point for your talk. You can refer to specific national events or to environmental turning points. Make sure to choose an historical event that means something to you; if your first debate on war, pro or con, stands out in your mind, use it. Our own lives are history; a speaker I heard recently outlined the technological equipment that marked the passages of his life, from the portable record player that could stack up to 10 records to his notebook computer.

SPECIAL OCCASIONS

Often our speaking date coincides with an important occasion: Persons Day, Deepavali, summer solstice, Groundhog Day. When you're asked to "make a few remarks" or "bring greetings" (such terms!), make those comments worthwhile. Referring to a special day and talking about it can add interest and substance to your greetings. Examples?

Persons Day. Canadian women were declared persons on October 18, 1929—what does it mean to be a person? Do we have full and equal rights under the law today?

Deepavali. The Hindu celebration of light. What kinds of light would you celebrate: spotlights on the unheralded, lamps of learning, candles for hope?

Summer solstice. What does the ritual change of season bring to the world?

Groundhog Day. While you had the television cameras of the world hovering to see if you cast a shadow, what would you say to them?

GLORIA STEINEM'S SPECIALTY—COMMUNITY DISCUSSION

At the end of this chapter are excerpts from a recent speech by Gloria Steinem. As she travelled North America on a book tour, she changed both the form and feeling of the traditional speaking environment by asking people to talk *to each other* and share concerns. By acknowledging the audience's worth, their ability to provide answers as well as questions, she turned the event into a community discussion: ideas, energy and information flowed around and through the hall. The speaker was *part of* the group. Although the audience was eager to hear Steinem's perceptions, each person also shared the power; other voices were heard. This is her introduction:

"Thank you all for taking time out of your busy lives to come here and take a chance on a stranger, or an outside agitator or whatever I am. And because of your generosity, we have something very precious here tonight—we have an hour together.

"So here's my plan. If all goes well, each of us, me included, will leave this room with one new organizing idea, one new troublemaking suggestion, one feeling of support, one new revolutionary comrade. In order to make that happen, I need your help. I need your help in overcoming this structure with you looking at each other's backs and me looking at you. It's a structure based on hierarchy which is in turn based on patriarchy which doesn't work anywhere, anymore, at all.

"During what's usually called the question and answer period, I hope you will help me overcome this structure and turn this into the organizing meeting it really ought to be. Please be thinking what answers you would like to give us, not just questions, organizing announcements of upcoming troublemaking meetings this group should know about. If you'd rather not say it yourself, pass me a note, I'll read anything—I'm leaving very early tomorrow morning. Because as all feminists say, if we come today and there's no trouble tomorrow, we haven't done our jobs."

WHAT NEXT?

After the grabber, you need a transition, a statement that leads into your thesis and overview. Such a transition might be:

"And one of the issues that stands out in this instance is the need for...."

"As so many people have observed recently...."

"And what Steinem has said about organizing is true for us as well...."

FINISHING STRONG: DYNAMIC CONCLUSIONS

Distance runners know the secret of a good race—finish strong. If you watch a 1,500-metre race, you'll see the best runners work for a position at the front of the pack; they hold that spot until the last lap when they give a final great push to pull ahead and fly to the finish line.

It takes planning and practice for speakers to save enough material, enough conviction and enough strength to avoid petering out and to *finish strong*. Don't put all your energy into the body of the speech and conclude by saying something like, "Well, I guess that sums it up and I can sit down now." Or worse, repeating every single point you've made until you've exhausted your resources and your audience.

Remember the frame—the idea of your grabber and conclusion tying your arguments together in a solid package? If you started with a story, outline a further development; a startling statement or humorous remark, refer to it, perhaps mentioning another aspect.

Sheri Alexander's feisty conclusion tied in well with her grabber: "Dr. Azouz is here today to make you aware of what you and your clients may be up against once they leave the country. And how you can save their lives—and your neck."

BUILDING YOUR CONCLUSION

The function of the conclusion is to reinforce your thesis, review your main points, if necessary, and finish solidly. You and the audience should think, "There, that feels complete." If you have already reviewed your arguments, a complete summary may be unnecessary.

Your aim is to remind the audience without boring them. You may wish to urge them to action or point to future possibilities. If it's appropriate, tie your remarks in with the rest of the evening or conference. Whatever you choose to do, end your speech. Wrap it up well and then sit down! Do not ramble or repeat yourself. Finish!

Ending on a high note may come naturally to you. There are also a number of sentence patterns that help your sentences rise to a crescendo. You can build your conclusion with alliteration, a series of parallel questions, or repetition. Jesse Jackson used alliteration when he promised to "compete without conflict and differ without division." Eddie Greenspan concluded his speech on the futility of the death penalty by referring to Donald Marshall, a New Brunswick native person convicted of a crime he did not commit. Greenspan asked: "Which of you, sitting here today, could have pulled the bag over his head? Which of you could have fastened the rope around his neck? Which of you could have sprung the trap door which sent Donald Marshall to his death?"

LISTEN TO YOUR CONCLUSION

When you practise your speech, listen to your final words. Do you sound clear and strong? Do you sound like yourself? Do you sound convinced?

In her conclusion, Gloria Steinem enters into her famous "organizer's deal" with her audience. In this excerpt you can hear her conversational tone, the humour, the feeling that she shares the experiences and quandaries of her audience and the joy of the revolution from within.

"Each of you here has to make a promise to me that within 24 hours beginning Monday morning, each of you will do at least one outrageous thing in the cause of simple justice. I don't care what it is—you know best.

"It can be as simple as saying 'pick it up yourself.' It can be deciding to run for political office; it can be telling each other your salaries where you work (they keep you from saying the one thing you actually know). It can be saying to your neighbours or colleagues, 'What are we doing in a white ghetto? We're culturally deprived,' or 'What are we doing in a heterosexual ghetto? We're culturally deprived,' or 'What are we doing in an able-bodied ghetto? Where are the ramps?'

"Whatever it is, I leave it up to you. And I must say, people do terrific things. I returned to a town where I had spoken before and this wonderful old woman said to me that she had heard my 'pick it up yourself' remark, and she was very concerned because her husband didn't even pick up his underwear. 'So,' she said, 'I found it quite useful to nail it to the floor.'

"... If you promise me that each of you will do just one outrageous thing in 24 hours, I promise you I will too. AND, there are two guaranteed results. The first is that by Tuesday, the world will be better. The second is, that you will have SUCH a good time, you will never again get up in the morning, saying 'WILL I do an outrageous thing?' but only 'WHICH outrageous thing will I do?'"

BALANCING YOUR SPEECH

The body of your speech needs careful attention. It's not enough to decide on your main points; you must still sift your research carefully, balance your sources, avoid even unintentional plagiarism, check that all your proofs are in three or four manageable sections, and that those sections are arranged in a suitable order.

SIFTING YOUR RESEARCH

"Gathering random facts does not necessarily mean obtaining information. Information is obtained through a process by which facts are gathered, organized, compared, and balanced in a logical manner."
—Stephen Overbury

Most often, your speeches will be on topics you know well. If you are speaking at work, or about social issues that concern you, chances are you are very familiar with the material. If you need to research further, libraries and first-hand interviews are the fastest and most complete sources.

Stephen Overbury, consummate researcher and teacher of research, considers libraries the best, although most often overlooked, sources of information: "There are at least three things you can be sure of about libraries: they collect information on every subject; the information can always be located; and the librarians who run them have been trained to meet your information needs."

Overbury also recommends phoning companies and organizations to get facts quickly—and then doing your job of comparing and balancing the information.

EVALUATING YOUR SOURCES

On a recent newscast, government officials said that no workers would be unfairly disadvantaged by proposed changes to unemployment insurance legislation. The alterations will make it impossible for any person quitting a job to qualify for unemployment benefits. A spokesperson for a national women's group says that the legislation will force women to remain in dangerous work environments rather than risk losing income while they look for another job.

Is there such a thing as "the truth?" David Suzuki thinks not: "There is no such thing as objective reality. We each select our experiences through the filters of our genes, values and belief systems. Ask a logger from B.C. and a Haida Indian to talk about the importance of a virgin stand of cedar trees, or a Bay Street businessman and a person on welfare about taxes and social services. You would swear from their responses that they come from different worlds."

Cross-testing information helps you to present balanced material. When you look at your sources, you should examine such things as the author, the tone, the publication and the date of publication. You are trying to identify bias, not to eliminate it but to balance it. Your awareness of the background of your sources will help you present a more honest picture to your audience.

AVOIDING PLAGIARISM

Sometimes, your sources are too good and they work their way, unacknowledged, into your speech. Plagiarism occurs when you *knowingly* pass off the work, words or ideas of others as your own. It is a mean-spirited thing to do. And it's illegal.

Basically, all information considered public knowledge can be used without specific acknowledgement. However, if you use other people's words or theories, you should give them credit. It weakens your presentation if several of your listeners have read the theories you are outlining expounded in an article by someone else. It is better to err on the side of caution.

ORGANIZING YOUR INFORMATION

Manageable, memorable statements. That's what you're after. Organizing your observations, arguments, steps, explanations or exhortations into three sections is simple and it's clear. Are you going to praise the attractions of the Costa Rican rainforests? How will you organize your mass of enthusiastic observations? Try three main categories:

1. The world of the rainforest—climate, fauna, etc.

2. The beings—human and animal—dependent on it.

3. Measures we must take to protect it.

This organizational technique will work for the mountain of information you have on the Chilkoot Pass, the gateway to the fabled Klondike Gold Rush Route. If you want to convey the thrill of hiking the Chilkoot you can concentrate on

1. The history of the Klondike Rush of 1898.

2. Scenery.

3. Climbing adventures.

Will the same system work for a speech to convince your cable television station to do special programming for Black History Month? It certainly will; talk about

1. Respecting and reflecting all members of the community and their heritage.

2. Excellent community interviews available.

3. Cable television's mandate for socially responsible programming.

Each major section has subsections so that you can work a considerable amount of information into your speech and present it clearly. To do this, jot down significant points for each main section, look for ideas or themes that go together, experiment with mini-plans, and you're ready.

FIVE-MINUTE WORKOUT

Practise taking an idea and breaking it into main ideas and supporting subsections. Soon you'll be able to do it quickly. If it's hard at first, remember that old exercise dictum—no pain, no gain.

Use your time on the way to work to do your mental exercises. Whatever you pass, whatever comes to mind, chart it into a workable plan:

- Is there a street musician on the corner?
  Instruments: guitar, accordion, saxophone.
  Success: money, crowds, general appearance.

- Did someone cut you off at the intersection?
  Reasons: Type A, fatigue, mindless wonder.
  Personality changes in a car: mean machine, status, eliminator.

- Having coffee in a doughnut shop?
  Doughnuts: calories, freshness, sugar powder on your face.
  Sociological studies possible: workers getting a sugar boost for the drive ahead, the homeless putting in time in a warm spot, regulars gathering for gossip and neighbourhood analysis.

Eventually, you'll be so good at this that the division of major topics will go smoothly.

ORDERING YOUR MAIN POINTS

The nature of your speech, the occasion and your common sense will tell you how to order the various sections of the body of your speech. Remember the audience—what order is best for them? Your aim is to approach the subject in a way that will make it easy for you to remember and your audience to enjoy.

1. Chronological order. Events that have a certain sequence, such as a marketing strategy or medical procedure, should be outlined in the order they occur. Reverse chronological order is also a clear way to organize your points. This approach is a natural one for detailing historical or political developments.

2. Flashback or flashforward. Add drama by starting at one point and casting forward or back in time to present the material.

3. Spatial order. If you're discussing the design of a wheelchair-accessible housing complex or the safest, most efficient arrangement of machinery in a plant, spatial ordering is most logical. Geographical order is easy to follow if you're outlining national concerns like weather or trade patterns, or tourist concentrations.

4. Cause-and-effect order. Do you want to illustrate the link between a smoke-free workplace and the reduction of employee sick days? Are you advocating the use of incentives to increase productivity or performance? How about free spay/neuter clinics helping to reduce the number of unwanted strays? Audiences are intrigued by this clear approach.

5. Reverse order. Two young chiropractors came to speak to a group of business people who have regular dinner meetings to discuss community concerns. The speakers wanted to get their audience involved so they started with a demonstration. With themselves as models, they showed postures and simple exercises that everyone could use during a working day and urged the audience to try them. Immediately, the group was active, involved and full of questions. Shrewdly, the speakers had question period next. Last of all was the theoretical explanation; by then the audience was more interested in hearing the theory behind some of the practical work they had just seen.

   For an audience with some common knowledge of the subject, this order works well. The group is involved and the atmosphere is one of lively exchange.

6. All-things-being-equal-order. Sometimes all the factors are equal and anything will work. Use the approach that makes sense and interests you.

7. When you're desperate. If nothing works, remember you can always discuss anything using the categories physical, emotional and psychological. It's an overused strategy but you may need it as a last resort. For example, the physical, emotional, and psychological

   • appeal of colour on cereal boxes;

   • impact of portable radio headsets in the workplace;

   • benefits of pets in senior citizens' centres.

SMOOTH TRANSITIONS

How do you move from point to point smoothly? Runners in a relay race know that the switch-over is a crucial moment, and they practise it often. In your speech, you need that same grace to move naturally from one idea to the next. If your overview is clear, your audience will know your main arguments and be ready for the switch. Here are words speakers use to make clear, logical transitions.

TRANSITIONAL WORDS

Adding a point

and	further	as well as
also	moreover	in addition
besides	another	by comparison
next	a second point	furthermore
or	likewise	in the same way
again	too	in addition

Emphasizing a point

above all	in fact	especially
certainly	to be sure	in particular
chiefly	without doubt	even more
doubtless	unquestionably	important
indeed	as my mother said	to repeat

Showing similarity

in like manner	in the same way	similarly

Introducing examples or details

for example	namely	specifically
for instance	such as	in particular
as you can see	that is	for one thing
to illustrate	the following	in fact

Restating a point

in other words	to put it another	if we look at it
in effect	way	from a different
similarly	in short	perspective
that is	that is to say	

Introducing a contrast or qualification

although	otherwise	even if
but	unlike	occasionally
conversely	while	whereas
however	yet	after all
despite	in contrast	admittedly
nevertheless	surely	in spite of
on the contrary	unfortunately	if
on the other hand	granted	still

Showing result/cause and effect

as	then	because
therefore	for	thus
for that reason	it follows that	since
accordingly	as a result	consequently
hence	so	

Showing connections in time

before	next	when
previously	tomorrow	thereafter
formerly	afterward	nowadays
once	immediately	then
earlier	soon	lately
now	in the future	eventually
presently	shortly	subsequently
meanwhile	at the same time	ultimately
at this time	simultaneously	final
after	at present	in the past

Indicating chronology or sequence

finally	in the first place,	moving along
first, second, third...	second place...	at the end
first, secondly,	at first	at last
thirdly... (don't	to begin with	finally
use firstly)	also	
next	then	

Concluding

(try to aim for something more original than "in conclusion.")

in brief	all together	consequently
as a result	as we have seen	accordingly
on the whole	to sum up	to conclude
finally	therefore	thus

with thanks to Robyn Knapp, Centennial College

MAKING THINGS CLEAR: ANALOGIES, STATISTICS AND VISUAL AIDS

Analogies help to make a point by offering a parallel example and asking the audience to make logical connections. Gerry Rogers tried to explain the neverending nature of political activity like this: "The whole process is sort of like doing dishes. They're never done—there's always another dirty dish! And it never stops. We have to continue to be vigilant."

Warren Burger, former Chief Justice of the U.S. Supreme Court, was once in a cab when the driver recognized him and offered his opinion on whether the justice system should rehabilitate criminals or just warehouse them: "You know, putting people in prison is like putting clothes in the wash without any soap. The clothes get wet but no dirt comes out."

A sports analogy works very well for public speaking. Good skiing and speaking have a lot in common; it looks so easy when you do it well. Only the speaker or skier knows the importance of practice, technique and coaching. Only she or he appreciates the rush of adrenalin that gives you the edge, the desire to go for it.

STATISTICS

Statistics are numerical facts; depending on how you use them, they can be clinchers or clunkers. When you use a string of statistics, even if they are impressive, the audience forgets the numbers before you are finished. Try for one or two astounding statistics the audience might remember. Even better, use stats on a human level. Consider these guidelines.

1. Do not overuse statistics! Gloria Steinem, in her book *Outrageous Acts and Everyday Rebellions,* confesses to "a habit that might be okay in articles but is death in speeches: citing a lot of facts and statistics." Her friend and lecture partner Florynce Kennedy told her kindly: "Look, if you're lying in the ditch with a truck on your ankle, you don't send someone to the library to find out how much the truck weighs. You get it *off.*"

2. Make sure statistics are accurate. Check different sources to make sure the statistics you are using are accurate and fair.

3. Use statistics comparatively whenever possible. There are fewer than 500 beluga whales left in the Saguenay River northeast of Quebec City. Their plight becomes obvious when you point out that a century ago there were 5,000.

4. Statistics should mean something to the audience. Isolated numbers will not make an impression, but examples will. In the case of the belugas, a marine mammal at the top of the food chain, recent

autopsies have shown levels of PCBs, cancer-causing agents, so high that the beluga corpses should be considered hazardous wastes.

The high rate of breast cancer in North American women is often lost when it is expressed as yet another huge number. It becomes very real when you say that one woman in 11, perhaps in 10, will develop breast cancer.

AUDIO AND VISUAL AIDS

A-V, as the techies call it, can add colour and drama to your speeches. In my experience, there are two rules you should always heed:

1. Back-up material is just that. It can never replace a good speaker.

2. Do it well or skip it!

Audio-visual material can enhance your presentation if you have spent your time designing and practising a clear, coherent, thoughtful speech. Choose your back-up material sparingly and ask yourself if it fulfils the following criteria:

- Is it necessary?
- Is it clear and colourful?
- Is it big enough?
- Is it a grabber?

When using graphs, charts, sketches and maps be sure that the colours are vivid and contrasting. The letters must be visible from a distance. Experienced speakers put their A-V material at the front of the room and then walk to the back of the room. The picture that looked perfectly clear when you held it in your hand is a tiny dot when you're in the audience. Remember, if it doesn't add to your speech, leave it out.

Do I sound negative? Perhaps just a little tired of people showing me tiny squiggles or trying in vain to pinpoint something on an overhead transparency? Why don't people practise?

On the other hand, speakers I admire use audio-visual material extremely well. Peter Jaffe says it keeps him right on track; he uses slides as reminders of his key points. Roberta Bondar is likewise enthusiastic: "There's nothing like seeing slides of the space program to make you feel enthusiastic. I find they're a good cue for you; if you know your material, you don't forget it.... If you're giving a general lecture, slides with a lot of writing can be distracting, but if you're giving technical talks, it's much easier to have the information on the slide than to ruffle through your notes to see if you've memorized something properly."

And yes, I do use slides and clips from video tapes both as a change of pace and as a way to communicate immediately. A set of slides from The Quilt or a video clip of first nations people talking about their experiences in residential schools is powerful. Again, the rule is to use only as much as you really need.

USING SLIDES AND OVERHEAD TRANSPARENCIES

In Chapter 9, there are checklists for using audio-visual material. For now, remember only the most important—and common—advice from people who use A-V material frequently:

- Practise your speech with the slides several times in advance.

- *Never* use material you've never seen or rehearsed with.

- Always carry an extra bulb, your own extension cord, and, unless you really trust the contact person, your own projector.

- Keep your upside-down or out-of-focus pictures for your own private shows.

- Explain the material as you use it. It may not seem as obvious to everyone else as it does to you.

- Have you ever felt frustrated as you watched the top of a speaker's head as he tried to find something on an overhead? Move to the screen to point something out on a slide, overhead, or film clip, and speak facing the audience. Do not talk to the slide or fumble with pointers or little flashlight arrows.

CRISIS CONTROL

Your speech and everything related to it is your responsibility. If you are using audio-visual materials, check that everything works before you are scheduled to speak. Trust no one but yourself when it comes to your speech!

Too many beginners suffer terrible humiliation as a result of the naive belief that technical stuff is someone else's responsibility. If your speech bombs because the machinery didn't work, who will look foolish—you or the unknown person who told you not to worry? It's your speech. Look after it!

THE SEVEN-DAY COUNTDOWN

Good speeches need careful design and practice. How do you practise speaking? OUT LOUD. OFTEN. The most common error speakers make is to agonize over piles of notes until the last minute. It doesn't work. This is a speech—your efforts should be on speaking. How do you calm yourself and make time to rehearse? Here's a seven-day countdown I made up years ago; I still use it when I get nervous.

THE SEVEN-DAY COUNTDOWN

Day 1:
- Check details with organizers.
- Talk to friends.
- Procrastinate, daydream, brainstorm.

Day 2:
- Brainstorm.
- Go inside yourself to discover what you really want to say.
- Formulate a thesis.

Day 3:
- Design speech—work on thesis and overview of main points.

Day 4:
- Add supporting arguments, examples, details.
- Make notes and start to practise.

Day 5:
- Revise notes; practise aloud.
- Do you like your speech?

Day 6:
- PRACTISE! PRACTISE! PRACTISE!

Day 7:
- Relax! Review notes one last time.
- Practise all or parts once more out loud.

GLORIA STEINEM

For more than two decades, Gloria Steinem has been a spokesperson and organizer for the feminist movement in North America. She was the founding editor of *Ms.* magazine, and has written, among other things, two bestselling books, *Outragious Acts and Everyday Rebellions* and *The Revolution Within.*

SB: You wrote a lot about your early "obsessive" fear of speaking. Do you like it now?

GS: *Speaking wasn't something I came to naturally or early in my life. It was late and difficult. If I had to choose a form of communication, I would always choose writing. But I have learned that there is something that happens in a room together, physically, that could never happen from a printed page.*

SB: People are reaffirmed when they hear you speak. It's a shared thing that's very strong.

GS: *I hope so. Perhaps that's partly a function of not having learned the "proper" way to speak because I never did really. My model of human communication is still sitting in a living room so I suppose that's good in a sense because you don't ever learn to "orate." You don't make the audience into something distant.*

SB: Do you still get nervous?

GS: *Yes.*

SB: What do you do?

GS: *I've learned over the years that you don't die which is the first lesson. Secondly, I try consciously to get my energy up and focus both on individuals in the audience and on what I'm saying, to try to lose myself in the content of what I'm saying.*

SB: How aware of the audience are you?

GS: *In many auditoriums they try to lower the lights so you can't see*

*the audience; I always ask them not to do that. I want to see peo-
ple there. Otherwise I start to imagine some disapproving giant.*

SB: So the audience is important?

GS: *Yes, and the kind of audience dictates to a large extent how nervous I get. The worst audience for me is an audience of establish-
ment males and the worst circumstance is one in which I have to
convince them on behalf of some very important issue. I feel
responsible not only for myself but for other people who can't be
there. I feel there's a lot resting on what I'm saying.*

    *The worst single instance I remember was addressing the
Washington Post editorial board. It's not a large group—fewer
than 12 people—and trying to get them to change their minds
and support the extension of the ratification deadline of the Equal
Rights Amendment. Kay Graham had asked me to do it and I got
completely nervous. I was terrible. I got that kind of dry mouth
where each tooth has a little sweater on it that you can't get your
upper lip over. My heart was pounding and I wasn't good and I
didn't convince them, and we won anyway.*

SB: Do you use notes?

GS: *Yes, I always use notes rather than writing a speech out word for
word. Unless it's a very formal situation like giving testimony or
a graduation speech.*

SB: But mostly you use notes?

GS: *To write it out word for word, you might as well send a letter.
There are things you think of or ways you express yourself while
you're standing there. The atmosphere and the circumstances
change what you say.*

SB: How much do you prepare in advance?

GS: *When I'm speaking on campuses or to community groups or for
benefits, I usually have a general idea of what I want to say.
Then I interview the people in that place, on that campus or in
that group, to try to find examples from the group. Even though
the points you make are similar, the examples will come from
that community.*

    *I never use the same set of notes twice. I make them over
again every time. I do repeat some of the same building blocks in
each speech, but each situation is different enough so that I make*

a different set of notes—although sometimes they end up drib-
bling off into scribbles.

SB: What speakers do you admire?

GS: *Eleanor Holmes-Norton is wonderful. She's very strong, very
powerful. She has a little bit of the Baptist Church with the style
of doing an incantation. I think she's very good. Alice Walker is
wonderful too, although she's a very different kind of speaker.
She does always write out in advance what she's going to do, but
that's a poet writing it out. It's different.*

SB: Do you think that women speakers differ from men?

GS: *Yes. I think women attempt to include the audience more. They're
much more considerate of the audience's time; that is, men wander on telling jokes, or making long pauses, or saying things that
are completely off the mark in a way that I think women are less
likely to do.*

SB: How did you develop your community newsline style? When
I heard you last year, you said you were bringing news from
women to women, news we didn't get from the media. You
acted as a rather extraordinary conduit for women's views.

GS: *I came to it in a natural way because I was travelling a great deal.
I often felt like a large bee carrying pollen from one place to the
next. I would be telling people in community X what people in
community Y had done to solve a similar problem, or sharing with
students on one campus what students had organized on another.*
   *I often found myself doing that in the discussion time and
then I started doing it in the speech itself because it was a way
of bringing in a lot of different subjects; it gave a framework in
which I could include a lot of things.*

SB: It works very well.

GS: *Often I've noticed that when we focus on one subject, we think it
has to be consistent. We often leave out the very thing that has
excited us the most in the last week. If we were sitting down
with a friend over coffee, that's the very thing we would tell her.
We need to make a place to include those things. If they excite
us, maybe they will excite others.*

SB: Women are often put down when they speak, not so much because of the substance, but because they're women speaking out. What advice do you have for people who are afraid of being put down?

GS: *Understand that you'll be put down for not speaking. When you approach a prejudice you can easily recognize it because nothing you do is right. So if nothing you do is going to be right anyway, you might as well do what you need to do. For instance, "if you're feminine you can't do the job—if you can do the job, you aren't feminine." Any double bind like that means that there's real prejudice at work.*

SB: Does speaking out have a lot to do with the achieving of self-esteem?

GS: *Yes, if you fail to use any part of yourself out of shame or fear, then the theft of self-esteem has begun. You have suffered the suppression of part of yourself. So, if you don't speak your thoughts, if you don't use your voice, your self-esteem is affected.*

SB: It is important to make the effort—even if it is intimidating.

GS: *Yes, and I also think that the physical stuff matters. You're almost always stuck in a room in which the structure is hierarchical—people are looking at each other's backs, and you're looking at them. I usually try to name it in the beginning and say that in what is usually a question and answer period, I would like others to speak, to help me overturn this structure, so that we can benefit from each other's wisdom.*

SB: How do you deal with those solid wooden boxes that pass as podiums and cut you off from the audience?

GS: *Sometimes you can break that down. You can sit on the edge of the stage, or stand to the side. But even if you can't change it physically, you can name it and say, "Let's figure out a way to change this together." That makes the audience already feel part of the process, not sitting there in judgement of you or just receiving whatever you say uncritically. Of course, the ideal group is one in which everyone can speak, which means a limit of five people.*

SB: But you try to approach that when you give the question period over to the audience. Many people who wish to speak have a chance.

GS: *That works quite well, and you know that it's going well if some-one on one side of the room asks a question and someone on the other side answers it. Because then the process is going on with-out you.*

But I think for me the ideal group is one in which everyone can speak right away, in which you're sitting in a circle and peo-ple go round and say who they are, and why they're there, and what they hope this meeting will bring. Just so everyone's voice is heard—because that immediately breaks down the hierarchy. It's amazing what a difference it makes if each person is heard from —even for just a sentence or two. It never ceases to amaze me.

SB: Anything else on speaking and why it has become a pleasure after the terror of the early attempts?

GS: *Not only is speaking different from reading because you are doing it in a group and communally (unlike reading a page when you're by yourself), but you also get a sense of intent and character from the speaker, from everyone.*

I never want questions written down. I hate that. Because you don't know what they mean as well as you do when they stand up and say it. Moreover, you're only hearing your own voice both reading the question and answering it. It's an unnatural human exchange. Every once in a while I get stuck with it. The worst thing that ever happened, and it only occurred once, was they not only had the audience write the questions out, but they asked them to write them out before I spoke.

SB: What is your advice to people, women and men, who want to speak, to be really good at it?

GS: *I think, first of all, each of us has a way of saying things, and things to say, that are unique: no one else can say them. That's our motivation for getting up there. I also think that there isn't a perfect model of what this speech should be like; there's our indi-vidual way of doing it. Once you take away the idea that there's a paragon we're supposed to meet, whether it's an ideal of physi-cal beauty or the way a speech should be given, then I think we put the power in ourselves instead of in external judgement.*

This is part of a large and endless and rich human conversa-tion. Some of that conversation will take place now in the very room that you are in, and some of it will take place 50 years from now because you spoke. It's the butterfly theory—even hard-nosed physicists acknowledge that the flap of a butterfly's wings here can change the weather hundreds of miles away. So your speech will have an impact through the people you speak to, in many other ways for who knows how long—forever.

Excerpts from Gloria Steinem's Speech

Toronto, February 7, 1992

In this speech, Steinem uses what she calls the "living room" model of discussion. She reaches out to the audience individually and as a group to share news and exchange information. She first calls on her audience to overcome the patriarchal structure of the hall and reach out to their sisters in the room and in the world.

Laughter and applause punctuated this speech; her organizer's deal was eagerly taken up; and the community meeting part was alive with different voices.

I know what I'm going to do with the rest of my life—live up to that introduction [given by Doris Anderson]. Thank you all for taking time out of your busy lives to come here and take a chance on a stranger, or an outside agitator or whatever I am. And because of your generosity, we have something very precious here tonight—we have an hour together.

So here's my plan. If all goes well, each of us, me included, will leave this room with one new organizing idea, one new troublemaking suggestion, one feeling of support, one new revolutionary comrade. In order to make that happen, I need your help. I need your help in overcoming this structure with you looking at each other's backs and me looking at you. It's a structure based on hierarchy which is in turn based on patriarchy which doesn't work anywhere, anymore, at all.

During what's usually called the question and answer period, I hope you will help me overcome this structure and turn this into the organizing meeting it really ought to be. Please be thinking what answers you would like to give us, not just questions, organizing announcements of upcoming troublemaking meetings this group should know about. If you'd rather not say it yourself, pass me a note, I'll read anything—I'm leaving very early tomorrow morning. Because as all feminists say, if we come today and there's no trouble tomorrow, we haven't done our jobs.

Before I talk a little more about the revolutionary potential of self-esteem, I thought I'd give you a few news bulletins from the States. I've been wandering around on this book tour. It's very different out there from what the media represents. There are a lot of smart, suffering people who are ashamed of a nation headed by George Bush and I would like to apologize for foisting on you, and on the world, Ronald Reagan and George Bush.

In fact, because the United States has such terrible and undue influence, it seems to me other countries ought to be able to vote in our presidential elections. I have a vision of CBS on election night saying, "Is Czechoslovakia in yet?"

.... Poor women and especially women of colour in both of our countries have always suffered from having two jobs. This is not new. They've always worked outside the home and in the home both. Now middle class women are suffering from the same problem, so perhaps now we'll do something about it. I suggest we need a new leap forward in consciousness similar to the one of 20 years ago which was to oversimplify that "women can do what men can do." And now we need to know that men can do what women can do. In fact, until men raise infants and small children as much as women do, women can't be equal in the world outside the home and children will continue to suffer the terrible punishment of fatherlessness, of growing up believing, whether we're boys or girls, that somehow men cannot be as loving and nurturing as women can, which is a libel on men. That divides up our natures into feeling we must put our identities solely in others if we are female, or being achieving in the world outside the home if we are male.

This, of course, is the beginning of the undermining of our self-esteem, the dividing of the self, the whole human self, into that which is acceptable to feminine roles, that which is acceptable to masculine roles, thus making each of us in different ways, to different degrees, feel ashamed of part of ourselves, that is our true and authentic self.

I think there is also a lot of misunderstanding out there in both of our countries. Essentially, young women are supposed to be the red-hot centre of feminist activity. Therefore, if there is some reluctance to call oneself a feminist in high schools, colleges and universities, this is taken as proof that the movement is going backwards. In fact, statistically, there are more young women willing and able to call themselves feminists than there ever were before.

But we must also remember that women's pattern of activism is the reverse of men's (except the men in this room of course). Women grow more radical with age and men grow more conservative with age. And it makes sense, when you think about it, because a young woman of 18 has more power, as women have power in a patriarchy, which means as a sex object, as a childbearer, as an energetic worker than she probably will when she's 50. But a man at 18 has less power than he probably will when he's 50.

Moreover, young women haven't yet experienced the great radicalizing events of a woman's life which are getting into the labour force and finding out what happens to you; getting married and discovering that it's not quite yet an equal partnership; having children and discovering that *makes it even less an equal partnership; and aging. If young women have a problem, I would only say it's that they think there's no problem.*

I want us all to know our history so we'll learn the lessons of organizing and struggle so we'll know how to win when we do meet barriers. I think it's great that young women have such enormous hopes and dreams because they're going to be mad as hell when they meet the first barrier. They're not going to be as passive as many of us were about giving in to all of this and thinking somehow it's all their fault.

Moreover, demographics are doing something interesting. There are increasing numbers of older women, at the same time the psychographics of rebellion are increasing among that group. For the first time, in the next 25 years or so, we're going to have a critical mass of older women who are uppity; who are difficult; who are accustomed to a certain amount of independence; who have become, as one of them said to me, "a woman who takes no shit." And that is where I think sociologists should be looking for the red-hot centre of revolution.

CHAPTER
4

THERE COMES A TIME:
TAKING A STAND

There is no innocence in the spectator.... If you're aware that something is unfair and plain wrong, you've got to act.

— *June Callwood*

It is pointless to make an important point in a boring fashion because it may be lost. It has to be made in an entertaining and dramatic way.

— *Eddie Greenspan*

▲▲▲▲▲▲▲▲▲▲▲▲

I t happens to us all—an issue, a policy, a family matter—something that causes us to take a stand. And when the subject affects us deeply, it gives us momentum and courage. How do you persuade people? First of all, you design the best speech you can. Then you deliver it with commitment. Your words, your eye contact, your use of notes, your presence—they all count.

If you really want to speak well, listen to the people who share their skills throughout the book and believe them! All the chapters in this book feature conversations with outstanding speakers but this chapter is a bonanza. There are four superb speeches—and the variety is remarkable: Rose Anne Hart, a former student of mine, talks about the golden rule; Thomas Coon, a member of the Grand Council of the Cree, explains his people's dependence on trapping; June Callwood, a journalist and social activist, gives a convocation address on the need to combat evil; and Edward Greenspan speaks out against the death penalty.

HOW DO YOU PERSUADE PEOPLE?

All speeches are persuasive; if you urge others to spend money on a major advertising campaign, adopt slo-pitch for their ball league or add anchovies to a Caesar salad dressing, you are persuading them. There are two important things for you to keep in mind:

- have something to say;
- make sure your commitment to the topic is sufficient to move your audience.

Your concern must be strong enough to give you the power to convince others. When you have a purpose you believe in, your commitment will give your speech credibility and strength.

Generally, your purpose is to move the audience to do one of three things.

- To adopt or change an idea. Convincing others that airbags should be standard features in all cars or exotic animals should not be kept as pets are examples. Once the idea is accepted, action may follow, but the focus of the speech is on the logical support of your thesis.

- To confirm or reinforce a concept or belief. Strengthening your audience's opposition to apartheid or their support of preservation of wilderness areas confirms widely held ethical and social principles. Does this type of speech always have to be so serious? Not necessarily. Convincing others that real Christmas trees are better than artificial ones, or that cats are better than dogs, are also themes I've heard lately.

- To adopt a course of action. A speaker concluded his presentation on Amnesty International by distributing information and forms for donations. Another asked group members to take out their drivers' licences and check the section concerning consent for organ donation. She asked everyone to give the matter deep thought and sign the form within 48 hours. In each case, the speakers gave good arguments and provided specific tasks for the audience to do. The time frame provided even firmer direction.

USE YOURSELF AS A TEST CASE

What persuades you? When the question of extraterrestrial visitors arises, for example, are you more convinced by the opinion of a scientist from NASA, statistics documenting the number of UFOs reported last year, or a first-hand report of one such encounter? Most people lean toward one type of proof or another and good speakers know that in order to touch all facets of each listener, and all segments of each audience, they must use a variety of appeals. The most common proofs are ethical, logical and emotional.

Look at your audience as a group of people who have come to eat at your restaurant. Some anticipate a good meal because they know the chef's reputation and appreciate the atmosphere of your restaurant. Others are more concerned with selecting food that will give them the balance of nutrients they require to be fit. The remaining diners are won by the meal itself: the presentation, the aroma, the taste.

In your speech, you require the same balance of credibility, solid information and emotional or gut appeal.

USE REAL EXAMPLES TO MAKE YOUR PROOFS CONVINCING

There is no better way to nail down each point than to give an example. References to real people, places, news events or job experiences familiar to your audience will help them understand your arguments. If you're talking about corporations taking responsibility for errors, compare the examples of the Exxon Valdez oil spill and the tuna boycott. Exxon's sluggish handling of the disaster resulted in public rage which remains undiminished; the name is still synonymous with messing up in a big way. On the other hand, Star-Kist, a company that faced a major protest by children and environmentalists concerned with the slaughter of dolphins accidentally caught in the drift nets, responded by changing its practices. In many supermarkets, you can now buy dolphin-safe tunafish.

People are less and less willing to accept statements that are not supported by good examples. Talk to people, read, use your own life to provide details to persuade your listeners.

ESTABLISHING CREDIBILITY

Your knowledge of the field and your qualifications go a long way in establishing your competence in the minds of the audience. Make sure that the program notes and the remarks of the person introducing you include any background information that will help. You can also forge links by talking about something in your own experience that shows you are trying to deal honestly with the subject at hand.

Showing respect for the audience is very important. Speakers who arrive on time, who are well prepared, and who have practised their speeches value their listeners. A speaking engagement is serious. You don't come to a business presentation with notes half-done and admit you threw a few ideas together in the car; don't do it for a speech. Take June Callwood's advice: "I assume I'm speaking to highly intelligent, well-informed people.... I prepare by giving a lot of hard thought to the audience, what experience they've got, and where they're at."

What is your intent? Your audience will wonder why you are so concerned. If you have personal motives, admit them. If you are presenting a plan that you believe is in the best interests of your listeners, make sure they know it. The more positively others perceive your motives, the more likely they are to listen to you.

What sort of impression do your words and your concern make on your audience? Do you cite reasonable examples? Are you fair in your treatment of opposing sides? Do your words include your entire audience, without making disparaging assumptions based on education, income, race or sex? Do you avoid belittling others? Are you committed to your own suggestions?

When you talk to people, you can have a direct impact on their lives. You may not think you're doing it, but your remarks can give others the courage to go on, a new idea, advice they need that very day. When you realize how important speaking is, the realization adds passion and energy to your words.

APPEALING TO THE HEAD <u>AND</u> HEART: USING FACTS AND EMOTIONAL APPEALS

What facts do you need? Consider your audience. Are you speaking to people who focus on dollars and cents? Will expert opinions convince them? Do some listeners have fears or biases that need resolving?

Once again, take the example of the woman who spoke on the need for organ donations. Her long-term goal was to make her audience more aware and supportive of organ donations; her immediate objective was to get them to sign their donor cards. She had done a thorough audience analysis: "I know Milene could only be reached with facts and statistics. Sanjay responds well to humour and Robyn would be looking to see if I had covered all the angles." She supplied statistics outlining the actual and potential numbers of lives saved and the reduction in health-care costs if donors are found quickly. A combination of humour, scientific fact and expert opinion helped her address the unspoken distaste some people have for losing parts of their bodies, even after death. Her conclusion was the clincher. In it she referred to the local drama of a small child who had waited for a transplant. Everyone knew the story.

WHICH EMOTIONAL APPEALS WORK?

The best advertising campaigns feature nostalgia, animals, love of family, examples of integrity, a sense of adventure and wacky humour. It takes skill and experience to assess which tactics work and which turn people off. You cannot manipulate your audience or take unfair advantage of their vulnerability. You can, however, make effective appeals to a wide variety of emotions. Here are just a few:

- protective instincts for children or environment;
- anger at insult or injustice;
- pride in a neighbourhood, firm or school, or in the audience's achievements or potential;
- competitiveness;
- empathy with and sympathy for individuals and groups;
- pleasure; and
- pride in having one's work or worth acknowledged.

GETTING YOURSELF READY

Last year I saw Gail Singer introduce her movie *Wisecracks* to an audience of 900 people in a packed auditorium. She told story after story about why she decided to make a movie about stand-up women comics (to disprove the myth that women have no sense of humour), and how brazen she had had to be to get agents at Cannes to view it. Gail Singer spoke to us like friends and accomplices; she told us her secrets, her hopes, her future plans.

Gary Potts, Chief of the Teme-Augama Anishnabe, also spoke to a group I was part of. He explained why first nations people and environmentalists had protested the development of the Red Squirrel Road in the Temagami region of Northern Ontario. The road would destroy the last stand of old growth white pine in that part of the province and it intruded on an area the Teme-Augama regarded as their birthright. Gary Potts's tone was low, unhurried; his determination unmistakeable. He spoke to us as possible allies, people worthy of careful explanation.

In both cases, these people spoke with their whole beings: their eyes, posture, hand gestures, the way they moved and paused. They centred their full energy on talking to us, reaching us—and they succeeded.

You can speak like this; it requires much practice to concentrate on talking to people, explaining things to them, rather than worrying about the next point you want to make. Good speakers, great speakers focus on forging the bond between themselves and their audience. When they succeed, you can actually feel the excitement of shared energy.

CIRCLES OF CONCERN

Jacinta de Joseph needed to give a speech at a dinner honouring social workers who had been working in the field for only a year. Immediately her long involvement in social work issues took hold and she was deep in a discussion of the responsibilities of their professional association. Her language and her issues were those of a person with long experience; they didn't match those of her audience. "Hold on," I begged. "Is this a dissertation or a dinner talk? These people are interested but not that much—you're not in their circle."

Picture the models of the solar system you used to draw: a series of concentric circles that grow smaller as they get closer to the sun, the heart of the system. Imagine the sun is your "heart issue," something you know and care a great deal about. Good speakers think about which circle their audience is in, how close they are to the subject. They talk to them there, with words, examples and intensity appropriate to their involvement.

If you have a particular point of view that is not generally understood by your audience, or is understood but not accepted, you have to work from the position where you and your audience have something in common and lead them gradually closer to your heart issue. If you neglect this step, if you speak only in terms of your involvement, you'll lose them.

The next time you design a speech, picture the circles in your mind—where are you? Where is your audience? Talk to them in their circle of concern and lead them to a fuller awareness of the subject.

FREEING YOURSELF

The new way of public speaking gives you an unexpected ally—the audience. The people before you want to hear your views, not to shoot them down, but to listen and compare them with their own experiences. Certainly, there will always be a few whose aim is to find fault but the majority are there to support you. Trust them. This is the new way of speaking—to give people a chance; to encourage, not intimidate. The audience has a responsibility to create a positive environment.

If what you have to say is important to you, believe in it! Believe in yourself and depend on the audience to help you. Ask them for support. Admit you're nervous. Change the seating so there is more of a group feeling. Take friends and know where they're sitting so you can look to them for reassurance. Listen for noise: hums of agreement, laughter. These people are with you. Speaking is changing because we are speaking to each other. Do not be intimidated by the size of the room; concentrate on the people. Reach out!

A NOTE ON NOTES

Once you have made notes, you have to use them. This seems self-evident but for some reason speakers who will read from a full script will not look at their notes. They equate notes with memorizing. It isn't so. Think of your notes as a grocery list; when you go to the store, you take a brief list: milk, cheese, salad fixings, avocadoes. You consult the list to see which items you need and if you forget to look, you find yourself at home without the very thing you went for.

So it is with speech cards: the highlights of your talk are there in order. A word, a phrase will remind you of the ideas you worked out and rehearsed. Take the time to look at them; it always seems longer to you than it does to the audience and soon you'll be able to do it so smoothly, they won't notice at all.

Inexperienced shoppers may need a slightly more detailed list: "1% milk, cheddar and ricotta cheese." And if they are very forgetful, a special notation—"old cheddar, not mild." What they do not require is a painfully detailed description: "The cheese section is distinguished by the word 'cheese' over the tray containing an array of various types of cheese. Find the flag that says 'cheddar' and you will note there are mild, medium, old and very old varieties...."

A foolish exaggeration, you say! How many of you have heard speeches in which an otherwise skilled person finds it necessary to read her own name? A popular veterinarian was speaking to a community group, about 20 of us, about work and role-modelling. She read the entire speech *including* the introduction, a brief biography: "Good evening, my name is Sheila Lee and I've got the only large and small animal practice in our region. I was born in West Bend and went to school in Stratford...."

This woman was nervous, too nervous to practise, too nervous to look up. Did she have to read her own name? It was a very distancing experience. Make notes and use them. Have a conversation with your audience; they expect your attention.

THE REHEARSAL

Once you have a firm idea of your speech, it's time to practise. Make a set of notes and go over your speech several times. Your aim is to have a good grasp of the main points and a sense of how the actual words will sound. Here are some pointers:

1. Know the grabber and conclusion well. These are the parts when it's essential to give full eye contact to your audience. Write them out in full if you wish—they took a lot of work—but use the writing as reference only.

2. Go over your entire speech three to seven times. You need to practise enough to be comfortable with the pattern of the speech, the flow of the ideas. All these rehearsals don't need to be aloud, just some of them. Develop the ability to look at your notes and know immediately where you are. It's important to do the entire speech several times—don't stop when your words get mixed up or it will seem to take forever. You may have to refine phrases or change ideas. If you sound confused, maybe you are. Work on it until it *sounds* clear.

3. Concentrate on the design, not the words. Get a feeling of the flow of your main points. With just a glance at your notes, you want to remember the story you're going to tell and the point it proves. Big, bright numbers will keep you on track—when you see the notation *#1: determination: story of Fox 40 whistle*—you know where you are in your speech and the point you wish to make. You want a feel of the overall design: the ideas and the order they're in. Don't try for the same words all the time; that's dangerously close to memorizing, the most alienating form of delivery possible.

4. Practise aloud for a personal sound check. Why? To make sure that the speech you hear in your head sounds as good out loud. Often, we're surprised by the very sound of our own words. You might have to change sentences or examples.

5. How does your partner/friend/colleague like it? Kitchen table rehearsals seem odd at first but they help. Ask people you trust to listen to you; they'll give you feedback about which examples work for them. They'll also tactfully mention nervous gestures of which you're unaware: hitching up your clothes, clicking a pen, fiddling with your glasses, jingling coins. As speakers, we often undervalue our own persuasiveness; friends reinforce the good points. I find this kind of practice hard but very helpful.

6. Practise with the actual notes. If you've made notes from a fuller script, or rewritten your notes, make sure you rehearse with the ones you will actually use. Notes are personal; we expect a certain order. Can you find the main points and important examples when you're under pressure? Is the numbering large and clear from a distance?

7. Include audio-visuals in your rehearsal. Your notes say "overhead 1." How long does it take to get the overhead in place?

Are the overheads clearly numbered? Is the significance of the visual to your speech obvious?

8. Time yourself. Finish on time. A few minutes over is normal; 25 minutes is boring. It can also upset the entire schedule of the event. Help the organizers keep to their timetable by keeping to yours. That's the purpose of your notes. If you add examples spontaneously, check your notes to see that you're still on track. Good speakers leave the audience wanting more.

9. Speak from the heart: use your own language. You should be able to deliver your speech and *feel* it at the same time. Find your own words; if anything is forced or stagey, alter it so that your personality comes through. Speaking from the heart means using words you understand and mean.

10. You can't be everything to everyone so BE YOURSELF! Whenever I make a speech I think of who will be in the audience and what my purpose in speaking to those people is. It's a combination of what I want to say and what they need to know. However, I sometimes get intimidated. Not long ago I was the keynote speaker at a conference I considered major. Indeed, I was so overwhelmed by who would be present, what should be said, what they might think, that I lost my focus. What did I do? I followed my own advice:

> calm down
> centre yourself
> talk about what you know.

SAMPLE OF A PERSUASIVE SPEECH

Rose Anne Hart

Rose Anne Hart was a student of mine. She's a college graduate, the mother of eight children, a community worker and a person now pursuing her third "22-year plan." Thoughtful and direct in most situations, she found it hard to talk to large groups. She used her natural skills as a story-teller to conquer her initial shyness and get involved in her material.

In her introduction, she heads off a "ho-hum" reaction and goes on to outline a clear three-part plan. In the last section of her speech, she anticipates being charged with oversimplification and provides a rebuttal.

I want to speak to you today about a very old-fashioned idea, one you've heard a thousand times. In fact, you've probably heard it so often that it's become meaningless to you. I want to talk about the golden rule, "Do unto others, as you would have others do unto you." I'm going to tell you a story to illustrate some of the errors we make in dealing with people, the consequence of these errors, and I'm going to tell you how to avoid ever making these errors yourself.

I had a friend named James; he was in his forties, had his own business, and was a loving and caring member of his community. I met James when we were both volunteers for a care-giving organization here in Toronto. I was a counsellor and he was in fundraising. In his spare time, James crocheted blankets for the people we helped; I remember one time he brought me a small red one and asked me to save it for a Chinese baby, because he had heard that to the Chinese red is a symbol of good fortune.

My friend was gay. He had many of the mannerisms we see parodied on TV and in nightclub comedy routines. He had a longstanding relationship with another man; they owned a home in the community; and they attended church regularly where they helped out with all the functions. At one point James's friend became very ill. In fact, the doctors told him that they didn't expect him to live very long. James phoned the church and asked the clergyman to make a housecall. The clergyman agreed, but a little while later, he phoned back and told James that he had thought it over, and he felt it would be giving scandal to the community if he was seen entering their home.

James's friend recovered, but James never did.

He fell into a depression which caused the breakup of his relationship and eventually caused him to take a bottle of sleeping pills. And as if that weren't enough, he wrapped a garbage bag around his head and secured it at the neck with tape. He was determined to die and he was successful.

Now, we all know that not every slight is going to have such tragic results, and we know too that James's death was not caused by a single incident but rather by a lifetime of small hurts piled one on top of another to form one unbearable burden. I don't expect my speech today will heroically save lives, but I would be delighted if it would save one of us from adding one more measure of pain to someone else's growing burden.

Being aware of the consequences of our actions is one sure way of guarding against ever having to use the saddest of all phrases, "I just didn't know." As the Roman philosopher Plutarch put it, "Boys throw stones at frogs in sport, but the frogs do not die in sport. They die in earnest."

I didn't tell you this story to make you feel sorry for James. I told you this story to make you think. When you meet someone who is different from *you because of nationality, or colour, or religion, obesity, handicap, or sexual orientation, before executing that clever imitation, before making that witty remark, before issuing that curt dismissal—think. Think about how you would want to be treated if your roles were reversed. If we follow this one simple rule, "Do unto others as you would have others do unto you," we can never go wrong.*

ETHICAL RESPONSIBILITY IN PERSUASIVE SPEAKING

Every time you speak, you have a responsibility to examine the ethical base of your remarks. When others give you time on their program, they accord you a special status. As a speaker, you hold a position of privilege and must consider what arguments are justifiable to prove your point. As you determine your own ethical standards, consider the following common guidelines.

1. Advocating dangerous or illegal behaviour is unethical. Arguing for the legalization of marijuana is one thing; suggesting that others use the drug is unacceptable. It is unethical to try to convince others to do something which may be harmful or unlawful.

2. Lying or suppressing information is unethical. Lying is universally unacceptable. During the Watergate crisis, Richard Nixon said, "I misspoke myself." His attempt to doubletalk his way out of a lie made the situation worse.

   If you know of major drawbacks to your plans, you must mention them and use the opportunity to present solutions or alternatives. This does not mean you have to include every single drawback or difficulty; common sense will help you make the distinction between a significant disadvantage and a minor problem.

3. Name-calling is unethical. Attacking another person or group by calling them names is unacceptable. A speaker who thinks he or she is speaking to a sympathetic crowd may attempt such inflammatory references as "welfare bums" or "liberal bleeding-hearts" but such attempts usually backfire.

4. Citing "technical ignorance" or "expert authority" as an excuse is unethical. If you are discussing reducing costs in your business and a colleague recommends using someone who sells soft-

ware at reduced rates, what is your response? What if your frugal friend says this person is a "computer expert" and knows what's legal or not, does that absolve you of the responsibility of verifying the legality of the action? Does your personal lack of computer knowledge make you any less guilty of wrongdoing?

What if you are asked to speak on behalf of a manufacturing company in your town that is in danger of being shut down? The company is accused of emitting PCBs, cancer-causing agents, into the atmosphere. However, they have several "expert opinions" that the emissions fall into the "safe" level. What is safe? Can you base your personal support on the reports of experts?

As Conrad Brunk writes in *Business Ethics in Canada*, "It does not follow... that the more facts you know or the more of the subject you have studied, the more *morally relevant* facts you know. Even in highly technical matters it is possible for the non-expert to obtain at least as good an understanding of the morally relevant facts as the expert. And, the non-expert may have a far superior understanding of the relevant moral considerations. Technical experts can be moral morons just as ethics experts can be technical morons."

JARGON AND BAFFLEGAB

Jargon is the language of insiders used almost as a short form to discuss common interests. Every industry uses it; movie theatres don't have commercials, they have "corporate trailers." When is jargon appropriate? When everyone shares the insider terms. If your objective is to present your ideas clearly and convincingly, *everyone* has to understand. Using jargon to impress people is inappropriate; such attempts at self-aggrandizement can fall flat. Such was the case with a conference organizer who said she was going to "kickstart a Q & A" after my presentation.

I admire people like David Suzuki and Tak Mak, two outstanding scientists who have no need to impress people with the esoteric nature of their studies. Rather, they concentrate on using analogies and language that everyone can comprehend. To explain how a T-cell receptor works, Tak Mak, one of the world's leading immunologists and the discoverer of the functioning of the receptor, uses the analogy of a handshake. T-cells work to keep the immune system of your body balanced; the T-cell receptor handshakes each cell in your body. "If it is a branch of your own tree," he says, "it's okay." If not, the T-cell receptor sends messages for help to destroy it.

This is an example of using language to include people; if you use jargon that excludes others, that interferes with effective communication, replace it with real words.

Bafflegab is worse; it is the piling up of words, especially long, impressive ones, to avoid actually saying anything. Bafflegab includes such devices as euphemism, substituting cosmetic non-specific language for direct words. Thus, you are not fired, you are "dehired," "released" or "non-retained." A fence becomes a "non-ecological boundary," and a world exposition features "guest relations facilities" (toilets) and "security hosts" (site police).

Listen closely and you'll find the phrase "at this point in time" a good indicator that bafflegab is being used. Airlines say "at this point in time, we're in a flight overload situation." *Translation:* the airline has sold more tickets than the plane has seats.

Similarly, the use of short forms or a series of initials like NFL, GNP, ANC, UFO, CEO, MVP, PMS, FBI, FLT is fine if your audience shares this shorthand. If there is a possibility they don't, use the entire phrase the first time around and then employ short forms. Once your audience hears you mention the African National Congress, they'll be ready for future references to the ANC.

IT AIN'T NECESSARILY SO: A BRIEF GUIDE TO INFORMAL LOGIC

One thing that causes audiences to fidget in their seats is a lack of sense. Logical reasoning is essential; it adds strength to a foundation of thought and good design. The most important step is simply to ask yourself, "Does this make sense?" Are the thesis, supporting arguments, examples and statistics reasonable?

As a speaker or as a listener, ask yourself if the statements being made are logical consequences of facts you know. Occasionally, something strikes us as not quite right but we can't identify the problem. Perhaps this brief summary of errors in informal logic will help you to recognize and beware of the most common pitfalls.

NAME-CALLING

Attacking a person rather than an idea is not a valid reasoning technique. Traditionally, this is called an *ad hominem* ("against the person") attack. Using words like "wimp" or "pinko" does not advance your case. If you have proof that a person advocating a gambling casino is a known criminal, that is a serious allegation and a sound attack on the proposal. However, gratuitous name-calling is irrelevant. It damages the credibility of the speaker.

GENERALITIES

Speaking about something in broad general terms suggests you don't have specific facts. A comment such as "All the studies show that children need two parents" is a signal that generalities are being paraded as truth. Have specific studies to back your points. Too general a statement leaves you open to contradiction.

CARDSTACKING

It's not fair to present your argument as if it's the only one. You don't have to argue the other side of the case, but you can't leave the impression that it doesn't exist. A balanced approach has more weight than one that stacks all the cards in your favour.

JUMPING ON THE BANDWAGON

"*Everyone* is doing it!" Despite what you told your mother when you were 13, the fact that *everyone* is shredding their pant legs and shaving one half of their heads is *not* sufficient reason for you to do so as well. It is deductive reasoning gone all wrong: all too often everyone *isn't* doing it. The group sampled may be too small to give reliable data; the research methods may be insufficient; the circumstances in which the members of the audience find themselves may be very different from "everyone" else.

RELIANCE ON TRADITION

This is another form of jumping on the bandwagon. The plaint that "we've always done it this way" is not a convincing argument. There may indeed be valid reasons for actions confirmed by tradition to be continued, but the pros and cons behind the tradition must be explored.

RIDICULING

Sometimes it is fun to make your opponent's ideas look ridiculous, and this can be part of a good argument. If it's your *only* tactic, however, think again. If in highlighting one facet of a position, you ignore other valid parts, your criticism of your opponent's position is weakened. Audiences sometimes throw their support to a speaker they consider to be under unfair attack.

EXPERTS

It's good to have experts to support your ideas, to have big names on your side. However, use experts with care. Be sure they *are* experts, recognized in an appropriate field and well known to your audience. Their comments must be up-to-date and appear free from bias. Balance your experts to include those who do not have such a strong identification *only* with the idea you are advancing.

Remember also that experts often conflict; your opponent may have an equally forceful expert to counteract your point. Thus, use experts only if they will really build your case.

If you are using an endorsement, that is, supporting your case with the statements of known authorities, avoid the appearance of bias. Be sure the endorser has some relevance to your cause and does not have an automatic obligation to support you. For example, a local group organized a panel to speak against the use of animals for laboratory experiments; it included *both* an animal rights activist *and* a fashion and beauty commentator.

CIRCULAR REASONING

Beware of circular reasoning, which doesn't really prove anything, and only brings you back where you began. If A is true because B is true, but the proof of B is A, watch out.

MISUSE OF ANECDOTAL PROOFS

Stories of how your cousin's divorce cost her the business she'd helped build, or how the lack of basics in your child's primary education ruined his chance at college, add force to your speech. But personal stories or anecdotes should not stand alone; additional reasons are needed.

CONFUSING OPINION WITH FACT

Take care to distinguish between facts and opinions and acknowledge the latter for what they are. Do not pretend that they are facts. Facts can be verified; opinions must stand the test of time to be found true or false. For example, fishing crews wear copper bracelets to protect them from arthritis and rheumatism. Is the effectiveness of these bracelets a matter of fact or opinion?

FALSE FACTS

The most logical, well-reasoned argument will crumble if it is based on false facts. Be sure your research unearths the most recent and reliable information to support your case, and evaluate your sources carefully.

FLAG-WAVING

Resist any attempt to convince people with an exaggerated appeal to patriotism. Good citizens support governments and organizations that use reason, not propaganda, to justify their actions.

FAULTY CAUSE AND EFFECT

If you are citing causes and effects, be sure that the cause does indeed produce the effect you claim. Have you considered all the variables that may lead to a particular result? Is it true that if you eat less, you will lose weight?

POOR ANALOGIES

Comparing your idea to something that the audience understands can be useful. However, be sure the examples and analogies you use do not detract from the credibility of your argument. For instance, is it auspicious to compare planning a wedding ceremony to mapping out a military campaign? Is marriage really war? Be sure the analogy works.

OVERLY EMOTIONAL APPEALS

Emotional appeals have a place in a speech, but not as the sole factor in a reasoned argument. A speech opposing nuclear arms that consists only of the spectres of nuclear winter, blasted landscapes and the end of the human race will offend, repel and alarm your audience. However, they may not be convinced. Avoid, as well, a maudlin approach, a sickeningly sentimental play for support.

CO-OPTING THE LANGUAGE

Using the language of a group to appear to agree with them will not work if your actions are at odds with your words. For instance, the manager of a timber company that clear cuts tried to overcome the opposition of an environmental group. In his presentation, he used words like "sustainability" and "biodiversity," the very practices advocated by his critics. And yet, his actions were quite different; he was using language to manipulate rather than communicate and it undermined his entire argument.

USING ISOLATED ABUSES TO ATTACK THE WHOLE POLICY

There are always individuals and groups who will abuse their rights. This is true of every aspect of our society from people who use student loans to finance their vacations to illegal immigrants posing as refugees. However, the fact that something can be abused is no justification for its being prohibited. The majority of the population will use the policy responsibly.

SPEAKERS' SPECIALS

In one of my desk drawers I stash clippings I know are going to come in handy one day: cartoons, political commentaries that are right on, quotations and household hints. I value this drawer—whenever I need just the right example, I know where to find it. This section is a speaker's repository of handy hints; you won't often have to speak as a group, make a campaign speech or talk to a hostile audience, but when you do—you may find just what you need!

SPEAKING AS A GROUP

Remember the game. "Choose the item that does not belong in this category"? Try it on this list:

1. holding a car wash to raise funds

2. organizing a blood donor clinic

3. stuffing envelopes for a mass mailing

4. making a speech.

You probably picked #4 and you're right. All the other activities involve working with others, either stuffing envelopes at a kitchen table or organizing the car wash with members of your organization.

Why not try the same technique with speaking? It works if you want to address an issue from several points of view. It's also effective if the situation is so daunting that the collective strength of the group is needed. We do so many things working co-operatively, why not speaking as well? The old way of speaking promoted the idea of a person alone in a room pondering mighty thoughts. Sometimes that works. But what about the kitchen table? What about planning a multi-faceted speech as energetically as you plan the car wash? Here are two examples.

RURAL POSTMASTERS FIGHT BACK

The federal government of Canada decided to close, amalgamate or privatize more than 5,200 rural post offices over this decade. A group called Rural Dignity spearheaded a campaign to debate with the senior administrators and fight the closing of rural post offices, the heart of small communities. One of the ways they did this was to ask me to go across Canada organizing the postmasters and their assistants, and members of community groups, to speak out. I was confirmed in my basic belief. *We are all good speakers.* Those who say they can't speak are often the ones who make the most moving remarks of all. When something touches us deeply, the words that come out may not be the most polished, but they are the most genuine—and often the most effective.

Newfoundlanders told me you had to have backbone as well as heart—courage as well as conviction—to face a powerful employer in a public meeting. And they did. Groups all across the country learned to combine their talents and their perspectives. They decided to speak in small groups, each person representing one aspect of the opposition: a senior citizen describing how necessary individual service can be; a town councillor outlining the economic value of the postal jobs to the community; postmasters demonstrating the need for confidentiality, training and loyalty to the community; townspeople detailing how important a social role the post office played in the daily lives of the inhabitants.

These group presentations took the same amount of time as one normal speech; the amount of time each person used varied according to her or his personal style. To see so many people willing to fight for their community, to rise up and make their views heard, was impressive. It made me realize how much their towns meant to them and how much small towns contribute to the well-being of the nation.

FROM BLACKBOARD TO BOARDROOM: TEACHERS RISE UP

What happens when a powerful supervisory group fires 28 non-unionized female support staff? In the past, the answer was often nothing. For a group of teachers' assistants in Northern Ontario, things were different; teachers came to their aid. A group of women staff members gathered at one person's home to talk with the TAs and plan strategy.

They were all distressed by the firings and the consequent danger to some students—it's no laughing matter to find a confused or handicapped child alone in the playground when it's −25°F. And they were upset by the callousness of the manner in which the women had been told of the cutbacks. They were also intimidated; they knew that if they spoke out, they would be accused of overreacting. Subtle reprisals would follow.

However, the teachers and secretaries were unionized; they knew their right to speak would be respected and they had faith in each other. Three of them volunteered to speak. The others pledged active support. A secretary spoke for one minute on how important the TAs were from her point of view; it was her first public speech ever and it was good: clear, precise examples, sincere and strong. One teacher spoke on how vital TAs were to her classroom and another spoke on the qualities of good assistants. The speakers were excellent. Their sincerity and even their nervousness impressed upon the audience the gravity of the situation.

What did both groups gain? A sense of self-respect. They stood up for what they believed in; they defended their co-workers and their community. As one of the TAs said, "I always knew I did a good job but before this, nobody had ever said they appreciated my efforts. It made me feel good as a human being to hear those women speak on my behalf." Three-quarters of them kept their jobs.

"PICK ME, PICK ME": THE CAMPAIGN SPEECH

By now you know my neighbour, Deb Murray, very well. She used the parallel of being picked for a baseball team for her campaign speech in her professional organization. The lessons she learned may help you as you prepare your own campaign speech.

1. Remain yourself. Do not lapse into jargon or stilted speech. Remember, your first aim as a speaker is to interest your listeners. Be interesting. Be organized. Speak from the heart.

2. A campaign speech is still a speech, not a shopping list. Organize your talk in the three-part format. Have a great grabber and a strong thesis. Most important of all, have a clear overview of your three main points and tell a story to illustrate each one. Your main sections can be:

   - you—your interests, beliefs, strengths
   - your professional experience
   - the challenges the organization faces.

   To focus more on the organization, discuss three major challenges and speak to each. You must, however, mention why *you* are well suited to deal with these issues.

3. Tough times in your organization? Yes, you can make references to the internal or external problems but judge carefully which approach is best. Remember your audience. If they've had enough of talking about the issue, approach it subtly. This time around, Deb Murray is going to announce that her lifetime aversion to cats has changed to grudging respect. Her reason? Cats always land on their feet and that's what her group has to do. Cats also love cream and, as always, Deb considers her organization the cream of teaching federations.

4. Do not, *absolutely do not*, read to people. They want to elect a person, not a stack of notecards. Make eye contact. Persuade them you're the one. If you can't look at a group when you talk to them, how effective will you be in a leadership position?

5. Give your listeners a sense of yourself. Tell stories that reveal a little of yourself to your audience. In the process, you'll sound relaxed, confident, likeable, funny, committed—just the person they should vote for.

6. Finish by reaching out to the audience. Enlist their support, talk about things you share, visions you hold. Finish strong!

7. Practise your speech. Go over it enough times that you can hear the conviction in your voice. It's all right if you also hear a few tremors; breathe deeply and go for it.

TALKING TO A NEGATIVE OR HOSTILE AUDIENCE

How do you define a hostile audience? Generally they are people who oppose an idea as vigorously as you support it. That's the key: *ideas* are in conflict, not human beings. By remembering that, you should stay clear of personal attacks and remarks that put down other points of view. Just because people do not agree with you, they may not disagree; they may be uncommitted. You can view the commitment of the audience to an idea on a sliding scale. Your aim is to bring the audience along the scale a little closer to your proposal. A 100% change of mind may not be possible *the first time* but you can attempt a process of gradual persuasion.

There are specific steps to remember in dealing with an audience opposed to your ideas.

1. Get yourself ready. What is your purpose? Do you want to add to the conflict or defuse the situation? If you go into the group in a combative state of mind, your body language will communicate your antagonism immediately. If you concentrate on a rational presentation of ideas, you are in a better position to convince rather than clobber your audience.

    Is your voice helping you? Concentrate on sounding courteous; use words that acknowledge the intelligence of your audience. Breathing exercises can help you achieve a sense of calm that extends to your voice; that evenness will gradually affect others.

2. Acknowledge your audience's position. A fire department facing new regulations that require them to hire minorities, vacationers forced to move to a smaller, less convenient hotel and home-owners facing expropriation are all naturally upset. Admit their distress and do not trivialize their situation by citing other, more dramatic crises.

3. Request a fair hearing. Try to agree with your audience on some points: the necessity of immediate action, the distress caused to everyone, the need for clarification. It's psychologically impor-tant to have something in common. Then firmly request a fair hearing. Most audiences are reasonable enough to give a fair chance to a speaker presenting an unpopular position.

   Explain that you have an ethical responsibility to present opposing ideas. If you can, compliment your listeners on their fairmindedness and remind them again that ideas, not individu-als, are in conflict. The search for a solution, not the passion of confrontation, should be the main objective.

4. Don't be intimidated. Every audience contains a few people who are waiting to criticize your point of view; they were programmed to be confrontational and they always will be—*no matter who is speaking*. If the whole group is negative, take comfort in the fact that your stand is important, your point of view is valid, even if it's unpopular.

   Do not argue with individuals; rather try to defuse the situa-tion by following some of the techniques Peter Jaffe outlines in Chapter 5: keep calm, keep explaining, tell stories that put you on a personal level with the audience and turn an aggressively phrased question back to the audience or the person who asked it. If someone heatedly disagrees with your stand on censoring violence in music videos, say to the person: "This is obviously an important issue for you. What would you do to control the violence?"

   Make your point of view well known, have proofs to back your ideas, but make it clear you're not up there for target practice.

5. Predict objections and take care of yourself. It's naive to assume that everyone will support such obviously good ideas as a guar-anteed annual income or a needle exchange program for drug addicts. If you realize that some people will be unsupportive, you'll be ready for those cold looks. Don't be put off by hostile

expressions or muttered comments. Somewhere you will find someone who will offer support; if necessary take a friend or share the platform with a colleague. You can also follow June Callwood's lead: "Usually, I find several faces that are sympathetic. I couldn't talk to a hostile face; I'd stop looking at that person. It would discomfit me too much. I look at fairly sympathetic faces, and I watch them carefully to see what's happening. I check them over and over again."

SAMPLE OF A SPEECH MADE TO A HOSTILE AUDIENCE

Thomas Coon, Grand Council of the Cree

Few issues are as explosive as the question of animal rights versus the trapping of furbearing animals. Thomas Coon, a chief of the Grand Council of the Cree and a member of Indigenous Survival International, made this speech outlining the need to protect native trapping rights and way of life. His audience included many members of animal rights groups.

Note the very personal introduction, the exchange of language, and his appeals to reason, to exchange, to non-interference. Coon provides background so that southerners can understand the native way of life and he draws parallels between native and non-native conservationists. This is a moving speech; it combines calmness of expression with the passion of belief.

> Sometimes, I feel that I and my culture, my tradition, my way of life are being questioned. This is why I would like to say a few words in my Cree language. Maybe you will learn some Cree words from me....

> Why is our traditional way of life tied down to the fur industry? There is always the concept of trading in the traditions of native people. I mentioned earlier that you must help each other, you must respect each other. In doing that, you trade. I trade my beaver with my neighbour and, in turn, he gives me moose meat. I trade my mittens with him, and, in turn, he gives me something else. That trading has always been there, and so has trade with the other parts of the fur industry—we do that. We trade the fur pelt for an income. And when Canada stops trading, then I will stop trading. The income that we get from fur pelts enables me to go to the trap-line when I am harvesting wildlife. But once that's gone, I will not be able to practise that, and many of our people will not be able to. You have now forced me, displaced me, from the land.

> The animal rights people... will not only destroy the fur market, but also our way of life, my culture. It will destroy my traditional life style. You

know, sometimes we really have to put ourselves in the place of the people who are suffering in order to get the real taste of pain and hardship. The families up north are very isolated, as I explained earlier, and they need this income and this market in order to survive. When we make presentations such as these, not only do we speak of protecting the market, but of protecting our way of life, our culture....

To me, wildlife is a gift of the Great Creator. These are the gifts of nature. Wildlife is the fruit of the land. Thank you.

SOARING

**"You reach out and you fly,
there isn't anything you can't do."**
—Rita MacNeil

If you've watched birds catch thermal currents and soar effortlessly in the sky, you'll know what can happen to speakers. If you follow the suggestions of the preceding chapters, you are ready for the thrill of catching the currents of audience reaction and soaring. Even more, you should be ready to *enjoy* it.

The secret lies in your preparation: the plan and the practice. By the time you're ready for a major speech, you know how to organize. Your notes are clear, colour-coded and precise, but there's more. *Advanced* preparation requires that you list your thesis, main proofs and supporting ideas the usual way, *and* list alternative or additional material on the side, in case it's needed.

Imagine you have prepared a speech on eating disorders for an audience of teenagers. However, as you circulate in the foyer, you notice a fair sprinkling of adults. Have you any information about parent support groups or anecdotes about families who were baffled for months by someone's odd eating habits? Get out your pen and jot down reminders of that information and **asterisk** them so you'll notice the addition.

What happens when inspiration hits? Two examples illustrate brilliant improvisation. A young man was speaking on shy rights, the need to protect the dignity of the reticent and scared-to-death. As he walked to the lectern, he suddenly ducked below it and started with the words, "I'd much rather make my speech this way than face you. Whenever I have to look at people to talk, I get so shy I can't say a word." He won his audience immediately.

A streetworker was speaking to a citizens' group on the financial reasons some people turn to prostitution. Looking at several obviously unconvinced men, she said, "Look around you. Can you be sure everyone here has enough money to pay the rent and buy food?"

Then, looking slowly at each member of her audience, she said, "I'm not so sure what I may have to do in my lifetime to care for myself and my children, and I'm not going to knock anyone else for what she or he may have to do to survive." She established very strong rapport with everyone in the room and the dissenters listened carefully to the rest of her speech. Agreement was not necessary, but open-mindedness was.

How do you soar without wiping out? Here are a few pointers. I can tell you from experience that you sometimes surprise yourself with how *good* you are. It's a wonderful feeling. That's the fun of public speaking: the hours of practice and the connection with the audience make great flights possible.

WATCH YOUR AUDIENCE CLOSELY

The way your audience sits, nods, nudges each other and talks to you with their eyes gives you clues to their reaction to your ideas. If you touch an unexpected nerve, there will be visible signs of agreement. Laughter is a sure indicator. Unconvinced audiences may respond to a plea for a fair hearing; watch the body language. Choose faces and eyes that will support you and give you a fair indication of how you are doing.

HAVE EXTRA MATERIAL ON TAP

Pretend you're a musician doing a set in a club. You know the musical taste of the regular clientele but you still have a list of "extras" and "standbys" taped to your guitar. Always have a few extra examples or proofs handy.

HAVE FAITH IN YOURSELF

You are good. Trust your own thoughts and feelings and experiences. Put a part of yourself in your speech; share something of yourself with the audience. You owe it to them to be honest and up front. And remember that everyone can rise up, everyone has the capability of making accurate, moving, convincing, superb speeches. When you decide to tell a story that just came to you, or you remember yet another and better proof, go for it.

USE YOUR PLAN

You knew it! First I say "go for it"; next is "use the plan." The plan is there to make sure that you come back to the topic, back to the thesis, back to the *reason you are speaking*. You may get carried away by your own remarks and get confused. "What was I talking about?" The notes tell you. Make good, clear notes and then use them! Pause and look at them. Good notes also help you to—

FINISH STRONG

Save enough of your energy and enough vocal power to come to a clear, convincing conclusion. Put your whole heart into your conclusion.

By now you know the secret of soaring is to prepare for anything. That way, if you want to improvise, you have the skills to do it. Your confidence will impress your audience and your reason, wit and logic will convince them.

THE 24-HOUR COUNTDOWN

In Chapter 3, there is a seven-day countdown; here's a 24-hour countdown. Let's assume you are speaking at 10:00 on Wednesday morning.

24-HOUR COUNTDOWN

24 hrs to go
Tuesday
10:00 a.m.
- Make a final copy of notes.

11:00 a.m.
- Rehearse with those notes.
- Make sure of examples.
- Wow your partner, friend or cat with your delivery.

11:30 a.m.
- STOP CHANGING THINGS!
- Experimenting's over; this is it!
- Concentrate on delivery.

22 hrs to go
12:00 noon
- Take care of yourself.

14 hrs to go
8:00 p.m.
- Your lucky friend hears the speech again.
- Which anecdotes work best?
- Can he or she identify thesis and overview?
- You need feedback and praise!

12 hrs to go
10:00 p.m.
- Relax—STOP PRACTISING!

2 hrs to go
Wednesday

8:00 a.m.
- Get ready: check notes are in order

1 hr to go
9:00 a.m.
- Start deep breathing for control
- Listen to yourself: is your voice relaxed?
- Rehearse introduction, conclusion and any hard spots.

BLASTOFF!!
10:00 a.m.
- BREATHE. RELAX. GOOD LUCK.

JUNE CALLWOOD

June Callwood is a journalist, novelist, indefatigable speaker and fundraiser. She founded Nellie's, Jessie's and Casey House in Toronto, and was an early advocate of palliative care. Her energy and her generosity are outstanding.

SB: Why do you speak? You must spend almost all of your personal time speaking.

JC: *Well, I turn down 15 to 20 speeches a week. I give them for two reasons: it's for a cause I support, like the opposition to the censorship bill, or for palliative care, or better services for children, or the problems of poverty and homelessness. I frequently speak at fundraisers for battered women's shelters.*

Public speaking is also my pension fund. As a freelancer, without a company pension plan, I have to plan for my own retirement, and I am paid for a number of my speeches. As an older woman, it will be a good income for me.

SB: You speak well to audiences made up of people of very diverse backgrounds. How do you approach your audiences?

JC: *I make a lot of assumptions. I see it as a very personal relationship, and that a belligerent or scolding tone, hectoring, or a critical approach is going to mean you're not going to be heard. People aren't going to listen to you.*

I also assume that no matter how people look (and I don't mean their physical appearance but the stoniness of their faces, or the fact that they don't look like an interesting group), there's going to be a lot of surprises. I never underestimate an audience. I assume I'm speaking to highly intelligent, well-informed people. I also make the assumption that they share my views, as long as I stick to the ethical component which is responsibility for one another. I urge them to open themselves to participating in their society more fully. It's a gentle message but it's very, very important.

SB: What public speakers do you admire?

JC: *Eddie Greenspan is probably the best in Canada. Alan Borovoy is dynamite; Julian Porter is a remarkably fine speaker. I once heard Ralph Nader, and understand why he is such an important consumer advocate. He's a great speaker. Rosalie Abella is one of the best speakers anywhere.*

   Pierre Berton is compelling; you pay attention. It's his size, the big voice, and big thoughts. He has a big view of the country that he communicates.

SB: How well do people do at introducing you?

JC: *I've had some awkward ones, including the ones where they get your name wrong. One student at the University of Toronto, Scarborough College, introduced me as the founder of NATO. It was a bit much. I have also been thanked and introduced with wonderful elegance.*

SB: How do you prepare for a speech?

JC: *I work only from notes. I'm getting five honorary degrees this spring, and four would like me to do the convocation address. They also want a print copy of the speech—but I don't have one. The second speech I gave was entirely written, and I nervously read every word. I found that I'd left the last page on the seat where I'd been sitting. I had to leave my seat and come down the stairs to get the page, and I've never had a written speech since. I prepare by giving a lot of hard thought to the audience, what experience they've got, and where they're at. I don't want to patronize people with information they already have.*

   I think about what kind of expertise I'm addressing and where it is that I've got anything that's useful or helpful. Most of the time, you're there because someone on the planning committee thought you have information that is useful for the group. They don't always know exactly what it is, but you take their ideas, and add your own judgement of where that group is at, and what would be useful to them from your experience, for you to talk about. I write in note form, sometimes full sentences, on folded pieces of white paper. Never any longer than five sides of notes. Just one word will sometimes remind me of a story. I take care with the opening and with the end.

SB: Can you see the audience when you're speaking to them?

JC: *Yes, I watch carefully; I watch faces. Usually, I find several faces that are sympathetic. I couldn't talk to a hostile face; I'd stop looking at that person. It would discomfit me too much. I look at fairly sympathetic faces, and I watch them carefully to see what's happening. I check them over and over again.*

SB: Do you regret any of your speeches?

JC: *In Halifax in the late 60s, I spoke at a luncheon for couples attending a service-club conference. It was a time when everything was very open and I was still in full stride as a hippie. They seemed very stiff and uncomfortable so I said to them let's touch one another, let's care about one another. People cried and gave me a standing ovation, and I felt I had manipulated them. I was sick with shame. Of course everyone is lonely, and people need to touch. To have pulled a real evangelical trip on them was inexcusable. It's easy to make people cry when you touch their loneliness but it's unethical. You open them all up, and when it's over, you're on a plane. To my credit, I knew it was awful and never did it again.*

SB: Do you still get nervous?

JC: *Some audiences. The convocations are nervewracking. I didn't finish high school, and was intimidated being at a convocation at all. I'm nervous of extremely well-dressed people; it always has bugged me. When I was a kid we were awfully poor, and clothes were a way you could tell we were poor. Teenagers with better clothes always made me feel vulnerable, and I envied them, so a room of extremely well-dressed people still makes me feel vulnerable.*

  I really sweated over a speech to the Canadian Bar Association, Ontario. It was a very prestigious group, and I worked all day trying to figure out what would be of interest to them. I spoke on altruism.

SB: What speech do you remember?

JC: *Psychiatrist John Rich, a friend of mine, once said there are two kinds of people: the ones who remember only their mistakes, and those who remember only their victories. Lamentably, I only remember the duds.*

  If I've misjudged things, or been picketed and gotten distraught, been attacked in question periods, I can't forget. I don't rise to that kind of challenge, I sink. I have a resilient ego, and I don't take it personally, and I believe they're wrong, but I can't take the anger in their looks, the bitterness. It's how they behave when they attack: the lack of compassion, humanity, generosity and civility. The bad manners depress me terribly. It's much more complex than what they're attacking; I feel the same way when they attack someone else.

SB: What advice do you have for beginning speakers?
JC: **Be prepared! Know the content.** The most nervewracking thing in the world is not being sure of what you're doing. It's awful to get up with notes half done, poorly phrased, not well thought out. It's terrible to get halfway through and have nothing more to say.

   Get the material ready and be sure you know it. Whether you're using notes or a prepared speech, be absolutely comfortable with it. You're going to be uneasy anyhow the first few times, so concentrate on knowing your material.

   You know your subject; you have a good reason to be there. Take heart from the fact that people asked you to speak because you do know your subject.

   People don't want to see you fail; nobody enjoys a speaker's pain. The audience takes no pleasure at all when a speaker can't find a place, or the voice or paper shakes. The audience feels so uncomfortable. They don't want to watch you make a mess of it. They yearn for you to do well, they're totally on your side, and there's very positive energy going for you.

JUNE CALLWOOD

Speech: It Might As Well Be You
This is a convocation address given at a community college. June Callwood spoke from brief notes, and used humour to engage her audience and build rapport.

   I take my cue from our oldest child's graduation 21 years ago from McGill University. When I asked her about the convocation address (which I missed while taking our four-year-old to the washroom), she replied, "It was superb. It was ten minutes long!" So, that's what I'm aiming at—to give a superb address. You'll be comforted to know.

   You'll notice I don't wear anything that indicates I graduated from anywhere; I didn't get enough education to qualify for this school, let alone graduate from it.

I hasten to assure all the graduates that not a moment you have laboured to reach this achievement has been wasted because the world is vastly more complex and alarming than when I began to work on a newspaper when I was 16 years old.

You've mastered technology, you're full of facts, and most important of all, you've learned how to learn. That's a process that begins with the awareness that there is something you need to know, then enough organizational skill to give that gap a heading so you know what it is you want to find out, some library skills to find a resource centre or a resource person, the nimbleness to assimilate and substitute.... So you're all set. Also you must be terrified. I've heard nothing but how few jobs there are—it's a most encouraging way to start a convocation. There is the yawning unknown that begins tomorrow, and that really is not so much a question of a job, but what kind of life you'll have. I can't speak of jobs and opportunities—I've been a freelancer for 41 years. I know a good many of you, maybe all, will succeed despite the odds. You may find another career path. But nothing is lost in the universe; whatever you've learned now— nothing is lost.

However, I can speak with some authority about how devastating it is to be a young person, to feel injustice as acutely as young people do, to have ideals, to believe that there is honour and consideration, and compassion, and that's what you want for yourselves....

What I ask is you don't lose that empathy. No one, no one is really a stranger to you. The commonality between men and women—and I'm a feminist; this is what a feminist looks like: this is the profile of a feminist, this is full-face, this is a feminist!—but there is commonality between men and women, between the races, and between religions, and between your parents and yourself, and between workers and management. What we all share is our vulnerability and our mortality. In that sense, there is nothing between you and anyone else you know, or have ever hated, or have ever admired. You're made of the same substance. You can be warm and caring but you've got to trust that people are like you, that inside people are alike. They have the same fears as you have. We humans are a tribe, we're herd animals. And we need one another, we need to trust one another, and we need one another's kindness.

One thing more. Hannah Arendt said this, it is the thing that has meant the most to me. When she was analyzing the evil of Eichmann during the holocaust, she looked to find the essence of evil. What is it? Six million people killed. What is the essence of that magnitude of evil? She came to the conclusion after a long time that the real evil is not so much what Eichmann was. The real evil was the apathy of people who did nothing, who were spectators.

*That's what I want to leave with you. There is no innocence in the specta-
tor. If you do not get involved in an accident, in a racist or sexist slur, or
someone being even mildly humiliated, or someone in need. If you don't
get involved, you are as much the cause of what is happening as the person who is actually doing it. If you're aware that something is unfair and
plain wrong, you've got to act!*

*You have to be non-violent, I think; you have to be calm, you have to be
resourceful, but don't just stand there. Everyone longs to be the good
person that is inside, and there is a splendid person inside. That's the person we want to come out, but it takes a little practice....*

*You start by helping a small child who is sobbing away about a broken
crayon. Easy to do, eh? Then you politely tell someone it's not fair to cut
in on a line-up for a movie. Then you protest in some visible way the pol-
lution in the drinking water. And so on.*

*Eventually you save the world. And if someone has to do it, it might as
well be you.*

*I salute you. I honour and I treasure you. May the wind ever be at your
back and the sun on your face.*

EDWARD GREENSPAN

Edward Greenspan, Q.C., is a defence lawyer renowned for his
championing of the underdog and his outspoken opinions of the
Canadian justice system. He is an entertaining speaker, and his clarity and wit make him a favourite commentator and TV host.

SB: What makes a good speech?

EG: **It must entertain.** *It is pointless to make an important point in
a boring fashion because it may be lost. It has to be made in an
entertaining and dramatic way.*

A good speech must be made in fairly simple language.
*It's senseless to use words that are not generally understood.
Maybe it's my training as a lawyer; I recall using the word "sur-
reptitiously" when I was addressing a jury, and I saw glazed looks
on the faces of the jury that caused me to conclude that they
didn't understand what I meant by that word.*

*When I'm addressing a gathering, I assume that I'm talking
to bright high-school students, always. In law school, in writing
law exams, we're told to write as though we were trying to explain
complicated legal principles to a bright 13-year-old. That's a
good rule when you're speaking—speak to a bright 13-year-old.*

***Making an analogy is vitally important to making your
idea understood.*** *It helps people know precisely what you mean.*

Humour is something I always try to inject. *No matter how
serious the speech, even when I was debating the death penalty,
if it was à propos I would make a humorous reference. In the
case of topics that are simply not funny, like the prosecution of a
hatemonger like Ernst Zundel, no jokes. There are things that
are too serious for any levity at all. For some reason, occasional
jokes during the death penalty debate were acceptable. But
wherever humour can be injected, I will take advantage of it. If
you lose your audience, speaking is a waste of everybody's time.*

*But if you're going to use humour, the depth of the rest of
your speech has to be that much better. You cannot keep the
speech at a superficial level or you're underestimating your
audience.*

SB: How do you prepare for a major speech?

EG: *Because I speak often, if I am attracted to an analogy that I read
in the press or in a book, or if I hear it on the radio or on television, I will make a note of it. I collect what I think are good examples of whatever point is being made. Of course, it is always on
legal matters. If I am given the task of addressing a group on a
certain subject, the first thing I do is gather up the major works
on that subject and I read them, so that I'm not missing some
issue or point relevant to that topic. I also read minor works or
essays so that I am fully aware of competing or opposing views,
and take from that material quotes that best sum up what the
writers are trying to say. I dictate a summary of my interpreta-
tion of what I have read. Then I outline in point form, what the
key issues in the area are, pro and con, and from that, I determine*

*what my views are relative to all views on the subject. That is, I
look at the popular position on any issue and look to the position of its detractors and dissenters and I try to determine where
I stand. I end up with a summary of the main issues and a clear
statement of what my views are on the subject. I then go to the
material I have collected to see if I can find any quote or story
that is appropriate and then I sit down and dictate my speech.*

SB: Do you like to know about your audience in advance?

EG: *I like to know the type of people I'm speaking to, in a general
way, so that I know where their interests lie and what part of the
community they reflect. Oftentimes while I'm there and I sense
the mood of the audience, I may change some of the examples
that I intended to use. I always speak to the head-table guests to
get a flavour of the organization and the audience.*

SB: How do you explain unfamiliar terms?

EG: *If I'm talking about a concept, like a rehabilitation model of
punishment, I won't use any expression unfamiliar to the general
public. Or, I'll stop and explain, I'll go back historically. If I'm
talking about the rehabilitation model, I'll go back and explain
how prisons began and why we have them. For a long time, we
thought prisoners were sick and needed to get better. Those theories have been questioned over time. I don't assume that the
audience is familiar with the subject of the speech.*

SB: What errors do speakers make?

EG: *Speakers often use terminology that they assume the audience
understands when, in fact, they don't. Speakers lose their audiences that way. They use those words to impress others with
their knowledge and erudition, and it's absolutely ineffective.
Lawyers do it; they love to use words like "purport." Now, I've
never sat in a bar and heard anyone use the word "purport" in
general banter. And so, I never use that word. I don't need to hide
behind my words, to say words that make me sound smart.*

SB: Do you get nervous?

EG: *I get anxious every time I speak. When I stand up, it's a question
of trying to win the audience. For the first five minutes of my
speech, I run the big risk of telling jokes; there's nothing worse
than a joke falling flat; recovering from it is very difficult. Yes,
I'm apprehensive about every public speech I give. I want the*

audience to be entertained and informed. Working toward that, I
will always look at my entire audience as often as I can, trying
to bring them all into the speech.

SB: Do you have notes?
EG: *I have notes. I write my speeches out in longhand or dictate*
them and they may go through two or three revisions. I learn my
speeches. I also have very good peripheral vision; I can look at
an audience and see my notes at the same time.

SB: Can you tell if a person is telling the truth?
EG: *I don't think that I'm any better or any worse than anybody else*
at the difficult task of trying to figure out who is telling the truth.
Every person has to make those decisions every day; if you talk
to a car salesman, you have to determine if he's telling the truth
or not; if you ask a waitress or waiter what's good on the menu,
you have to decide if they're telling the truth or not. You have to
learn to trust or not to trust what's being said to you by the
demeanour of a person or other things that help you in your truth-
seeking mission. When you watch television, you have to decide
if you're being told the truth or not during every news report.

SB: What don't you like in speeches?
EG: *I don't like the heaviness of some speeches in which people wade*
through statistics. If you can't prove your point simply by making
an analogy from the statistics, and you go on and on, the audience
just listens to large numbers.

SB: What speech did you enjoy giving?
EG: *I enjoyed speaking to the Empire Club about the role of the*
defence lawyer. There was a good feeling in the room, and the
Empire Club is the World Series for a speaker. In fact, I said that
to them, that I could now die and go to heaven having reached
the height of a speaker's goal, addressing the very prestigious
Empire Club. I think people really liked that. They like honesty,
humility, sincerity and self-deprecation, a very Canadian char-
acteristic. I think it's important to make the audience happy and
feel good.
    But let me also point out that I've said things to audiences
that they clearly don't like; in fact, I may infuriate and I may
upset. But they don't walk away not liking me or not talking
about what I've said. I think it's important to be controversial

and to cause an audience to think about how they feel about the subject matter. I will never hold back from my audience my true feelings on a subject and I will not tone down my language to the point where my beliefs are not crystal clear. I will call it as I see it. I owe that much to my audience.

EDDIE GREENSPAN

Speech: The Futility of the Death Penalty

In 1987 Eddie Greenspan spoke out against the death penalty in a series of nationwide appearances. This is an edited version of that speech. Note especially the power of the conclusion.

In Canada, capital punishment was abolished in 1976, but it has never lain still in its grave, and continues still to raise its ugly head from time to time. Each time a police officer or prison guard is killed, we hear a clamour for its return. . . .

It is my purpose to hopefully persuade you first, that capital punishment is no deterrent to crime and therefore an unjustifiable weapon to deter potential murderers, and second, that the state wants to continue to kill its victims, not so much to defend society against them—for it could do that equally well by imprisonment—but to appease the mob's emotions of hatred and revenge.

. . . To attempt to abolish crime by killing the criminal is the easy and foolish way out of a serious situation. Unless a remedy deals with the conditions which foster crime, criminals will breed faster than the hangman can spring his trap. Capital punishment ignores the causes of crime just as completely as primitive doctors ignored the causes of disease; it is not only ineffective as a remedy, but is positively vicious in at least two ways. In the first place, the spectacle of state executions feeds the basest passions of the mob. And in the second place, so long as the state rests content to deal with crime in this barbaric and futile manner, society will be lulled by a false sense of security, and effective methods of dealing with crime will be discouraged.

. . . And yet some people misperceive rising crime rates and say that if we had capital punishment—if we could literally put the fear of death into these criminals—the problem would all go away. Now that doesn't make sense, of course. Crime rates have nothing to do with capital punishment. In this capital punishment debate you will hear lots of statistics. You will hear people talking about crime going up and crime going down when there is or is not capital punishment. This is not a topic where it is possible to find the one definitive study which concludes, once and for all, that

capital punishment is a deterrent, has no effect, or, indeed, that it cheapens life and encourages people to kill.

... It is easy to be in favour of revenge in the abstract. But if something happened to someone you know, and that person got angry with another family member, went out and purchased a weapon and killed his victim, would you really want that person—automatically—to be hanged? Don't think about it in the abstract; think about a real person. We don't hang abstractions, we hang real people.

... Now some people say capital punishment is justified because it prevents a murderer from ever again committing the same crime. In Canada, less than 10 people who have been found guilty of murder by a Canadian Court were ever convicted of murder again.... No one knows whether visualizing and hearing of the effects of punishment of one deters others or induces others; or whether, even if it served to deter in this particular way, it might not render men, women, and children callous to human distress.

Only one thing is certain about capital punishment or its effect—that it is administered for no reason but deep and fixed hatred of the individual and an abiding thirst for revenge. Are we so lacking in hope for the human race that we are ready to accept state-sanctioned vengeance as our penal philosophy? Capital punishment is too horrible a thing for a state to undertake. We are told, "Oh, the killer does it, why shouldn't the state?" I would hate to live in a state that I didn't think was better than a murderer.

There isn't, I submit, a single admissible argument in favour of it. Nature loves life. We believe that life should be protected and preserved. The thing that keeps one from killing is the emotion they have against it; and the greater the sanctity that the state pays to life, the greater the feeling of sanctity the individual has for life.

We stopped taking human life in 1962. That's the last time the hangman in Canada practised his terrible trade. And for those of you who regret that situation—who lust for the return of that rope, let me remind you of this: Donald Marshall was convicted for a crime he did not commit. Which of you, sitting here today, could have pulled the bag over his head? Which of you could have fastened the rope around his neck? Which of you could have sprung the trap door which sent Donald Marshall to his death? Because that is what capital punishment is all about. It's not just another news story on page 10 of your newspaper. It's the coldblooded killing of a human being. The next time you hear that bloodthirsty cry for revenge, I ask you to remember that.

CHAPTER
5

DON'T HOLD BACK:

TOUGH TOPICS, QUESTION PERIOD
AND EQUIPMENT

In my mind I have a responsibility to speak out on the issue of violence in the same way that my parents wished more Germans had spoken out, had taken those risks back in the '30s.

— *Peter Jaffe*

This morning my doctor called to reschedule my appointment; her incest survivors' group was holding a special meeting that she wanted to attend. For a moment I couldn't concentrate on the alternate time she was suggesting. I was too startled, too busy trying to deal with her unexpected disclosure. This is what I call buzzing. For many people, talking about tough topics—incest, rape, child abuse, wife assault, HIV/AIDS—causes a physical reaction to set in. For some, it's a visceral or gut feeling; for others, it's a mental buzzing. We can't hear what follows. Depending on how powerful the impact of the words, we may not be able to concentrate for the next few seconds or for the next few minutes. Our nerve endings are abuzz with the power of certain words.

THEY'LL HEAR YOU WHEN THE BUZZING STOPS

In the last ten years, many social agencies have participated more actively in the field of public education. From presentations in schools and businesses to community information nights, volunteers and professionals speak on a variety of difficult topics. But there is a difference between speaking and being heard! Specific strategies are needed to discuss emotionally demanding or frightening subjects. Let's be very clear, this is not counselling in clinical areas; this is public speaking, presenting your material in a public forum.

Dana was a colleague of mine who volunteered in a hospice which provided a haven for people who were terminally ill and wished to die in a caring atmosphere where their rights were respected. Some of the residents had cancer, others had AIDS, still others were losing a battle with chronic heart disease or leukemia. Dana believed in the hospice movement and volunteered to talk to her department at work, the personnel section of a large insurance company. To her disappointment, the response was lukewarm. Several people even accused her of hurting morale by dwelling on the morbid aspects of life. Dana was earnest; she was also naive enough to assume that her co-workers shared her enthusiasm for compassionate care-giving. She did not understand that some of her audience

- *did not want* to hear her. They refused to acknowledge a subject that frightened or repelled them.

- *could not* hear her. Her first words set their inner beings in turmoil. They could not hear or accept information. They were, literally, deaf to her topic. Afterwards, many could not remember the presentation. Still others were angry about wasting their time.

Are there strategies to make such presentations effective? Yes, there are. Several years ago I volunteered at Casey House, a hospice for people with AIDS. Profoundly affected by the people I met, I decided to speak out about HIV disease wherever I went. For a while I was not popular. I assumed that everyone I spoke to shared my concern. My vocabulary, my references, my intensity were for people in my innermost or heart circle. I had to figure out how to reach others in their circle of concern. I learned to talk to teachers about HIV by talking about children who might have parents or siblings with HIV/AIDS and how they needed to hear the disease discussed with compassion, not loathing. They also needed information delivered clearly and competently. Children provided the way in to talk about HIV. Eight years ago, few people I talked to considered themselves or their children at risk.

After that I talked to people working in the areas of violence and sexual assault. They too wanted to know how to reach their audiences. Gradually we developed a way of speaking that enables others to listen—it's a process that requires careful attention. Here is the approach: first there's a summary and then a discussion of major points. The aim is to make speakers on tough topics effective and keep them safe. Peter Jaffe's interview on talking about violence concludes this chapter. Read it and learn—Jaffe is one of the finest speakers I have heard!

THEY'LL HEAR YOU WHEN THE BUZZING STOPS: ENABLING OTHERS TO LISTEN

1. Think about your visible and invisible audiences. What do they need to know?

2. Find the way in with a story. Join them in their circle of concern.

3. Say the hard words five to ten times in the first five minutes.

4. Tell stories until the buzzing stops.

5. Discuss the subject in terms of the group's interests.

6. Bring support—a co-worker, a sympathetic organizer, a friend.

7. Use audio-visual materials to say things you can't.

8. Provide a hand-out. As well as being interesting and organized, make sure you give every person a hand-out that includes telephone help line numbers.

9. Take care of yourself/predict opposition/wear something for good luck.

10. Provide plenty of time for questions. Questions that seem off topic may be someone's only chance to get information.

11. Follow through—stay around long enough to deal with the stuff stirred up. Provide phone numbers for more help.

12. Keep confidences!

VISIBLE AND INVISIBLE AUDIENCES

When you speak on tough topics you face the visible audience, the people you see, and the invisible audience, people with needs they may be unwilling or unable to reveal. In some cases, it may be unsafe for them to talk. It's up to you to know the levels of need of most audiences.

Let's take a group of 30 high school students; your topic is wife assault. In our region

- four or five live with violence in their homes. They need to know there is support for them in the community; they need information on how to get help; and they need reassurance they didn't cause it.

- some will encounter violence in the future. They will experience violence in dating or in marriage. Your remarks may be the only reference they have.

- several know of violence. Their friends or relatives of friends experience violence. Your remarks will be passed on. Teenagers have excellent memories when it comes to relationships.

- the teachers in the school may live with violence. Consider staff rooms a good place to leave pamphlets.

- several are perpetrators of violence or potential perpetrators. Some do not recognize what violence is; behaviours acceptable in the home are challenged by your presentation.

TELL STORIES UNTIL THE BUZZING STOPS

Once you have introduced the topic—date rape, racism—give your listeners an opportunity to catch their breath. Tell stories, give examples, recount personal experiences, until the group has had time to recover. This also gives you a chance to say the hard words enough times to normalize them.

How does this work? A family counsellor is making a presentation to a large company that is under pressure to enact same-sex spousal rights, meaning that gay couples will be entitled to the same benefits as straight couples. For many, the words "gay," "lesbian," "lover" and "homosexual" cause a buzzing in their heads; it may be shock at hearing the words or difficulty coping with the concept. The speaker is wise enough to use the words calmly and say them slowly. He knows that repeated use neutralizes their sensational aspect. At the same time, he tells stories about the families he works with, showing that their hopes and problems are similar to those of more traditional families. Gradually, the buzzing stops and the group calms down. Most are now able to listen to the presentation.

AUDIO-VISUALS THAT SAY WHAT YOU CAN'T

Consider these scenarios; in each case you are the resource person:

- you're speaking to a group of high school girls aged 15-18. It's obvious that popularity is very important to them all. A number of them say that accepting a little hitting is okay if that's what it takes to keep a boyfriend.

- a men's group is having a discussion on violence. Several men say that pushing and shoving or slapping their wives keeps them in line.

- a group of volunteer youth leaders is learning about HIV/AIDS. For some this is their first formal education session on the subject. Several ask if kissing is safe; others worry about cutlery at camp.

- an all-male college class is discussing safe sex. No one objects when two of the men say using condoms is wimpish.

This is where you need videos that speak out. You are familiar with the technique of using a film to give information and spark discussion, but consider short video segments or clips as back-up support for various parts of your presentation. Use three or four different clips to say things you can't.

As a discussion leader you emphasize that hitting is never acceptable; you're expected to say that! But what about adding a clip of five young women, all saying violence is not allowed. Use members of the peer group to send the message home. Similarly, I've seen a five-minute video by a variety of really big men saying that strong men never use their strength to hurt. A three-minute segment on "the AIDS nerd" describes a "cool guy" who becomes the victim of ridiculous AIDS rumours. Suddenly, the audience is laughing at their own secret fears. The resource person can't ridicule unfounded and harmful fears but the film can! And hearing young media stars, male and female, advocating responsible use of condoms reaches many people; younger audiences pay attention to their peers and older groups are impressed by their frankness and absence of embarrassment.

Machines can also take hate better than you can. Tough topics can provoke extreme reactions. It's better to have the vitriol directed at the speaker in a video than at you.

Video clips cannot replace the concern or the warmth of a real speaker, but they do provide wonderful allies. And some pictures are so poignant, they stay with the audience for a long time.

PROVIDE A HAND-OUT

Give everyone an easy-to-read hand-out that includes helpline phone numbers. It's important that you give the pamphlets to each person. If you leave them on a table and invite people to help themselves, some will be unable to risk being seen taking the information.

TAKE CARE OF YOURSELF

When I became a volunteer team leader at Casey House hospice, the woman who trained me gave me advice I've never forgotten. "Find support," she said. "When I started, the job appeared so simple. I'd been an organizer in the Peace Corps and had done some very hard work. This looked easy. Within a year I was exhausted from the pressure—you can't do it alone." No one who works in a difficult environment underestimates how draining it is. Speaking is also very demanding; you're talking about your heart issues and it often touches you unexpectedly.

As well as the usual advice about pacing yourself, I also advocate taking a friend if you think you might face a hard audience. There may be other community groups interested in similar issues who would like to attend or set up displays. Predict audience reaction; if someone explodes at you, can you handle it? Have you arranged to take a break afterwards in a safe and peaceful place? I always wear a lucky pin or shirt with a slogan I like; it helps me.

Predict audience reaction. You may think you're talking about a principle that is widely accepted and be taken aback by an unexpectedly angry reaction. Once you've worked in a field for a long time, you think your ideas are normal. Think again!

TIME FOR QUESTIONS

Your topic is family violence and someone asks you how many police officers are on duty in your town on a weekend. Where did that question come from? Allow digressions; sometimes the information being sought is vital to that person. If the group trusts you, they may ask seemingly unrelated things, off-topic questions that still get information to the people who need it. Ask yourself:

- what do they want to know?
- why did they ask you to speak?

Encourage the group to talk to each other; they need to discuss their concerns, provided it is safe to do so. When you value the process as much as the message, your presentations will be better. If you have your main ideas well organized, then you'll know how to work them into the discussion when the talk takes off. And anyone who facilitates true communication is considered a great presenter!

QUESTION PERIOD

Query, comment and confrontation. Most question periods have some of each. Once your speech is finished and the applause dies down, a different kind of speaking occurs, one which requires you to think—and speak—on your feet. In most audiences, there will be people who want more information, some who wish to share their experiences or expand the topic, and a few who, as Jaffe says, "see it as a competitive situation."

If you know there will be questions, prepare yourself—think of possible remarks and your replies. Anticipate how you will deal with aggressive comments and watch how participants in televised debates and interviews manage.

Once again, the difference between the old and new ways of speaking surfaces. In the old way, the very asking of a question is confrontational; even if the intent is not hostile, the tone may be. People who persist in jockeying for status feel they have to start a question by attacking the speaker.

"Well, I've got a bone to pick with you on that first point."

or

"I think you've got your figures all wrong. In the report I did..."

and even worse,

"I've never been so insulted—your entire presentation is wrongheaded and unnecessary."

Often, you can deal with people who start like this by realizing that behind the bombast, their real question may be quite simple. They just have to score points by trying to find fault.

Compare this verbal bluster with more collaborative remarks like:

"Please elaborate on your first point. I'm not sure I agree."

or

"How do your stats compare to the ones done by...?"

and sometimes
—nothing.

QUESTIONS

You're a landscape gardener and you've just made a speech on environmentally safe insect control at a regional conference. Here are some basic pointers for dealing with questions.

- Listen carefully to the question and repeat it for the audience. Determine the intent of the speaker: does he or she just want information or are they trying to use question period for their own purposes? If you recognize folks who sell chemical products in your audience, you can predict their remarks and deal with them in the body of your speech.

- Present facts directly and briefly. Some speakers try to sidestep requests for basic information by hedging. If asked for the components of a spray, give them. If an explanation is in order, present it afterwards.

- If asked for an opinion, give it clearly without bafflegab and back it up. Don't preface your remarks with empty phrases and lengthy preambles.

- Be honest in your replies. Carole Edwards, a wellness consultant, faced many difficult questions in her work in health promotion with the Cancer Society. She says some presenters couch words in platitudinous statements; they offer political and diplomatic replies. Her approach is more forthright. In response to a question regarding breast screening for women under 50, she says, "There is no right or wrong answer. I don't tell people what to do. I give them the information and empower them to make their own decisions."

- Divide long questions into parts and deal with each briefly.

- Don't know the answer? Admit it and promise to get back with the information.

- Made a mistake? Admit it. Don't over-apologize. People can accept a mistake; they get impatient when you refer to it often. Move on: "Now we've dealt with this matter, let's discuss other sections of the proposal."

- Be fair in calling on people. Give as many people a chance to ask questions as possible. Enlist help in spotting those who wish to speak and in determining who comes next.

- Give notice that you're wrapping up. When the chair gives you the sign that time is almost up, say, "I have time for only two more questions; I think the man in the centre and then the woman on the right were next."

COMMENTS

Gloria Steinem turns her question periods into community organizing sessions; she invites her audience to share concerns and notices of political activities. Your own question periods will be enriched by those who wish to add to the information presented or give a different perspective on the situation. Beware, however, of those who wish to make their own speeches. As Steinem said to one speaker who was presenting the convoluted route of his own philosophical development, "If I were you, I'd quit while I'm ahead." It was a gentle reminder to finish up. When he ignored it, she was more direct: "State your question please."

When someone makes a good point, acknowledge it. They've contributed to the gathering and good speakers share power, information and credit.

CONFRONTATION

When I wrote my first book on public speaking, two of the people I interviewed gave me *the big test*. This is an old male power exercise in which the person to whom you are speaking overwhelms you with a torrent of belligerence. One such gladiator yelled, "Why the hell do we need another book on public speaking? My shelves are full of books on power selling and power speaking." I was taken aback both by the volume and by the vehemence. I replied firmly that my book was on speaking to make a difference in the world, not just the wallet, and there were no books with Canadian and/or female content. With that he sat down and we had a very pleasant interview. I had passed the test. Some otherwise fine people still use this tactic; don't be startled by it. Hold fast to your best instincts and speak out for what you want.

Rehearse question period. Ask your friends to devise some likely questions and go over both content and delivery, what you'll say and how you'll say it.

Best of all, read Peter Jaffe's approach in the interview that concludes this chapter. He says: "There are people in every audience... wanting to destroy you, waiting to ask the embarrassing question or dispute your statistics. They see it as a competitive situation.... I look to support from the audience. I used to try to deal with these things [hostile questions] alone and I'd just sink deeper.... What I do now is say, 'That's a really interesting question—let's see how other people in the audience feel about that.' It's a better way of doing things. And it also says you're not up there for target practice."

No one is up there for target practice. Talking to each other, not attacking, is a precept of the new way of speaking that not everyone has learned—yet.

VALUE AND VALIDATE YOURSELF

This year I was on a panel and the issue was an emotional one. A man rose to ask me, "Don't you think that, considering the gravity of the issue, it would be better to vote yes now and work to change things later?" This was a loaded question. I was supposed to answer "yes, of course" or give a similar knee-jerk response learned in girlhood. However, I let my own experience stand as validation of my argument. "No," I answered. "I cannot vote yes. In my experience, people are rarely motivated to alter something once the pressure is off."

It worked; once I validated my own opinion, others accepted that validation. You can't base your entire argument on your own perception, but you can and should acknowledge your personal expertise.

WHAT ABOUT HECKLERS?

"This is my very first time on stage. Could you please come back when I have more experience?"
—Rita Rudner, stand-up comic

Hecklers are rare. However, there are *some* determined to call out in the middle of your talk, to disrupt. If the comment is valid, repeat it to the audience and deal with it. If the remark is rude or inappropriate, ignore it. If the speaker is disruptive, offer to speak to her or him afterwards and *do not* dare the person to join you on the platform. There's a version of platform chicken that requires the speaker to say to the heckler, "If you know so much, why don't you come on up and join me." This macho challenge is an invitation to disaster. Remain cool. Try remarks like, "Look, why not allow me to finish. I was *asked* to speak here." On the other hand, don't be overly sarcastic; if you are ruder than your attacker, you'll appear to be a frightened bully. You may even lose audience support. Generally, once you stand your ground, the audience will back you and the heckler will subside.

SKID SCHOOL LESSONS FOR THINKING ON THE SPOT

Have you ever panicked when your car started to skid? I have. A few spectacular doughnuts later and I was off to skid school, a program that teaches drivers how to handle treacherous situations and perform well under stress. The rules are simple and they also apply to speakers facing slippery conditions. The primary rule is to avoid the skid. Predict the situation and take precautions to avoid going out of control. However, if you do start to slip, follow the basic rules of skid school:

1. Don't panic.

2. Take your foot off the brake and steer.

3. Steer in the direction you want to go.

Translated into speaking terms, they read:

1. Don't panic. Breathe—get oxygen to your brain. Pause—assess the situation.

2. Get your brain in action. Think of what you want to say.

3. Have a thesis, one main idea, and steer toward it.

For those who do a few spins before they acquire the knack, skid school has a large uncluttered lawn. Your livingroom is your practice track. Don't worry if you freeze the first time; follow these rules for:

HANDLING UNEXPECTED QUESTIONS

Questions that you didn't anticipate or are slightly offbeat may knock you off balance. Sometimes, that's the intention. If you forecast questions, you have a good chance to develop and rehearse your responses. But, if you're caught off guard, the following technique works; practise it all, especially point four.

1. Pause. Think. Don't panic at a silence. A pause is good for your image; you appear thoughtful rather than glib, you show respect for the question. Get comfortable with pausing.

2. Clarify. Ask questions for clarification. This gives you time to think and ensures you are on the same track as your questioner. If I ask, "When is civil disobedience acceptable?" you may ask me to clarify what I mean: nonviolent actions? in time of peace or war? public or private? Often being asked to repeat their question causes people to notice their tone and make it less combative.

   If it is clear you are totally ignorant, *don't bluff*. Admit you're not sure (you needn't apologize) and promise to get back with an answer within a specified time.

3. One point plus amplification. Make a clear statement, with some examples or explanation. In effect, this is a thesis and one or two supporting points. Under pressure, one point is sufficient. Don't ramble.

4. Involve the other person. Ask for a comment in response. This works well to turn attempted confrontation into communica-

tion. Under pressure, it's hard to remember phrases that elicit a response; stockpile a few of these: "This works in our agency, how do you handle it?" or "That's my experience in a small company, how does it compare with yours?" or "Does this hold true in your situation?" or "Does this match your experience?"

Here are some skid school questions for you to try. It's unlikely you'd face any of them at a meeting but they're good for trial runs.

- What should we do about people who help themselves to bulk food while shopping?
- How old is middle-aged?
- Which are better, American-made cars or imports?
- How common is drug abuse in amateur and professional sport?
- If you were asked to mud wrestle for charity, would you?
- If a major disaster occurred and you had one hour to live, how would you spend the time?
- Should T-shirts with obscene sayings be banned in public places?
- Would you rather be called "bland" or "pushy"?
- Should the minimum driving age be raised?
- If you found bags of money on a highway, would you try to return them?
- Is Elvis alive?

IS THIS ON? USING EQUIPMENT

"Trust in God but tie your camel."
—Sufi saying

Picture this—a speaker walks jauntily up to the microphone, blows into it and bellows "IS THIS ON?" The audience reels in pain at the noise. Why is it that the most experienced speakers take the time to do an equipment check while the very people who need the help a good sound system offers never give it a thought? Here is my best advice—if you want to be a good speaker, *check your equipment.*

How often have you seen speakers approach a microphone, look at it and then stand back a full foot. You can't hear them at all. The judge awarding prizes at our local sled-dog races was too macho to speak directly into the microphone; he stood to one side and pretended he didn't need it. The names of the winners were inaudible. The equipment is there for a purpose; use it to your advantage.

IT'S YOUR SPEECH—DO THE WORK

All the preparation in the world won't help you if the equipment isn't working. Beginning speakers are often undone because they assume that "somebody else" has made all the necessary preparations. Just remember, this is your speech—if the mike isn't working when you stand up, who will look like a jerk, you or the person who said, "Don't worry; everything's taken care of"? Check every detail. This is insider advice. You may not believe any of these things really occur—until they happen to you.

a. Take a private moment. Arrive in good time, perhaps 30 minutes in advance, to get yourself ready, meet the group and do an equipment check. As soon as you arrive, and before your hosts introduce you to everyone, go to the washroom to arrange yourself. You may not have another chance. Comb your hair, check your clothes, make sure your notes are handy. Halfway through your introduction is not the time to make sure your zipper is done up.

b. Check the microphone. The most common response to a request to test the microphone is a vague but pleasant, "Oh, I'm sure everything's all set." Understand that for the organizers of an event, "everything's set" when the speaker arrives and the meal is ready. They've done their part. It is your job to check equipment essential to your presentation. The mike may have been ready two hours ago when the technician went home. Check it yourself now.

c. Is the slide projector working? Now is the time to be sure your slide holder fits, the bulb works and the cord reaches the outlet. Say to the technician, "I'd like to check the first three slides. May I see them please." If anything's wrong, you've got time to get help. If you're using a film or video, be sure it is ready to go and you understand the controls.

d. Don't hold back! If the equipment isn't available yet, or the technician is on a break, stay there until everything is in place. You may need to return in a few minutes. Don't be distracted if your host seems impatient; he or she has other things to do. Assure them you'll be along as soon as all is well. If it requires time to get things as you wish, take it. You are the speaker—it is your job to ensure that everything related to your speech is ready. It is not rude to insist on changes or a sound check—it's responsible.

MORE ON USING THE MICROPHONE

We're all familiar with movie images of people horseback riding, canoeing and using microphones. These activities look so simple, we assume anyone can do it with ease. It is a shock when the horse runs away and the canoe zigzags endlessly. People approaching the microphone for the first time often look foolish as they crouch low or stand on tip-toe to speak. The mike seems too close, pushing into their faces, so they step back and become inaudible.

Modern technology has made microphones more sophisticated than ever. This means that everyone can be heard; public speaking is no longer the domain of the person who can boom to the back of a hall. You can lower your voice to sound confidential; you can hold conversations with your audience. But microphones only work well if you use them properly.

- Ask for a microphone when you make your arrangements. Microphones make public speaking possible for everyone. People with soft voices may be wonderful speakers; people with strong voices no longer have to strain them in order to be heard. A whole range of expression is possible. However, some groups still belong to the old holler and boom school of speaking. As a speaker, you deserve equipment to make your job possible—a microphone is essential.

- Become familiar with the equipment ahead of time. Find a microphone to experiment with. Mikes on floor stands or lectern clips have flexible necks. Floor stands have a centre join that will loosen to allow you to adjust the height a foot or more. Grasp the stand with one hand, unscrew the centre join (you may have to apply pressure), adjust the stand and tighten.

- Handle the microphone firmly and look confident. Tilt the head of the mike smoothly. Do not hesitate to adjust the angle of the mike when you first come to the lectern—the previous speaker is almost always three feet taller or shorter than you are.

- Determine the sensitivity. Some mikes are omnidirectional and will pick up your voice from all sides and the top. With others, you must speak directly into the head, at close range. Say a few words directly into the head, "Hello, this is Tuesday and I'm in Toledo," and move slowly back. You'll find how close you must be to get the best tone. If you stand too far back your voice will disappear or get very soft. You need to experiment. Ask the technician or a friend how the sound is. They should assess the volume and clarity at various points in the room.

- You're in trouble if the sound system fails. If there is no techni-cian, you will manage if you do your own sound check and learn how to turn the microphone on and off. If the sound starts to buzz or shriek, pause and try again. The next time it happens, look at the co-ordinator and see if anyone is sending for help. If the system continues to malfunction—stop. Turn off the micro-phone or walk away from it and try to speak without it. How-ever, do not yell at your audience. If this doesn't work, if most people can't hear you, stop again. Be sure to ask if you are audi-ble—don't just talk to the first three rows. There is no point in speaking if most of the audience cannot hear you. It's a frustrat-ing waste of time for everyone.

- Private is private. We've heard of television hosts who lost their cool when they thought their mikes were off. I remember Oprah Winfrey asking her crew what the heck was going on when she was interviewing Michael Jackson and the heat sensors went off. Much worse things are possible. Do not finish your speech and say to a friend, "Oh, do I have to pee." Wait until you have walked away from the lectern to make any remarks. That's also a safe time to cought or sneeze. Do not ever sniff into a microphone. It is an incredibly loud sound. If you have to perform any private function, excuse yourself and turn away from the open mike.

- Treat the technician with respect. Sound technicians are patient, meticulous workers who spend hours setting up equipment and monitoring long speeches. If you're working with a technician, she or he will make sure you sound good; the equipment works smoothly and changes are made quickly. If you're under pressure before a speech, take it out by exercising, not by ordering the technician around. If your speech is being translated simultaneously, thank the translators; they make you sound good in a language you can't speak.

REACHING OTHERS: LECTERNS, SEATING PLANS, FLOOR MIKES

Before Kahn-Tineta Horn began her speech on the Mohawk Crisis, the organizers performed a sweet grass ceremony to prepare the room for the event, to bring a feeling of unity to their midst. Afterwards, they smudged each person with sweet grass to purify their spirits and open their minds and hearts. It was an unusual way to start an address at a university, but they wanted to extend their traditional ways to a larger community, to widen the circle. Vera Martin, another native woman, decided to thank an organization that had supported her studies. At a luncheon of 300, she taught the Buffalo Yell and asked everyone to "use the gift of voice to make a difference in the world." This is the true purpose of my book—to share methods, to rise up, to make a difference. And, as usual, the way you do things is as important as what you do.

There are basic changes we must make if we wish the act of speaking to make community. The lecterns we use and the very way in which we set up a room make a difference in what happens. The kind of speaking I believe in widens the circle; it reaches out and makes a community of everyone in the room—speakers and listeners together. These changes are very simple; however, they challenge the status quo; to make them happen takes shrewd negotiation.

LECTERNS

Old-fashioned podiums are useful only if you want to block connection between audience and listener. So much of communication depends on body language: the way you move, your gestures, the energy you hold in your body.

Who advocates these boxes if they're such an impediment? Speakers of the old school. They don't want communication; they want to deliver their position. If the box masks their true emotions, so much the better.

Graceful lecterns on slim pedestals are the norm on television award shows and political presentations. But the rest of us may have to negotiate to get them. Specify what you want when you book a conference centre. It's more than a preference; it's a question of access, a basic way of making successful speaking possible for more people, regardless of race, size, gender.

What happens if you encounter the pine box? This was my most frustrating speaking experience last year. I was the guest speaker at a conference on women's issues. After I arrived late the night before I went to the conference room and found—a huge pine box. When I stood behind it, I was visible only from the neck up. Moreover, I could not see the first 12 rows of the audience—the barricade worked both ways. My first choice was another, smaller podium—there was none. My next was a free-standing microphone but the platform arrangement did not permit it and I really did need something for my notes. My last choice was a desk lectern that rests on the table. The hotel staff promised it would be in place for my nine o'clock speech. My back-up plan involved the case the A-V technician kept his sound board in; he promised to leave it handy.

When I left the room at midnight, I thought all was well. Next morning I found the full pine box had been reinstated. I thought this odd; almost all the speakers were women, many of them would not be visible. When I spoke to the woman who had ordered the change, she said, "Three men are bringing official greetings to the group. They're all over six feet—they'd look silly at a smaller lectern." It was too late to argue; I grabbed the technician's case, a sturdy box that offered 6 inches of additional height and lots of room to move about. Several other speakers used the same case but a few preferred to be invisible rather than risk challenging tradition.

SEATING PLANS

How can speaking be a conversation when most of the group is arranged in rows looking at the backs of each others' heads and one person is elevated above the rest? Steinem calls it a "hierarchy which is in turn based on patriarchy which doesn't work anywhere, anymore, at all." The solution is to replace all the traditional auditoriums with circular or semi-circular ones. Until this is done, ask that rooms with moveable chairs be arranged on that basis. That way, the audience looks at each other, as well as at the speaker. They feel more of a group and the speaker is part of the community, not elevated above it.

When you try a different seating plan, briefly tell the audience the reason for it. Encourage them to see speaking in a new way; we're dancing to the sun—together.

FLOOR MIKES

By now you may be asking, "Is this woman crazy? Does she really pay attention to all this detail?" The answers, in order, are "no" and "yes." I am not as naive as I was, or at least not as often. And yes, I do a lot of work to ensure that my speeches go well. All of these reasonable suggestions that require very simple alterations mean change. And change, especially when it involves the old order of doing things, is usually met with adamantine intractability.

Which brings me to floor mikes. Imagine a large hall with a speakers' platform at the front, the chairs arranged in straight rows and two centre aisles. Where are the floor mikes usually placed? The standard arrangement is one mike at the front of each aisle, about five rows back, and one mike in the back third of each aisle. How do the speakers stand? With their backs to the audience and their faces turned to the deities on the platform. Imagine the resolution it takes to go to either of the front microphones; you may have to stand for ten minutes or more with the rest of the group gazing at your backside. Is it any wonder so few women come forward at question period?

Why not put the two forward microphones on the outside of the circle so that the speakers stand facing the group with their backs to the wall? They can make eye contact with the whole audience when they speak and get support from their friends. This creates community and reduces stress for speakers and questioners.

It's a good suggestion, easy to implement technically. When I suggested it to the organizers at the conference I described earlier, they said no. By negotiating with the same unflappable technician, I got the microphones moved "but only," as the woman in charge said, "for your speech. After that they're going right back to their proper places. All the other speakers want it that way." No, I'm not naive. And I do know when to speak out; by the time I had explained to the audience how important it was to share power, to enlarge the circle, figuratively and literally, the floor mikes stayed in their new places. A number of people said they felt more confident in coming forward; it was easier to stand beside others than be isolated before the whole group. Change is like building a house; you work from the bottom up. Physical arrangements are a good place to start.

IF I ONLY HAD THE WORDS

When Alice Walker was asked to give a convocation address at Sarah Lawrence College, she "had no idea what one said at such gatherings." The president suggested she speak on writing, her life, war, poverty, the plight of women, anything; he told her it needn't be fancy or long, just "speak from the heart." So she called her talk "How to Speak About Practically Everything, Briefly, From the Heart." It's excellent advice for speakers—speak about everything, briefly, from the heart. When you need to find the words, the examples to move your audience, shut your eyes and go deep inside yourself. Find the words you carry inside and bring them out. They are powerful; they will touch others.

Use Walker's term; she called it a "talk." Use your own words; don't lapse into speakerese. Talk as you would to a neighbour, in personable, conversational tones with illustrations drawn from your own experiences.

USING SIGNALS: LANGUAGE AND ATTITUDES

Words are like icebergs: on the surface are the words we know; underneath are years of privilege and prejudice. All the biases that we absorbed in our early years, sexist, racist and homophobic, linger there, hidden and dangerous. If we are not careful, they show up in our speech, hurting some listeners and insulting others. Even if you normally advocate inclusive language, the old words, ones you would never use in normal circumstances, pop out under the pressure of speaking. A high-ranking civil servant confessed to me that she had asked a group to dismiss "the black cloud of suspicion" with which they had viewed previous administrations. She was humiliated by her thoughtlessness. Only by hard work can we hope to achieve language that reflects and respects all people.

People still ask me if language matters. It is hard to understand how deep-rooted words are in our lives and how very much they matter. If you want to send positive signals, to be perceived as fair, *never* underestimate the impact of words.

We know that terms have changed in an attempt to avoid sexist stereotyping. Jobs no longer belong to one sex or the other: there are firefighters, councillors, cleaners, police officers, chairpersons, stunt artists, camera technicians, sales representatives and news anchors. Speech patterns must also change. Thus phrases such as:

professionals, their wives and children,
help for mothers and children,
publisher Jack David and his daughter Maxi,
see your bank manager; he will discuss it

become:

professionals, their spouses and children,
help for parents and children,
publisher Jack David and his daughter, Maxi David, an
ornithologist,
see your bank manager; she or he will discuss it.

Just as we strive to avoid sexist stereotyping or putdowns in our language, we need to eradicate the systemic racism of our vocabulary. Although we recognize overt racial insults, we must also examine the prejudice inherent in very common phrases. When is a simple dwelling a "quaint cottage" and when is it "a primitive hut"? Who follows a "religion" and who is a victim of "superstition"? What's the difference between a "skirt" and a "costume," or a "neighbour-hood" and a "ghetto"? Every speaker needs to read and internalize the examples found in books on inclusive or non-racist, non-sexist language.

But there is more to do. It's not enough to eliminate sexist, racist terms; we must banish homophobic references. Words like "queer," "faggot" and "dyke" can no longer be used as weapons. These taunts, so common in schools and lockerrooms, wound not only the people they're directed at, but also their friends, their families and the invisible gays within hearing. How can we have a healthy society when some groups are trashed? Gays and lesbians have the right to be acknowledged and valued in our speech. Phrases like "the lesbian and gay community," "partners" rather than "husband and wife," and "family" rather than "mother, father and children" contribute to a fairer society.

SOUNDING GOOD

You're doing a sound check. What's the first question you ask the sound technician? If you're typical of most speakers, you'll say, "How do I sound?" How do you want to sound? "Like Whoopi Goldberg or Robin Williams" are my first choices. After that I want my voice to be relaxed, vital and strong; I want to sound like myself at my best.

For the first minute of your speech, listen carefully to your voice —especially to the pace, pitch and resonance. It's important to work hard, especially at the beginning, to get a sound you like. If nerves have closed off your airway and your first three words sound like you just got out of bed, pause, breathe deeply and continue. Listen carefully to yourself and aim for a voice you like and believe.

It's wise to start more slowly than normal: it helps you focus on your voice and the audience; it gives you a chance to relax. After that, your enthusiasm and energy will naturally cause you to speed up. Remember, this is not voice class. You want to sound good but not artificial. The voice you use on stage, no matter how hard you have worked on it, must be a faithful reflection of your personality. This is no place to sound phony.

When you rehearse your speech, your friends will give you advice like "slow down," "emphasize that point a little more," "I liked that pause," "you're rushing that word," "that part sounds just like you." This is the advice that can really help a speaker. Get people you trust to listen to you and follow their suggestions.

If you want to know terms used in voice books, here are a few. What they all add up to is sounding good.

- resonance: the richness or mellowness of the tone
- volume: controlled and appropriate loudness
- pitch: the highness or lowness of your voice
- pace: the speed at which you speak
- enunciation: the clear formation of sounds and words
- inflection: the use of your voice to create mood and meaning

You are not aiming for a constant pace or pitch; you are trying to use the full range of your voice. By varying the pace, volume and inflection you will maintain audience interest.

BREATHING EXERCISES

Have you ever seen a man yell until the tendons in his throat bulge and his temples pound? Or a woman race on and on until her voice is high and she seems breathless? This happens when speakers run out of air. *Air* is what makes our voices work; anyone who breathes only in the back of the throat ends up foolish and gasping as the air runs out. The best exercise to relax and control your air supply is the one used by speakers and actors everywhere.

In a relaxed position—standing or sitting—pull your chest up and your back straight. Now, shut your eyes and breathe: *In-2-3-4, Out 2-3-4.* Concentrate on nothing but your breathing. Continue for three to five minutes; as you breathe, your muscles and your mind are getting ready. Imagine yourself in a tranquil spot if it helps to calm you.

CRISIS CONTROL

Never speak without doing this exercise—In-2-3-4, Out-2-3-4—it relaxes your airway and larynx, calms your mind and sets a breathing rhythm. You can do it at a lectern or a conference table, or in your office.

VOLUME

Volume comes with air; if you hear your voice fading, pause and breathe. How much volume you need depends on what effect you want. Linda Tillery, a San Francisco-based musician and entertainer, offers excellent advice: "I want emotion, but not necessarily volume —keep it in context."

RESONANCE AND PITCH

By making a conscious effort you can improve the resonance of your voice. Imagine someone has fed you a large spoonful of liquid honey. Roll it back in your throat and swallow slowly. Speak again and see if the golden richness has reached your vocal cords. Together with rhythmic breathing, this is my favourite exercise. I use it often just before media interviews; the actual rolling back in my throat takes away the tension and leaves my voice and my nerves relaxed.

ENUNCIATION

You don't want to sound like Eliza Doolittle—or Dr. Higgins—primly repeating "the rain in Spain stays mainly in the plain." So do not be overly precise in ar-tic-u-la-tion. Conversely, you don't want to resemble my uncle telling his joke about swallowing his teeth. The secret is practice; if your friends say you mumble, concentrate on more precision. Your aim is to be clear but not affected. In private, you may want to experiment; repeat the following words slowly, giving full sound value to them: rec-og-nize, tart, prac-ti-cal-ly, marsh-mallow, orn-ery, Arc-tic, per-am-bu-late, crank-case, rat-chet, Pon-ti-ac, meg-a-lo-ma-ni-ac, and poop.

What happens if you make a mistake, you mispronounce a word, mix up names or use a wrong term? Don't apologize. If it's a matter of an incorrect pronunciation, continue; people know what you mean and most won't nitpick. If you have gotten important facts wrong, correct yourself without making a fuss and without repeating your error—"Excuse me, I think the correct term there would be assessment."

INFLECTION AND PACING

"Where I got the monotone that you're listening to now, I don't know —probably from the Canada goose." Northrop Frye jokingly criticized his own voice on a radio program but his comment is valid. Too often we use the same note for everything we say, and yet it is our voice that gives real meaning to our words. Do you want to express determination, curiosity, outrage? Your voice does it. Frequently, men with very deep voices fall into a lulling monotonous hum if they forget to breathe. The best exercise is to experiment with speed and inflection; slow down or speed up part of your speech and listen to how you sound. Exaggerate your inflection to limber up your vocal cords.

EMPHASIS

In English our voices go down at the end of a statement. Why do some people's go up? Under stress, a few speakers have a tendency to make statements sound like questions; they appear unsure of themselves and the situation. Practice, coaching and experience can treat this speaking emergency.

GET THEE HENCE: A NOTE ON GESTURE

If you have seen old movies, you know the melodramatic use of gesture favoured by so-called orators and thespians. Clasping their hands in anguish, covering their eyes in shame, averting their gaze in resolution were common. Gesture should be a natural use of your body to illustrate or clarify a concept or emphasize a point. Most important of all, it gives the audience a sense of you; it's an integral part of communication. Use gestures that are natural; again ask your rehearsal audience what they think. They'll warn you about distracting mannerisms like shifting your feet, pulling on one ear or putting your glasses on and taking them off. They should also tell you if you look like you're frozen, if anxiety has caused a warm, expressive human being to tense up.

There are two additional points to remember. If you need a gesture to illustrate a point—how small your dog is, how big a drop the stock market took or how positive you are that your advertising concept will work—make sure your movements are big enough, simple enough and clear enough to count. Nervous jabs and flutters don't tell your audience anything except that you're nervous. Rely on friends to assess your movement; anyone who has tried to rehearse while looking into a mirror knows that it's distracting and prevents concentrating on your speech.

If you tense up when you speak, bear in mind my second hint. People get as much from your body language as they do from your words. Eye contact, tone and gesture are essential parts of your speech. If you were to attend any of the outdoor competitions that are the highlight of our community—heavy horse-pulls, skating shows, skate board contests, clogging and line-dancing, sled-dog races, cross-country ski races—you'd hear French, English and Ojibway. We know what's going on by the intensity of the competitors' voices and the clarity of their movements. Don't cut part of yourself off from your audience. If your gestures are conversational and natural, they will be effective.

Good speakers use their entire beings to get their message across. Practise hard and believe in what you're saying. You'll be heard.

PETER JAFFE

Peter Jaffe is the director of the London Family Court Clinic, a children's mental health centre dealing with children and families in the court system. He also holds an appointment in psychology and psychiatry at the University of Western Ontario. His book, *Children of Battered Women*, deals with the impact on children of witnessing violence at home. In September 1991, he joined the Canadian Panel on Violence Against Women and travelled from coast to coast hearing presentations in church basements, women's shelters and rape crisis centres. He speaks often on violence against women; his style is warm, courageous and honest. His wry humour makes him a great favourite with audiences.

SB: Audiences are completely involved when you speak; how do you do it?

PJ: *A speech has to be a conversation; it has to be something you would say to someone one to one. You need to connect with an audience individually and speak to them the same way you would talk in a conversation. A common error is overpreparing, having fairly detailed material that you read from; the sentences are far too long with too many words that the audience can't actually follow. Sometimes less is better.*

SB: Do you prepare your presentations on violence for men or women?

PJ: *They're supposed to be for both men and women but mostly women come.*

SB: You have so many stories and statistics—how do you decide what to use? How do you put a speech together?

PJ: *I try to think about the essential points I want to make. There's a core of the speech that I think about—four or five things that I want to say that I can put down in one word or one sentence that helps me remember.*

SB: And you rely on four or five words or sentences?

PJ: *I also have stories with every one of those words. I don't know exactly what I'm going to say until I actually say it. I do that because it's more spontaneous, much more like a dialogue or conversation with the audience. When I was younger, I used to write things out but I found I was tied to my notes; it became an old story. This way helps keep me a bit on edge.*

SB: How many speeches do you do?

PJ: *Two a week on average, about a hundred a year.*

SB: How much back-up do you have?

PJ: *The five words or maybe five sentences. But I always speak about things that I know about. I get into trouble if I get off into somebody else's topic. I've learned a few lessons. Sometimes a very determined committee wants me to talk about something specific that is different from what I usually do. And I know now I never do that. I speak on my own stuff. You can't get away from your area of comfort. As a speaker, you have to demonstrate a level of commitment to the area and a level of knowledge.*

SB: I admire your use of humour. You tell such honest and personal stories.

PJ: *I think humour is very important. In any speech I always try to think of how I open. I want to make sure the audience is relaxed and humour relaxes people. So I pick something specific about a situation I sense around me. I also find that it's appropriate to talk about my son or something in my family or in my work environment. Something that exposes a piece of me. Audiences need to be able to relate to the speaker as a real person who's struggling with the same issues they are. No one likes a know-it-all, an expert.*

And I find that if I open with things I worry about every single day with my son, everybody who has a child or a niece or nephew, somebody they worry about, or a question they worry about—it defuses things. If you open by being honest and say you don't know everything, people relax and follow you.

SB: How else does humour help?

PJ: *Humour defuses things, especially with men. Some men in the audience will sit there and think, "I'm going to ask a question* *that will pull this presentation apart. I'm going to find a mistake with the statistics or something else to do it." But if you admit you're struggling with the same issues, it eases the pressure.*

SB: Do men have that combative approach because you're an expert, because you're a man, or because of the topic?

PJ: *All of those things. There are people in every audience, especially a professional audience—teachers, doctors, lawyers—there are 10 percent of them sitting there wanting to destroy you, waiting to ask the embarrassing question or dispute your statistics. They see it as a competitive situation.*

SB: So even with heavy-duty academic audiences you start with a story or a personal recollection?

PJ: *The more professional the audience, the more down-to-earth the story has to be. I don't want to be their competition. It gets defused from the start. Also, any audience you talk to has a similar level of expertise, anybody who's alive knows what's going on—so I like to feel like I'm joining my audience.*

SB: How does that work?

PJ: *If someone asks me a really hard question, my answer now is, "That's a really good question—how would you answer it your-self?" Or I'll ask someone else in the audience to answer it. It's very effective, even with audiences of 500.*

SB: Is this to save your own skin or is it a better way?

PJ: *It's a better way of doing things. And is also says you're not up there for target practice. Even if you're at the podium and ele-vated, you're not better. The people in the audience can think of good answers.*

SB: You use a lot of stories. Why?

PJ: *That's what people can relate to, even very sophisticated and academic audiences. If I need to, I can put on some complex bar graphs to let people know I've been doing the research for 20 years.*

SB: You know so much and have heard so many stories, how do you fit your remarks into a 20-minute slot?

PJ: *I've done the same presentation in a two-day workshop or in half*

*a day or maybe 20 minutes. Last week I was asked to speak to the
staff at my son's school during a ten-minute break in their lunch
meeting. The topic's important enough that I take whatever time
people give me. If you're given 10 minutes or 20 minutes, it's a
chance to raise some issues. Obviously, they don't value the issue
as much as I do. For me, it's a challenge to raise those questions
and hope they invite me back. Usually they do.*

SB: You use slides very effectively. Do you find them helpful?
PJ: *I use slides as memory cues. I have a collection of hundreds of
slides and I'll pick as many as I need. They help structure my
talk from my introductory personal disclosure to those relating
to my topic. If we're talking about violence in the media, people
have to see that material.*

SB: You do a lot of work with police officers. How do you speak
to them?
PJ: *I speak to them in a direct way. Most of them like kids so if I'm
talking to them about violence against women, I concentrate on
the effect on kids. It means getting to know your audience and
seeing what their perspective is. If I'm talking to business people
… I make sure they know there's an economic cost to violence.*

SB: What happens when you get a very hostile question?
PJ: *I look to support from the audience. I used to try to deal with
those things alone and I'd just sink deeper. I'd get into a debate
with one person. What I do now is say, "That's a really interesting question—let's see how other people in the audience feel
about that." I need to check out if just this one individual is having a hard time and he also has a hard time at work, or if he is
reflecting the mood of the audience. And also because other people in the audience might be able to explain things to him that I
am not able to.*

*For example, a police officer says "laying assault charges
doesn't work. The women won't co-operate." I'll say, "Has everybody here had that experience? Has anyone had a successful
experience where there was support from the judge and the
woman did co-operate when there was support?" and then other
officers will answer. That way I don't feel I'm there for target
practice. I also gauge audience reaction.*

SB: You aren't talking about target practice in an abstract fashion. I've heard you get death threats often.

PJ: *I get threats all the time. I get letters after presentations. It comes with the territory.*

SB: Do you get frightened?

PJ: *Yes. It's something I worry about. I think, whatever threats I live with, many of my clients, many of the women in the country live with a great deal more danger every day. It's a reminder of the importance of the issue.*

   My parents were German Jews who escaped to Canada from Nazi Germany in 1938. I was raised not to condone any kind of discrimination. My dad often told me stories about some of the early warning signs—they sensitized me to any form of discrimination. I think there's an analogy with the experience of women. In my mind I have a responsibility to speak out on the issue in the same way that my parents wished more Germans had spoken out, had taken those risks back in the '30s.

SB: Do you have advice for speaking about this kind of hard issue?

PJ: *Trust your own experience. No one can argue with you about what you've gone through in your own life or what you're dealing with. People should stick to things they know about, including themselves and their reactions to things, their own thoughts and feelings. There also has to be a piece of themselves in the talk for it to be honest and genuine. Think about your own experiences. Never, ever read. If you can't think about four or five points that are really important to you and that you can remember with four or five words, or four or five slides or transparencies that you use as a structure, you need to practise more in small groups, in meetings, with colleagues. There's got to be a conversation.*

CHAPTER
6

NICE GIRLS DO:
SPEAKING FOR WOMEN

I speak very calmly;... I say what I mean and say it with force. I guess that scares people because it's the truth and it's right out there in front of their face. I am a warrior and a woman.

— **Waneek Horn-Miller**

Every year my high school had a contest to crown the posture queen. We'd be herded into the gym to watch the lucky finalists walk up and down, balance books on their heads and sit properly. If you remember these contests, you know that these "girls" did not swagger, swing, march or run. Any exuberance, any sassiness and any street-jive was forbidden. The emphasis was on correctness, not strength; femininity, not fitness. The girls who won could blend in anywhere; that was their virtue—they looked good, walked nicely and sat with their ankles crossed, legs angled to one side and toes just touching the floor.

This same emphasis on form, rather than real power, extended to speaking. Girls were praised for good grammar, articulation, pertness and "excellent vocabulary." When it came to speaking out in class, however, they turned into mutes. Arguing, answering questions and giving opinions were the domain of boys. Just like the posture queens who would never compete in track and field, girls with perfect elocution rarely raised their voices in debate.

But women are good speakers; we are eloquent and honest. We work hard to connect with our listeners. Are we still afraid to speak out? In many cases, yes. The girls who argued in class were not asked on dates; they were called "aggressive" and "bitch." In the early '60s *Life* magazine featured typical teen-age girls whose talking was done on the telephone as they lay with feet propped up on the bed and their heads on the carpet planning for the big prom. Where were the young women who worked to stay in school, who dared to desegregate the schools in Little Rock or who struggled to find the courage to stand up to sexist counsellors who advised them to take typing courses instead of chemistry? We still hear the internal voices urging us to "be nice," "be agreeable," "ask about his hobbies" and "don't interrupt."

In many places, nice girls don't speak out. As a rural postmaster said to Nellie McClung during her speaking tour in 1916, hearing a woman speak in public is "sorto' like seeing a pony walking on its hind legs; it's clever even if it's not natural."

Speaking programs for women often follow the posture queen model; they place pride in correctness, not conviction. A speaking workshop offered this month by a women's professional association features sharpness of vocabulary, orderliness of organization and correctness of grammar.

Where is the practice in standing up in a room to express your opinion with your hands sweating and heart pounding? Where is the reassurance that "they" won't like you any more for staying silent than speaking out? Where is the empowerment, the sisterhood, the delight in our own voices?

RISING UP—A NEW SENSATION

Try an experiment. Lock your hands by interlacing your fingers. Now look down and see which thumb is on the top. Relace your fingers so that the *opposite* thumb is on top. How does it feel? For many people, it is awkward; it causes a sensation of physical discomfort—a visceral flinch. Now, go back and forth from the comfortable position to the relaced one. Does it feel any better with practice?

There is a speaking parallel. Imagine you are sitting in a room full of people. A speaker has just finished and she invites members of the audience to go to floor microphones for questions or comment. What is your comfort position? Some people look straight ahead, some study the pattern in the carpet. Others nudge their friends, "You go—you're good at it." Many do the big twist; they turn their bodies and strain to see who is going to the mike. A few stand to speak; this is their chance.

If your comfort position is looking straight ahead or twisting round to observe, have faith in your ability to speak out. Step by step, inch by inch, like interlocking your fingers in a new way, you can feel more comfortable on your way to the microphone. And soon, we will see more women rising up and using their voices to make a difference in the world.

Is it worth the pain? Susan Faludi describes her metamorphosis from terror to triumph:

"The dreaded evening of the Smithsonian speech finally arrived. I stood knock-kneed and green-gilled before 300 people. Was it too late to plead a severe case of laryngitis? I am Woman, Hear Me Whisper.

"I cleared my throat and, to my shock, a hush fell over the room.... I began to speak. A stinging point induced a ripple of agreement. I told a joke and they laughed. My voice got surer, my delivery rising. A charge passed between me and the audience, uniting and igniting us both.

"... I knew public speaking was important to reform public life—but I hadn't realized the transformative effect it could have on the speaker herself. Women need to be heard not just to change the world, but to change themselves.

"I can't say that this epiphany has made me any less anxious when approaching the lectern. But it has made me more determined to speak in spite of the jitters—and more hopeful that other women will do the same."

"GO FOR IT"—CHEERING EACH OTHER ON

When we do decide to stand up and speak our minds, will there be support? I hope so. I hope women call out to each other "right on," "you've got it," or nod their heads vigorously in honest agreement. The women I work with comment constantly on the isolation they feel when they speak. Maybe we do need more obvious demonstrations of encouragement. Take your cue from gospel choirs—when a sister is singing, the others urge her on. I feel so good when I hear someone laugh or say "right on" or applaud when they agree. And I watch for the faces that register understanding and agreement. Sisterhood is not a passive thing—encourage each other with words and gestures. Speaking is a feeling of understanding and mutual communication.

BREAD AND ROSES: A TRADITION OF SPEAKING OUT

Hearts starve as well as bodies:
Give us bread, but give us roses.

This anthem of women working for change was first made popular during the bitter textile strikes in the early years of this century. It has been sung at labour rallies, memorials for women who are victims of violence, at demonstrations for reproductive rights, at immigration hearings.

Women have always spoken out—ours is a tradition of daring to risk ridicule in order to be heard. The early movies of suffragettes and organizers in the textile industries feature dozens of women speaking with passion. The temperance movement relied heavily on women speakers as did the movement to regulate and reform factory conditions for women and children. And yet, many of these movies are silent newsreels: the women march in the exaggerated style of early film; speakers rush to the stage, bob quickly at the microphone, smile justifiably at their accomplishments and hurry away. Where are their voices? Mother Jones, a dowager of formidable courage, was a brilliant labour organizer; we have her pictures but not her voice. Perhaps the technology was unavailable or the speaker more of an oddity than a force to consider; either way, we have very few recordings of the women whose voices rang out in the name of equality and fair treatment.

FUCHSIA AND OTHER BAD WORDS

Fuchsia isn't a bad word—it's a colour. But not so long ago colours like teal, magenta and sage were suspect. Women were told, "Don't use such *feminine* sounding colours like peach and baby blue. Use good clear colours like red, black, navy, brown." But so many words were bad. We could not rely on feelings or domestic examples or the truth of our lives to illustrate our speeches. As women have reclaimed the right to use words like "fuschia" and "peach," they have also established the right to use words like "intuition" and "feeling."

In the last few years I've also heard women say a lot of previously "bad" words. When Judy Rebick and Patricia Ireland, former head of the National Action Committee on the Status of Women and head of the National Organization for Women, respectively, are featured on the evening newscasts, I admire their directness. Rebick's response to whether or not confrontational tactics cost NAC support was, "We do not choose to be confrontational. When we are asked to participate in the process, we work hard and co-operatively. If we're not included, then of course we'll insist. We have to get over our fear of being confrontational."

Patricia Ireland speaks of fighting racism and heterosexism within the organization and credits the power of women: "In this season of discontent, it will be women who can transform the national rage and demoralization into hope."

Many women speak daily, sincerely, bravely. Sylvia Maracle confronts racism and speaks out for native rights; Anita Hill stood up to the badgering of the Senate subcommittee hearings; Ursula Franklin dared to ask why men didn't intervene during the Montreal massacre; and Aung San Suu Kyi spoke passionately for democracy in Burma. Although the Nobel committee awarded her the 1991 Peace Prize, the military rulers of her country did not allow her to accept it. She remains under house arrest.

Young women are rising to speak. Waneek Horn-Miller, a 17-year-old Mohawk, speaks with a quiet anger about the struggle for native self-government. Severn Cullis Suzuki was 13 when she spoke at the Earth Summit in Rio de Janeiro and the Global Forum of world leaders in Kyoto, Japan. Their purpose is clear—to speak, to explain, to convince.

NEW SOUNDS AND STYLES

Five years ago I was threatened in my classroom and believed myself to be in danger. When I complained, I started something that changed my life profoundly. Last year as part of a presentation, I decided to tell people that speaking out carries with it danger. As I took my notes from the filing cabinet, I recalled the long months of fear and disbelief. I turned cold as the memories came back. It was a very hard speech to make and I wondered if anyone else found it interesting or if I was still too caught up in the events. That story turned out to be the highlight of my speech.

My own focus was the recognition of danger, even in an educational setting, and the conflict I felt between my professional responsibility and my growing dislike of the systemic sexism and racism of the institution. The audience, however, was absorbed by the threat itself and its effect on me. They shared the shock of the initial encounter and the subsequent struggle for safety.

This interest in the process has always been part of women's lives; I have a friend who frequently prefaces her remarks with the explanation that she has "to start at the beginning, to spiral in. It's important to get the feel of the situation." If she's told "skip the details and get to the point," she loses interest; the details *are* the point.

This has a lot to do with the new way of speaking. Previously, the emphasis was on information and who controlled it. Facts and figures were the central issue for a male-oriented audience. The new way of speaking, for women and men, involves building rapport with your audience. By exchanging stories we can locate the information *and* each other.

SHE WHO LAUGHS—LASTS

The thing I notice in all the workshops I do with women is the laughter. How nervous do we feel before a speech? Laughter. Why do so many people check their zippers and straps before they start to speak? Laughter. Even in the midst of despair and anger there is laughter. It rises up irrepressibly—it's powerful. How often does it bubble up outside the kitchen, the coffee break, the all-female gathering? How often can you talk about things that concern women and feel confident that your audience will be interested—and will show their interest?

Gail Singer's movie *Wisecracks* is about women and humour. It features performances by, and interviews with, stand-up comics who talk about their jobs, their jokes and what it's like to be a female comedian. To see this movie is a liberating experience. The comics themselves are brilliant, their routines are wonderful. Even more amazing is hearing a large audience laugh at jokes that have a female perspective.

This sense of freedom to laugh out loud at things women find funny is the subject of Regina Barreca's book, *They Used to Call Me Snow White... But I Drifted*. Women do tell stories more than jokes, use humour as a way of integrating rather than putting somebody down. I've heard thousands of women laughing when Gloria Steinem talks about the one outrageous thing different women resolve to do. It's the laughter of recognition. And I know that for all-female audiences I have told some of my best funny stories.

Recently, I resolved to have faith that women in a mixed audience will laugh at something they do find funny—even if the men don't understand what's going on. As a speaker this was daring—what if I told a joke and nobody laughed. And what if they remained silent because in the old way, audiences only laughed at things men would find funny. I decided to experiment. During a speech to a large group of businesspeople, mostly women, I said that our words were "powerful, like fire and yeast." I continued, "No, this is not a gynaecological discussion—we're not into yogurt at the moment." There was a ripple of laughter that grew to a wave and rocked on for some time. Afterwards, one of the women told me that she had laughed not only because it was a good line, but she "had never heard anyone even mention the word yeast in public. It was like seeing my own street on television. It was mine."

In that speech I mentioned the word often hurled at women who speak out. When we overcome our jitters and speak up, doing our best to sound firm, someone says to us, "Oh, you sounded so bitchy." It's the all-occasion putdown. I told them about the hospital administrator I had seen wearing a T-shirt under her jacket. It featured five letters:

B old

I rrepressible

T orrid

C omplex

H APPY

Take back the word and enjoy yourself while you do it. Have faith in women's sense of humour and take a chance. If, as Barreca says, you make a witty remark or tell a funny story, and not many others laugh with you, "what you've made isn't a mistake. What you've made is a beginning."

TEARS OF CONCERN: CRYING WHEN YOU SPEAK

Many women cry when they first speak about something that truly matters to them. It's an emotional double-whammy. First, there is the deep concern for the issue involved. Coupled with that is the release of speaking, of breaking the tradition of silence and acquiescence. To hear your own voice in the world, to hear your own thoughts is a profound physical and emotional release. No wonder we cry. But do not let the tears stop you. If necessary, face your audience and say, "These are tears of concern, not of weakness." And continue.

At a recent workshop, several women rose to speak and two of them cried as they spoke. It was so powerful to hear other women call out, "That's it, Lynda, keep on going," "take your time," "you'll do it." Of course they continued; the tears were a surprise to them but not a defeat.

When the tears come—Risk and Trust Yourself and Breathe. And we will support you—with words and willpower.

TAKING OUT THE TRASH

It's time to do some housecleaning, to toss out speech patterns that were necessary in the old way of speaking in order to keep the peace and the status quo. Let's get rid of tag endings, disclaimers, cute words and BT (before therapy) jokes.

TAG ENDINGS

"It's a great movie—isn't it?"

"Let's have pizza—should we?"

"I'll order it tomorrow—is that okay?"

People have traditionally expected women to be more tentative in their speech. They also expect women to tag end more, to ensure their opinions are always phrased in such a way that someone else can veto the suggestion. Voicing your own ideas is good; speaking confidently, even exuberantly, is part of you.

DISCLAIMERS

"This may be a dumb idea but..."

"I would go this way, but I don't know, you may know a faster route."

"This may not work but..."

Why do some speakers put their own ideas down? It's a way of giving information to someone who considers himself or herself to be in a superior position. By denigrating their own ideas, people of a supposedly inferior status can offer information. Once the question of power is set aside, everyone is free to make suggestions without being considered a rival. No ideas are "dumb." Give yourself credit.

CUTE WORDS

"Could you squinch this over a smidge?"

"There's a thingummy to do that."

"This is really swell, meaningful, cute."

If you were watching movies in the early '60s, you know that women had to call everything "peachy," "keen" or "peachy keen." Saying "move this over a quarter of an inch please" is infinitely more helpful than the request to squinch anything anywhere.

BT AND AT JOKES

"Nice of you to show up at last, Georgette."

"Well, Sheila, written any more profound songs lately?"

"A rocket scientist to be sure—that's really bright, Juba."

"Any more brilliant ideas?"

Do you remember the barbed language of the '60s? Women used it in the name of humour, often as an opener. If you confronted the speaker, she always said she meant it as a joke—couldn't you take a little kidding? Unfortunately, some people think this is still funny. After a long day at work, you skip dinner, get through rush hour, gather your notes and make it to a meeting. Just when you need a cup of coffee and a kind look, someone makes a sharp remark.

I call this BT or Before Therapy language. As I get older and more vulnerable to the stresses of everyday life and human heartache, I find myself needing more positive care in my working day. Astonishingly, my contemporaries are also making the same discovery. Years of therapy may also have helped us. They have certainly resulted in more AT or After Therapy talk. It's a calmer, more thoughtful way of speaking to others Now, when I come into a meeting frazzled, someone says to me, "Welcome. Take a minute to get some coffee or juice. Someone will catch you up."

Next time you are tempted to make a sharp remark as an opener, reconsider. Abrasive jokes are nothing more than attacks calculated to give the speaker an edge. If you don't know how else to greet people, "hello" works well.

MEN: ADVOCATES AND ADVERSARIES

In a society based on power and status, men have traditionally been the ones to speak in public. Even in question periods, men speak more than women. At forums on women's issues, men often speak first and at length. They have no qualms about presenting their views on questions entirely beyond their range of expertise. Recently, I heard a male sociology professor declare that he felt quite capable of setting up a women's studies program without the usual fuss about discussion and collaboration.

Speaking is power. That's why question periods are sometimes so unproductive—men who want to demonstrate status go to the microphone to make comments, not to extend the discussion but to mark their territory. That is also why women who speak are so often trounced; by speaking out, we are challenging the power base.

Not all men guard their territory so jealously. Some are working hard to open the circle to women; to people of colour, both men and women; and to those who for reasons of class or different abilities have not previously been heard. Often, it's a matter of style. When men speak on panels, they refer to each other by name, may even joke about the others' remarks, even if they have never met before. Using the names of other panelists reinforces their insider status. When I was on a panel last fall, my opinion was opposite to those of my co-speakers, all of whom were men. It was only after the moderator, a man who believes in sharing power, acknowledged one of my statements and called me by name that two other men followed suit. The moderator's remarks made me more of an insider.

WHY ARE MEN SO MAD?

There is no way around it. Many men are angry. And anger is one thing that women who contemplate speaking out fear. They cannot accept the notion that because they voice their opinions, someone will get angry *at them*. And these women are right. Why should they have to face ridicule or censure because they want to speak? It isn't fair but it's true. When women speak out, they rattle the status quo.

Do nice girls speak out? We certainly do—and in some places we are still punished for it. A woman called me last fall in great distress. She was co-ordinating a discussion on family violence for key people in her board of education. As long as the sessions were handled by outside resource people, things went smoothly. But when this woman said that the same issues of power and control were problems within the board, the situation blew up. No! No! No! Such a thing did not exist; talking about it was not allowed. To prove there was no power struggle, six of the seven male principals in the group signed a letter saying this woman had hijacked the committee for feminist purposes and they would like her to step down.

"I feel so bad inside," she said. "I tried to be nice; I tried not to be confrontational; I tried not to attack them; I tried to make it acceptable." The lesson is clear: as long as the old ways are still in force, as long as old beliefs prevail, *there is no right way*. As Gloria Steinem says in her interview in Chapter 3: "Understand you'll be put down for *not* speaking. When you approach a prejudice you can easily recognize it because nothing you do is right. So if nothing you do is going to be right anyway, you might as well do what you need to do."

If the old ways are still in power, there is no right way. The very fact that you are speaking is the cause of the distress. Do not remain silent—your silence will not protect you. Rather, take heart and speak out. Your community needs you: the world needs you.

WHY ARE THEY DEAF TO YOUR SUGGESTION?

"When I make a suggestion at a meeting, it sinks like a stone. I wonder if anyone has even heard me. Fifteen minutes later, the guy next to me says the same thing and the other men say, 'Sound idea, Bert, good work.' Am I not speaking clearly or what?"

Why does this happen? Whether or not the suggestion was phrased properly is not the issue—it's the quality of the response that is so disheartening. Men are either not aware that women need comment and support or more tuned to their own network. Why don't women on the committee speak up? They may be waiting for the men to speak first or they may belong to the group who say, "I don't usually speak at meetings." There is work to be done.

First, give yourself a refresher course in group interaction. Men who are aware of the politics of meetings know the rules. If you can make a supporting statement for one person's suggestion, he is more likely to back you the next time. If no one responds at all, you can ask for input: "Joel, what do you think of that idea? Can we use it?" or "Before we move on to Bede's point, I'd like some feedback on my suggestion."

There will probably be some banter at this point but the group will get the message—you want acknowledgement.

We can all work to be more verbally supportive of women who speak. The next time a colleague gives a suggestion, recognize her contribution. You don't have to agree. Simply saying, "Sounds like you've worked hard on that, Jean. Could you explain it a little more," is a big step. You can go further and invite others to comment, "It may be what we need in this situation. What do you think, Rebecca?" Supportive interaction is normal for many of us. For others, it's a whole new way of being. Speaking plays a big part in the evolution.

LIBBERS, BUBBLEHEADS AND CASTRATORS: DEALING WITH PUTDOWNS

You've all seen the cartoon—one woman says to another, "Whenever *I* think I'm assertive, *they* think I've got my period"—or PMS or menopause. The list of putdowns is endless; they spring from unreasonable resentment. The first time I heard a man refer to a female administrator as a "castrating bitch" I was shocked. She was pushy and I disagreed with her, *just* as I had differed with her bossy male predecessor. But such rage was irrational. The woman's lack of distress was also puzzling; apparently she'd heard it before. I decided that was the worst possible insult.

Then I spoke with women in the fashion industry. They were angry at being dismissed; women who managed large retail businesses were tired of being called "bubbleheads." No one listened to them—so they thought. If no one was listening, why were the put-downs so vehement?

What are common putdowns? "I don't believe what I'm hearing" or "You can't believe that." And there's body language—eye rolling, helpless shrugging of shoulders, blank looks.

For many the worst F-word is f-f-f-f-FEMINIST. Want equal pay for work of equal value, harsher sentences for sexual abuse of children, access to birth control *information*? FEMINIST. How can such a reasonable word cause such outbursts?

More to the point, what can you do about them? Hold the line. When someone says, "Two women promoted in one week. That's too much female power for one office," stand your ground, firmly. Say, "It's fair as far as I'm concerned." Step forward if you can, but don't step back. Hold the line.

You can also refuse to be drawn in—"That's uncalled for, Ed"—or use humour for a sharp retort. Some of us still suffer from the notion that answering back is unladylike, but we're learning. A teacher's aide with fifteen years' experience was rebuked by a young teacher. "You should have referred that question to me," he said. "I have a degree in education." "Oh," said the woman, "didn't I tell you? I have an M.A. in common sense."

Right now I think of good comebacks in the car on the way home but I'm getting faster. If Saint Joan can do it, I can try. The 17-year-old girl, on trial for hearing God in her own head, was bold. With her life on the line, Joan never hesitated. Her tormentors thundered: "How do you know that the spirit which appears to you is an archangel? Does he not appear to you as a naked man?"

Joan's reply: "Do you think God cannot afford clothes for him?"

The list of Top 10 putdowns would not be complete without the accusation of brainwashing. Counselling badly beaten women in a shelter? Their partners yell that you're brainwashing them. Circulating a petition for more women's studies courses? You're brainwashing the female students. Why is educating considered brainwashing? It's frequently a matter of removing brainwashing.

HYSTERICAL WOMEN: A LIFE-AFFIRMING FORCE

Have you ever spoken with intensity about an issue you cared about? And were you then branded "hysterical"? That's a word we need to reclaim. It comes from the Greek word "hustera" meaning womb. If we speak with conviction, our critics label us hysterical, once again attributing our passion to our reproductive organs and invalidating our opinions.

What if we honour our hustera, our life-affirming force? The next time you object to an unfair hiring policy or a pitifully inadequate sentence for rape, and someone calls you hysterical, why not reply: "That's right. My hustera, my life-affirming force, gets all riled up at unfair, sexist hiring policies. I'm hysterical and I'm going to do something about it."

Imagine a throng of women taking back the words: a community of happy life-affirming "hysterical bitches."

PLAYING PLATFORM HARDBALL

The government is closing down our agricultural college and research laboratory. Rallies, tractor parades and petitions are planned and a series of community meetings is underway. A woman in a neighbouring town called the steering committee to ask which farm women were going to be on the next panel discussion. "What farm women are you talking about?" she was asked. "We don't know any to contact." Just like they don't know any women athletes, scientists, inventors, fire fighters. It's not so much exclusion as a total absence of awareness that we exist independently of men. Getting there is half the job. Whenever important discussions are planned, make sure your interest group is represented and be ready to supply the name of a speaker—or speak yourself.

Once you're on the panel, you have two groups to deal with: the audience and other panelists. If you follow the advice of this book and have a conversation with your listeners, you'll establish a link with them. If someone tries to pepper you with shotgun questions, turn the attention back to them. Ask for their ideas and solicit contributions from the audience.

What about the other panelists? Some of them are used to the old way of scoring points by attacking their opponents. You are supposed to be able to take care of yourself. Let's take an example. I took part in a panel that spent considerable energy discussing the wording and intent of a document. The man on my left, who did not speak to me before or during the event, was evidently miffed that someone he did not know opposed his point of view. Patronizingly he said, "I am very familiar with this document and I assure you that to come to the conclusions you have reached, you must have done some very creative reading."

As platform slams go, this was mild, but I still wondered how to respond. It's like a classroom. When rowdies act up, other people may disapprove but they still expect you to handle the situation. Your credibility is at stake. When my next turn came, I reaffirmed my earlier position and said, "I can assure my colleague that although I teach creative writing, my reading skills are precise and logical. This proposal does not protect our rights." There was a nod of approval from the audience.

I saw far more direct action from two women representing a rape crisis centre. They were on a panel at a "Stop Rape" meeting. Also speaking were several representatives of community action groups and four men from the police force. When an audience member rose to complain that officers who responded to her call had trivialized her concerns and failed to follow up, the senior officer on the stage replied at once, "No, none of our men would have done such a thing. Perhaps you misunderstood what was going on. I'd like to get to the bottom of this. See me after the meeting—we'll soon find the truth of the matter."

His remarks discredited and intimidated the woman in front of an audience of 800 people, many of them her neighbours. She was visibly upset. Seizing the table microphone, one of the crisis workers spoke: "We believe you. We hear this all the time. And we also hear this sort of denial. We'll be available afterwards for anyone who wants to speak to us."

TIME LIMITS AND INTERRUPTIONS

It's very hard to concentrate when someone in the front row is pointing to her watch and whispering "time, time." Even worse is the person who tries to slip you a note. Be courteous of others and share the platform. Go over your remarks at home so you have some idea of how long they take and remember to place a watch with big numbers right in front of you. Monitor your own time—and don't be intimidated by others. Often, it's your political opponents who are trying to rattle you by calling time at least a minute early. Listen for and co-operate with legitimate time signals.

Your response to interruptions depends on who is interrupting and how often it has happened. The first time, you can say, "Excuse me, Mercedes, I wasn't finished." A more forceful reaction is to look at the person interrupting, put your hand up in a stopping motion and say, "Just a minute, Ramon, it's my turn." If you speak in an even tone you keep audience support.

You can avoid interruptions by putting your remarks in a reasonable context. Nurjehan Mawani, the chairperson of Canada's Immigration and Refugee Board, was recently on the hotseat when she announced that the board is the first in the world to formally recognize domestic violence as a basis for refugee claims. Anticipating attacks of extremism, she introduced the changes with the remark, "I certainly feel that we are on the leading edge here but I don't think we're out of synch with the international trend."

KEEP ON WALKING FORWARD

When women rise up to speak, how does the quality of life alter? Put simply, it is kinder and more inclusive. There is more laughter, laughter based on community and sharing, not on ridicule. There is more emphasis on self-esteem and self-affirmation.

To make this world better we must keep on walking forward—together. We can do it. Bernice Johnson Reagon, in an interview in *Ms.*, speaks of her work in the civil rights movement. She says this about finding courage: "Day by day, I found courage to be who I was. This was different from who people wanted me to be. Finding courage. Taking the risk.... But I found that if you avoided everything that was a risk, there would be many things you'd never know about yourself.

"… If you stay in the safety zone all the time, you'll never know about your strength, you'll never know yourself at your most brilliant."

KAHN-TINETA HORN

Kahn-Tineta Horn is a 53-year-old Mohawk woman. She first came to public attention 30 years ago when she spoke out for native rights and sovereignty. For almost 20 years she worked as a civil servant with the Department of Indian Affairs and rarely spoke publicly. In 1990, she went behind the barricades at Oka where, as part of a handful of Mohawk women, men and children under siege, she was held behind the razor wire by the Canadian Armed Forces. At the centre of the dispute was a grove of sacred pines and a burial ground that the local townspeople wanted to destroy to make a golf course.

Since the siege at Oka, Kahn-Tineta Horn has spoken often on native rights. Her actions at Oka have cost her dearly and she would do it again—without hesitation.

Her gift of speech has been passed to her daughters. One of them, Waneek Horn-Miller, was with her mother behind the razor wire. She is now 17 and still carries a long scar on her chest as a result of a soldier's bayonet. I interviewed Kahn-Tineta Horn and Waneek Horn-Miller at the Kahnawake Pow Wow, an event held annually to commemorate the blockades of 1990. Both participated in the ceremonial dances; Waneek is a joyful dancer. Both mother and daughter speak calmly, with a sense of immense power. Often they smile. This is the gift of speaking. Across the stages of one's life, across the generations. They will never quit until the aboriginal people are free.

SB: After 20 years, what brought you back to speaking?

KH: *I got involved with the Oka crisis and the media asked me to explain the issue. I was able to provide background because I've worked with those issues. After that I was interviewed and spoke publicly. That's what happened.*

SB: Were you behind the barricades with your family?

KH: *Yes, about half the people in there were members of my family. Two of my daughters were also there. Waneek was 14 and Ganyetahawi (now Kanieti) was four.*

SB: What happened as a result of your being at Oka?

KH: *I got fired from my job with the government and lost custody of my younger daughter. I had to fight to get her back. I had criminal charges laid against me. I defended myself and was acquitted.*

SB: Did you have some idea that the consequences of taking part in Oka and giving interviews would be that severe?

KH: *I wasn't doing anything wrong so I didn't think anything would happen. I eventually proved I didn't do anything wrong. I even sued the government and won my job back. Just my being there upset the government because we wouldn't back down. They decided to treat us with as much severity as possible.*

SB: You said that you thought you were going to die. Did you mean that literally?

KH: *Yes. I was glad to get out alive. All of us, my family and my kids, thought about dying. It's taken me about three years to get over it, to rest up for the next stage of my life.*

SB: Would you do it again?

KH: *I will always do what's right, always, without hesitation.*

SB: Even with severe consequences?

KH: *Probably.*

SB: In your speeches to non-natives, you don't mince words. What is it like to tell your whole audience that they stole your land?

KH: *I guess that's what has gotten me into trouble. I've always been very blunt. The reason is that the Mohawk language is very direct and when I express myself in English, I speak the same way—very bluntly. I think at first people were upset with the way I expressed myself. But they have gotten used to it and they can take it better now.*

SB: Do you like speaking?

KH: *I feel it is my duty and I have a gift, so I do it. Some experiences I enjoy more than others. Some academic audiences are apprehensive. They expect to see a terrorist with an AK-47 and instead they see a middle-aged woman who smiles a lot and makes jokes at serious things. After that they start listening.*

SB: The humour helps?

KH: *The jokes have to be relevant and you have to be fast on your feet. You have to size up the audience and decide ahead of time what you want to leave them with. I want them to feel better toward Indian people; I want them to see our side. And I want them to be so confused they'll go out afterwards and learn things on their own—especially our true history.*

SB: Do you think they take it better or worse from a woman?

KH: *The men don't know how to take me. I show no fear—of anybody or anything—because of what I have been through in my life. So somebody with my cockiness and assurance—many men can't relate to that. The women love it.*

I'm from a matriarchal society; we have a different way of relating to men. I think it throws them. Their comments tell me that. Also I'm older now. I'm 53 years old. And I always remind them—I'm 53, not 23; I'm older than everybody else in this room so now you have to listen to me. I tell them I'm an elder even if I do not look it. Maybe that helps.

SB: How much do you prepare your speech ahead?

KH: *I prepare every single word ahead of time. I like to think through everything. I always think of new things. I like to grow as I go along, research new issues in the places where I'm speaking. I'm super thorough. If it's a formal speech, I will carefully write it and deliver it but often I work from jot notes. I can do it both ways.*

SB: I saw conference organizers do a sweet grass ceremony before you spoke. Does it make a difference?

KH: *It makes it much better for me. It sets the tone, relaxes people and makes them more open to what I have to say. And they take me more seriously.*

SB: When you were a fashion model 30 years ago, did you speak out?

KH: *Yes I did. The same as now. I really hated being stereotyped as a "princess." I didn't consider myself radical. I was born into it. For maybe 10 or 12 generations, we have spoken out. I'm just doing what I'm supposed to do. The Great Law tells us we have to carry out our work until we win. We can't lose; when you're doing something that's right you may have some setbacks but it's still right. You never quit.*

My daughters speak out. Waneek speaks. Kahente, my 19-year-old daughter, was working last year at Banff at a museum that was supposed to depict the life of the Stoney Indians. She wrote a report and as a result, she was asked to be the keynote speaker at the annual conference of the Canadian Museum Association.

SB: What advice do you give people who want to speak out?

KH: *I tell them not to go into anything like this unless they are prepared for the hardships and the suffering because they're fighting a system that is based on white, male superiority.*

    After that I tell them what I tell my daughters. Be very knowledgeable. Keep your ears open. Speak directly from the pit of your stomach because that's where you get your wisdom and guidance. It goes to your head, then it comes out through your mouth. When you do that, it will come out right.

I N T E R V I E W

WANEEK HORN-MILLER

SB: How do you feel when you talk to people about the blockade at Oka?

WH-M: *I talk about what it meant to me. I was only 14 and I made the choice to be part of it. I got tired of not taking a stand and not doing anything about it. I try to tell others about the history and politics behind it, not just what happened. People are afraid of using force but they don't understand we've used diplomatic ways for hundreds of years. Now they'll take a second look at Mohawks and at all native peoples. We are prepared to back up our traditions and our love for the land.*

SB: Does speaking make you nervous?

WH-M: *It makes me excited when I speak about things I know. I like informing people. I don't want them to go away not knowing. When people come up to me afterwards and say they are sorry, I say that I don't hate them if they try to correct what their forefathers did. But if they continue racist practices, I don't like them.*

SB: Are people afraid of you when you speak?

WH-M: *Some of them are. I've been told I speak with a quiet anger. I speak very calmly; I don't yell, scream or swear. I say what I mean and say it with force. I guess that scares people because it's the truth and it's right out there in front of their face. I am a warrior and a woman.*

SB: What advice would you give people who want to speak about political issues?

WH-M: *You can be angry but don't let others in a debate make you yell or scream. If you want them to hear you, speak in a calm voice, look the other person in the eye and say, "I respect what you have to say but this is what I want to say." You have to respect each other's point of view.*

SB: Do you think this kind of speaking will change the world?

WH-M: *Yes, but you also have to back it with action. I was 14 when I first spoke out; it was right after Oka and I spoke at Carleton University. The experience was fresh in my memory. If you put feeling into your words, people feel closer to you.*

   When I speak on native issues and rights I look around and see kids and my little sister. I want my kids to live the life my mother tried to create for me. I don't want them to have to grow up fighting and being angry like I am. There's a lot of feeling inside me: politics tie in with the threads of my life. I live politics and I act politics and I speak politics. I get very emotional about it.

CHAPTER 7

You've Got a Friend:
SPEECHES FOR SPECIAL OCCASIONS

When you're making a groove it's like making a gumbo base; it's got to settle, you've got to have the feeling. And if you hurry it up—you'll mess up.

— Linda Tillery

▲▲▲▲▲▲▲▲▲▲▲▲

A 17-year-old inventor named Rochan Sankar bounded to the microphone to accept the YTV Achievement Award for Innovation. With television cameras focused on him and thousands of people in the audience, he was affable, enthusiastic and funny. Eyes shining, he thanked his parents and the sponsors of the award and went on to talk of the excitement of having an original idea—the energy and the rewards it brought him. He was a superb speaker. Not so the bureaucrats who presented the gift. They found it necessary to read directly from the teleprompter. Hard stuff like "It's wonderful to be here tonight."

Special occasions hum with spontaneity and good will. Why do some speakers find it necessary to inflict empty phrases and wooden delivery on their friends and associates? Two weeks ago I sat in disbelief as the head of a national youth group addressed a banquet of 500 volunteers, many of whom she knew personally. She *read* the words: "I am so pleased to be here tonight. It is a pleasure to share this celebration...."

If you are asked to introduce a speaker, make a toast or present an award, concentrate your energy on connecting with the people in front of you. If you're nervous, reach out. Look at them. It makes all the difference. Know your material well and draw on the vitality and joy you carry inside. Your speech will make the event richer.

THE ONLY RULE: GET THE NAME RIGHT

Can you imagine mispronouncing Sinéad O'Connor's name? What about Elaine Wabi, Foluke Akinremi, Laurene Boileau, Iggie Praught or Duc Banh? What we consider easy depends on where we live and what we hear in the media. During Olympic competitions, we talk about various athletes as though they were old friends—and never once consider their names difficult.

Getting the name right is always essential, but even more important when the whole purpose of your speech is to introduce or honour the person concerned. Don't rely on someone else's version of the name or even your own experience—my friend Iggie pronounces her last name Pratt; her cousins say Prowt. It's spelled Praught. Find out for yourself.

STRATEGIES FOR TRACKING DOWN CORRECT PRONUNCIATION

1. Advance warning. The president of the local chamber of commerce has asked you to introduce the speaker at the annual banquet. She hands you a sheet with a few details about the speaker, a designer of wheelchair-accessible shopping facilities, and gives her version of the name. It's an easy one: Haley. What is your next step? Contact the speaker to check the background information and the name. Haley looks simple, but is it pronounced Hal-ee like the comet or Hay-lee like the author? If you mispronounce a name if front of 200 people, do they care that someone else fed you wrong information? Check the name.

2. Surprise—you're it. Your boss meets you at the registration desk with the news that you're doing the introduction. What next?

Relax—you've read this book. Organize your thoughts, practise breathing, wait by the door for the speaker to arrive and check the name and important details when you greet him.

3. Smooth work. The speaker arrives after the proceedings have started. You're on the stage and the president is outlining this year's achievements. You see the speaker walking toward the stage. Slipping smoothly from your chair, you move to one side of the stage, greet your guest and quietly check the name.

4. Deceptively daring. This situation makes even experienced speakers check their pulse rates. You're on the stage and the guest appears before you can make a move; soon you're called upon to introduce a speaker called Haley (or Cachagee, or Ayuyao). You have several choices: guess; do it wrong and apologize; embarrass yourself with a remark like "Gosh, I've never seen a name like this before"; or walk over to the speaker, shake his hand and very quietly say "Do you pronounce your name Hay-lee?" You are away from the microphone and no one can hear you. Furthermore, guest speakers will co-operate; they want to have their names given accurately. Having to correct you makes an awkward start to their own presentation.

TOWNS AND CITIES ALSO NEED RESEARCH

Last week the production crew of a local radio station mocked the announcer who referred to Gan-ann-ook: that's Gananoque (Ga-na-nok-way) to most of us. It's unnerving to stand up to introduce representatives to a conference and discover that the list of places represented reads like a quiz in pronunciation. How would you manage with these: Nanaimo, Ucluelet, Kluane, Kananaskis, Tuktoyaktuk, Batoche, Gimli, Sault Ste. Marie, Penetanguishene, Etobicoke, Stouffville, Percé, Chibougamau, Miramichi, Margaree, Malpeque, Middle Mosquodoboit, Baie Verte, Port aux Basques? If you are ever in desperate need, call your reference library or the newspaper in the town concerned.

GRACIAS A LA VIDA: THANKS TO LIFE

Most of us will never get an international award, but we will be touched when someone takes the time to express appreciation of our work or our lives. If you're asked to make a speech, don't hesitate because you are embarrassed. Focus your thoughts on the other person and make use of an opportunity that may never come again. Give thanks to life.

NEVER MISS AN OPPORTUNITY

Imagine your mother is celebrating her 75th birthday and your family says to you, "Say, you read the book; you make the speech." If you toss away the chance with an offhand remark like "Great going, Mom," how can you be sure that there will ever be another time for your family to acknowledge to your mother and to each other how much she has meant to you? The effort you take to speak is a tribute in itself.

MAKE IT REAL

Never make an empty speech. If you've been asked to bring greetings or present a brief overview of your organization, work hard to find something interesting to say. Select one or two features you value to share. The next time you hear a speaker string together a series of hollow remarks, ask yourself what might have worked. Could she have told a story she heard at the store and related it to the group? How about reflecting on the way the organization has made her daily life richer? In other words, take the time to say something solid.

This takes more work. Look at the almanac to see if your speech falls on the anniversary of a special day; does it have significance for the group? Are the seed catalogues piling up on the kitchen table? Does the ritual of planting and growth apply to the event? Think. Feel. Go inside yourself to find an idea to share with your audience —give something of yourself.

BE BRIEF, SINCERE AND SPONTANEOUS

Special occasion speeches are short and specific; they pave the way for the main event, wrap up the proceedings or accentuate an important occasion. If you are well prepared, you can be brief and the occasion will retain its excitement. Never let your speech overpower the main event; a longwinded introduction can deaden the momentum of the occasion.

The key to sincerity is finding the way in. What has brought you all together? What is special about the gathering? Find a tone that is you—tell a story that reveals your own appreciation or excitement. Avoid trite space-fillers such as "this cherished heritage," "our valued supporter," "this priceless opportunity." Speak simply and with warmth.

How can you be spontaneous and well prepared at the same time? On social occasions, your audience expects you to know the person you're talking about and to be enthusiastic. Do not read the name of the speaker or recipient of an award. If you need to look at your notes to remember that you have known your friend Jack David for 18 years and think he's brilliant, how convincing are you?

RESEARCH

You get information for a special occasion speech in the same way you do for other types: *Research*. Specific, concrete examples enable your listeners to see the value of a co-worker or understand the amount of work done by the co-ordinator of the Heart Fund. Dig for stories, examples, numbers and comments. Ask family members and colleagues for details to illustrate your remarks. If your mother came here as a war bride, recall her experience of arriving in a strange country. If a friend is receiving the George Wicken Writing Award, find out who Wicken was and why the award was established.

Research involves common sense as well. If you're presenting an award to a co-worker who is deaf, and it's appropriate to mention the fact, how do you find out what word to use? Does she prefer the term "deaf" or "hearing impaired?" Ask the person concerned. That's research.

PATTERNS FOR SPECIAL OCCASION SPEECHES: THE ADDED TOUCH

Special occasion speeches follow the same general outline given earlier:

- seize the attention of the audience and outline your topic or thesis;

- deliver the goods;
- reinforce your point and make a strong finish.

In other words, you need an introduction with a grabber and thesis or main idea; a body to flesh out the overview you provided directly or indirectly in the intro; and a conclusion to wrap it up.

The added touch is a special mood or reference. Take the basic pattern and tailor it to the ambience of the group; add glitter, insert gracious sincerity, trim it with humour. Your job is to have a feeling for the group and the occasion and to design a speech to match. The finishing touch is a specific *signal*. Your final words give the cue to applaud, the words of a toast, the signal to start.

THE INTRODUCTION

Quirky, unpredictable, boring. The speech of introduction is one of the hardest to predict. It's often assigned at the last minute and no biographical material is available. But you can make the difference. You can give a good speech that arouses interest in the guest speaker and presents an idea in a clever way.

Your job is to establish a link between the audience and the speaker. You should make the speaker feel welcome in that group and give the audience notice that they will benefit from the speech to follow. You can help the speaker by outlining the appropriate credentials and creating an atmosphere of anticipation. How long should the speech be? In most cases, two to three minutes.

PATTERN

1. Address the audience. What does everyone in the room have in common? Is the community meeting to learn about changes in environmental regulations or is a club gathering for its annual awards banquet? Set an appropriate tone for the meeting. If the speaker is intended to provide humour, inform the audience. I once sat through quite a humorous address that was received in silence; the audience did not know if it was polite to laugh.

2. Direct attention to the speaker. Answer the questions who, what and why. Mention the name early and repeat it two or three times in your introduction. Remember, the audience is hearing it for

the first time and wants to know who the speaker is, what his or her credentials are and why they should listen. Ask the speaker for background details they want mentioned and choose the ones appropriate to that group. Do not read the entire bio found in the program notes.

It is also your job to check your guest's title. You'll introduce a county court judge as "The Honorable Judge Jeanette Goulet," the archbishop of the Greek Orthodox Church as "His Eminence, the Archbishop of the Greek Orthodox Church of North and South America," an English professor as "Dr. David Kent" and the officer in charge of community relations as "Staff Sergeant Kim Oshida." Once again, a telephone call will give you preliminary information that you can check with the speaker when you meet. If you are introducing a couple, check both their names and titles.

Nothing is more awkward for a speaker than to have to make corrections in the introduction. At least get the name right. Then aim for precision regarding qualifications, interests, the topic to be presented. Accuracy reflects well on you and your organization and is worth the time you take to contact the speaker in advance and check all the information before the program begins.

The surprise technique: If you want to surprise your audience and your guest is truly well known or well respected by your group, you can use the surprise introduction. Give all the significant details and then say, "and I'd like you to join me in welcoming...."

3. Focus on the topic. Your co-workers may not be very interested in the most recent outbreak of rabies unless you focus on the danger to family pets and small children. If you mention that last year rabid foxes attacked farm dogs and school children, the importance of vaccinating domestic animals and implementing a drop-bait program is more apparent.

4. Give the signal—in this case the name. Use your voice to build to a climax and make eye contact with the guest. Then, speaking directly into the microphone, give the cue: "It is with great pleasure that I present Dr. Michael Kamakaris."

BEWARE THE KILLER INTRODUCTION

What's the worst introduction possible? The one that bills you as the "world's greatest speaker" or "a person guaranteed to make you laugh." Comments like this ensure audience resistance; they vow not to respond. Recently, I found myself in the middle of a nightmare. I was replacing a well-known political figure as keynote speaker and the woman introducing me said, "Who is Sandie Barnard? She is the *great* communicator." I could see heads hunching into shoulders and sensed the unspoken challenge, "Well, just see if she can reach me." Peter Jaffe, a man who can laugh and sympathize at the same moment, said it would have been more humane to introduce me as a complete unknown, an untried substitute who deserved some measure of patience. I recovered the situation by saying I appreciated the tongue-in-cheek introduction and was not necessarily a great communicator but a determined one.

Another approach that causes more work for a speaker is the no-trace lead-in: "Our next speaker needs no introduction, so here he is, Howell Gottlieb." Howell had better think fast or the group will have no idea why he was asked to speak. In a light-hearted manner he can say, "My colleagues only mention my qualifications when we're applying for grants," and proceed to outline the most significant of his achievements. The audience needs to know why he was asked to speak.

If you have had to sit attentively while someone reads out every degree earned, every job you've ever held, every award won, you can revive the audience with a touch of self-deprecation: "The detail that most impresses my cat Kodiak is how fast I operate the can-opener."

OTHER BLUNDERS TO AVOID

1. Don't make a speech about yourself, how you know the speaker or how difficult it is to make a speech about a person you admire. It's like a high school student writing an essay on how hard it is to write an essay. The approach is overused. If you know the speaker, mention it briefly and modestly.

2. Don't make the speaker's speech. Perhaps you were asked to do the introduction because you are interested in the topic. Good. You can state its importance with sincerity. Then stop. Do not give your view of the situation or cover the material the main speaker may have built into the speech. Stick to the basics: who is this speaker? what is the topic? why is it relevant to this group now?

3. Keep the humour low key. For a reason hidden deep in the sub-conscious, we blurt out inappropriate remarks when we get nervous. Our attempt at humour can alienate both the audience and the speaker. If someone is coming to speak on employment equity, it is no time to poke fun at the inclusive language policy. Stick to the basic information and be as gracious as possible.

4. Don't forget the name of the speaker. Write it out in big bold letters to save you if you fumble. If you can't imagine stumbling over the name of a speaker you know well, just wait. The more certain you are, the greater the risk of a complete blankout. If your speaker is accompanied by a partner or spouse, make sure that person's name is also given in full. Banish trite references to "lovely wives" and "distinguished husbands."

5. Demonstrate active listening. The audience's gaze will occasionally shift to you during the speech; your body language says it all. Don't be a chairperson who makes an introduction and then spends time making notes, whispering asides to colleagues or checking details with waiters. Keep your eyes on the speaker and generate support and appreciation.

THE SPEAKER'S RESPONSE

Gloria Steinem replied to a warm and admiring introduction by saying, "I know what I'm going to do with the rest of my life—live up to that introduction." She had listened carefully to the introduction and replied generously.

It's surprising how many people ignore the comments of the people introducing them and come with their thanks written out ahead of time. "Thank you, Mr. Chairperson. Your remarks were kind and I am thankful to be here today to mark this occasion. It is a delight to see how many people have taken time to join us." Clichés topped with insincerity—what a way to start.

Good speakers are recognized by their very first words. Leave time at the beginning of your speech for a reply to the introduction. The secret to a gracious and obviously spontaneous response is listening. Plan to finish your last-minute mental rehearsals of your three-part plan and first lines before the speech of introduction. Then focus on the welcoming remarks and find a reference, an image or word to pick up on. If you can do it smoothly, you distinguish yourself as an accomplished and thoughtful guest. Thus, when the person introducing you says they trust your remarks will "fortify our spirits and rejuvenate our depleted energy," you can respond with the remark that "energy and hope are like embers in a campfire; they lie quietly until a breeze comes to fan them." Then you have a choice depending on the audience: joking—"who knows what a gust of wind will do?"—or encouraging—"let's hope our discussion tonight will result in flames that rise up to warm us all."

THE THANK-YOU SPEECH

These are short but sincere remarks. Your preparation may involve advance research or on-the-spot attention.

PATTERN

1. Reason for the thanks. If you are thanking a speaker your function is clear. You need to mention one or two points from the talk that you found helpful or interesting and remark on them without repeating or interpreting the original address. If you are thanking a conference or group co-ordinator, you need to give the audience a specific idea of this person's function. Statistics sometimes provide a clear picture: 386 air flights booked, 2,300 meals planned and ordered, 465 name tags lettered.

2. Try for a balance of brevity and sincerity. Whether you have advance notice or must plan your thanks in two minutes, take time to make thoughtful, specific remarks. Concentrate on the concrete to avoid rambling. The key is to be sincere. Dwell on the idea you found appealing and let your enthusiasm show.

3. Signal—thank the person by name and pronounce it correctly. Finish your speech, then turn and applaud the speaker. A quick, witty thank you needs timing and practice. Jane Buck was asked to thank Carole Bertuzzi Luciani, a high-energy woman who had wisecracked her way through an hour's presentation to a women's organization. Jane went speedily to the microphone, thanked Carole warmly and then said, "You know Carole gave this same speech last night for our male colleagues. Of course it's different working with a live audience." She did the impossible; she thanked a speaker without breaking the feeling of excitement.

Jane's aim was to say thank you while they were still laughing and get off the stage. It's better than the laboured slow-as-molasses format: speaker/pause/laughter/pause/thank you/pause/applause/pause. The pattern she uses is simple: a funny line at the beginning, a joke in the middle and a way out. She advocates personalizing old jokes to suit the audience. With this approach, she says, "There's no way I can miss."

How do you thank an unpopular speaker? The speaker who has come to justify the government's decision to close the local hospital is not going to get a pleasant reception. Your job is to thank the unlucky civil servant for the time spent with your community group. You may not like what was said but you can appreciate the time and effort that individual gave. A simple statement is sufficient: "Thank you, Mr. Trudel. We appreciate the time you took to explain the situation to us."

PRESENTING AN AWARD

When you combine your own enthusiasm with some clear organization and add the sparkle of good will, you have a good speech of presentation. If you outline clear cause for the award, the audience will not only perceive the worth of the recipient, they will also enjoy the energy of your speech. Its function is three-fold: to honour the recipient, to present the actual award and to give the person being honoured a chance to express thanks. The speech should be three to five minutes in length; brevity is the key.

Why was the local owner-operator of a cycle shop voted citizen of the year? If the announcement of the award is the main idea or thesis, what follows? Three supporting reasons, which must be illustrated with anecdotes, quotations from neighbours, telling examples.

PATTERN

1. Set the stage. Discuss the purpose of the award, its background or history and the conditions concerning its presentation. You can include a mention of previous recipients but do not dwell on them to the point of overshadowing the present winner. You may need to brief your audience on such details as when the award was first made, why it was started, how recipients are selected.

Like all speeches, you need to have an attention-getter that is more creative than "It's a privilege to be asked to present this award." Talk about the person—"Five years ago, this individual had never heard of our town. In response to an advertisement, she came 1,500 miles to set up shop and has since made an invaluable contribution to our community."

2. Talk about the recipient. Tell short, accurate stories that provide snapshots of the person's worthiness. Use specific examples discovered during your formal or informal research and be sincere in your remarks. It's better to have a few real stories than a list of generalities. You may point out how you know the award winner but do not go on about yourself.

3. Explain the award or gift as a symbol of the group's esteem. Even though you all contributed, you need not dwell on the monetary value of the gift. Rather, explain that it is an honour for you to present the award and you are paying tribute to the recipient. You might include a description of the organization making the presentation, its background and a brief summary of its aims and achievements. If you are giving a trophy or plaque, it is appropriate to read the inscription word for word and to explain significant artistic details that might otherwise be overlooked.

4. Give the signal. The highlight of the speech is the naming of the recipient. Say the name clearly, slowly, with a sense of honour. Ask the cycle shop owner to come forward, give her direct eye contact and perhaps a personal word of congratulations. Then, speaking directly into the microphone so that everyone can hear clearly, present the award on behalf of the group. "All of us think that Winnipeg is a happier, more free-wheeling place to live because of your contribution to our community. It is with pride, Kit Creek, that we name you citizen of the year. Please accept this plaque and our best wishes."

5. Help the recipient with the gift. It takes practice to speak into the microphone, make eye contact, shake hands and accept an award in one smooth motion. Kit Creek might manage a small plaque and a certificate but what about the person who receives flowers, a letter and a six-kilogram Inuit sculpture wrapped in three metres of paper and secured with an entire roll of tape? Help with the gift. In most cases, it is expected that the person being honoured will unwrap the gift. In that case, a small table

is useful. The person preparing the parcel should show mercy by wrapping shoebox style—the box and lid are wrapped separately and the lid comes off easily. The whole thing is recyclable. Years of watching happy but flustered award winners trying to support an overweight prize with one hand, shake with the other, and search for words prompt this plea for assistance at awards ceremonies.

ACCEPTING A GIFT OR AWARD

No one expects you to have an acceptance speech planned and rehearsed; that might seem just a little too slick. If you have been notified in advance, prepare a general acceptance but try to keep your words spontaneous. If you are completely surprised, take a deep breath and speak from your heart. Take the opportunity to make a short, warm thank you and remember that the audience must hear every word you say.

PATTERN

1. Express appreciation in simple, direct language. Be sincere and pause, if necessary, to think. Remember that just a sentence or two is enough.

2. Don't apologize for being unprepared. You are supposed to be surprised and happy. Enjoy the honour and be yourself.

3. Thank the key people who helped you. Many successful efforts are the result of teamwork. Share the praise but do not list every person you've ever met.

4. Again, thank the organization presenting the award. A citizenship award is established to recognize community awareness and participation. What impact does receiving the award have on you? If there is cash involved, how will you use it? Where will you display the plaque?

5. Open the gift if that is expected. Someone may have worked hard to find a gift to delight you. Join in the spirit of the occasion by unwrapping the object as gracefully as possible. This is no time for flip remarks; respect the efforts of the organization that is praising you.

6. Accept the gift and say thank you once more.

LESSONS FROM A PRO

When Rochan Sankar appeared on television to accept the YTV Innovation Award for inventing the cardiogauge, he was told to prepare a speech that would be put on the teleprompter. But he was also told it would be better if he worked only from a plan and tried to be spontaneous. Rochan heard other winners table long lists of thank yous and decided to try a different approach: "I really wanted to give a message, something personal that applied to other people in the audience. So after the first few sentences on the teleprompter, I winged it. I spoke from my experience about what I really felt. It came from within."

Speaking directly to the audience, he shared his vision and his humour: "There is nothing more precious than an original idea; seeing it translated into reality is truly an exhilarating experience. It's extremely rewarding—intellectually *and* financially."

CREATE YOUR OWN CEREMONIES

Every time I do a workshop on social speeches, people ask me, "Who is supposed to speak? What is the correct order of speakers? Correct for whom? Create your own traditions, your own protocols, ones that are based on sharing the circle of power and recognition. Someone whose heart is full makes a wonderful speaker. And many times we want to acknowledge publicly the significant events of our own lives. It is truly a time to rise up.

Liane Sharkey is a woman who reclaimed her history and her faith by celebrating her Bat Mitzvah as an adult. I am proud to be her friend. Along with other women in her synagogue, she prepared for the ceremony and, although a very private person, wanted to make this speech. She uses the tallit or prayer shawl as the concrete object on which to base her remarks: "And so here I stand—a woman wearing her grandfather's tallit—an unusual privilege representing a future he probably did not foresee…. My grandpa's Bar Mitvah and my Bat Mitzvah are 83 years apart—worlds apart too—but united by the same tallit, the symbol of a commitment I am publicly declaring today with the same passion and love of Judaism as he did in his time. This tallit has become an integral part of what the Bat Mitzvah ceremony signifies to me—as an adult, a woman and as just one generation in a family of countless generations. The reconstructionism as practised here at Darchei Noam has been pivotal for me as a woman of my time, in being able to shed the restrictions of the past and embrace the evolution of a Judaism in which I can include myself fully."

THE FUNERAL TRIBUTE

This speech taxes your heart. On the one hand you want to give a final gift to a friend or colleague who has died. At the same time, you must find enormous personal reserves to put your memories into words. It is the speaking aloud, the actual words, that make a friend's death so real and so hard to talk about. But it is a tribute, a remembering that each person deserves. Take heart when you are asked to do this speech—and take time to work through the process.

In formal terms this speech is a eulogy. Traditionally, it dwells on a person's attributes and accomplishments, and is sincere and simple. Here are two examples. One outlines the characteristics, achievements, and charm of a devoted teacher and scholar, George Wicken. It was delivered at his funeral by his associate, David Kent. Present were many colleagues and students, friends and family. The second is more informal; it was planned and rehearsed in my kitchen when my neighbour, Deb Murray, was asked to speak about her "extra dad," the father of her closest friends.

A FUNERAL TRIBUTE TO GEORGE ROBERT GRENFELL WICKEN

Given by Dr. David Kent

> *George Wicken was many things, variously accomplished. He was a remarkable person in so many ways. His profound sympathy for other people—that reaching out from himself to the other we all experienced in relating to him—that sympathy was at the heart of his teaching gifts.*
>
> *… He was a trusted, valued person. No one who knew George was neutral about him. Everyone liked him. The presence of students here today tells us in what affection he was held by those he taught.*
>
> *But reaching out is tiring when combined with such a sense of responsibility and duty as George had. In his book on the Canadian poet Wilfred Campbell, itself a major contribution to scholarship on Canadian literature, George writes of the "personal spiritual experiences in nature" that*

Campbell's poetry describes. His annual vacation at the family cottage must have brought George the kind of self-losing experiences which gave him peace, rest and renovation. This communion with nature allowed George to return to the academic wear and tear each August with renewed vigour.

Sympathy, or identifying with the other, is probably related to George's love of the theatre, too. He delighted in organizing a theatre outing for students and faculty....

George was a sociable person. He loved to tell jokes. He certainly had a sweet tooth. He took great joy in rounding up tardy faculty and heading for Hospitality Place, the college restaurant. Or, he liked to use his powers of persuasion to convince us that there could be no more convivial place for lunch than at "Feathers," the English pub on Kingston Road. One of my dearest memories is the sight of George moving from cubicle to cubicle in our department office, greeting each one of us and stopping to chat as long as we wished.

Above all, George was a teacher. He loved teaching. It was his vocation, his calling, his fulfilment. Out of that love came ideas, innovative techniques, and imaginative exercises, all of which he generously shared with his colleagues.

... Another remark George made in his book on Campbell is pertinent here, and a reflection of his own personality. George wrote: "Commitment to others, through loyalty and love, can give life meaning." In that sentence George is still speaking to us now, speaking of commitment, dedication, enthusiasm, love. Those are values he embodied.

... If we could have told George something a few days ago, I wonder what each of us would have said. I'd like to end with a quotation out of a letter Leigh Hunt sent in 1822 to Joseph Severn, the man who was caring for the dying English poet, John Keats. I think some of us might have wished we could have said this to George, even if through an intermediary. I say it now on behalf of us all: "Tell him (Hunt wrote to Keats's friend) that we shall all bear his memory in the most precious part of our hearts.... Tell him that the most sceptical of us has faith enough to think that all (of us) are journeying to one and the same place, and shall unite somehow... again face to face, mutually conscious, mutually delighted. Tell him he is only before us on the road, as he was in everything else, and that we are coming after him."

A FUNERAL TRIBUTE TO WILLIAM CAVANAGH

Given by Deborah Murray, Haileybury, April 1993

William was my extra dad. He was my friend. Together we were dedicated

Blue Jay fans and tomato farmers. As farmers we knew the importance of a root system that would nourish and support the plants. To me Bill's life was a system like that, a system of roots of love and support and dedication to his family and the communities in which he lived.

Bill's personal roots were as one of eight brothers and sisters who had a happy childhood on the family farm in Perth, Ontario. He wandered north to Haileybury and met his beloved wife, Hallie. They had six children and the farming connection finally drew them back south. At Grand Valley their farm grew and grew because the livestock all became pets. Five years later the severity of Bill's allergies caused the family to return to Haileybury. At his garage he worked long hours from 7:00 a.m. to 11:00 p.m. and often went out at night when people called. But this did not prevent him from taking days off to have special celebrations and picnics with his family.

He faced the challenge of raising his daughters; they were all equally special to him and he stood by them: Priscilla, Marg, Anne, Jane and Sue. In turn, they gave him a ball team. He was very proud of all of his grandchildren and loved them deeply.

He had a great love of sports both as a participant and a viewer. He was a ball player and last week at the seniors club, he was high scorer at darts. Most of all he was an avid watcher of TV sports of all kinds. Watching a game with Bill was a kind of sporting event in itself; he would sit on the edge of the seat gesturing, leg up in the air, calling the shots. It was quite an experience.

There are the little things that we all remember and have pictures of. Bill kept involved in many things. In our community he was one of the initiators of the seniors club. He got it off the ground and kept it going. He was involved in the horticultural society and volunteer firefighters. In all these activities he would attend to details, big and small. Just like at home when at Easter for his family he would make rabbit tracks that came right up to the back door. Someone said to me that Bill will not just be missed; he will be really, really missed.

Plants have names, some of Latin origin, some common names, and some we make up when we forget. Bill was known by many names: Mr. C, William, Uncle Bill, Grandpa Bill, Dad, and Pa. In the routine of his days he was addressed in these ways by many people—at the post office, in philosophical discussions at the hardware store and doing Meals on Wheels.

There was a special name reserved by Mrs. O for him—that of sweetheart. The picture I have of them and their relationship is one of intertwined roots; the days and trips and times they spent together. Our thoughts are with you Mrs. O.

... It's been said he was a lucky man to have such a loving family. We were lucky to have him. When I think of the memories of us starting our tomato plants and the teasing that went on back and forth about whose seedlings were largest and whose began flowering first, I know we both had hopes of a wonderful crop. All of us here, family and friends, know Bill was the pick of the crop. We will miss him very much.

BEFORE YOU START—WORK THROUGH YOUR OWN STUFF

In recent years I have made and helped others plan several of these speeches. As a teacher, I was saddened by the number of students who were faced with making this kind of speech. Students or teacher, we all have the same job—to work through our own stuff.

As I was writing this chapter, my neighbour Deb, whose progress as a speaker I have followed as this book developed, was shaken by the unexpected death of her friend. She wanted to do the speech; the hard part was to deal with her grief. She had two days to get over what she called that "I think I'm going to throw up" feeling. Her own shock at losing a friend and her own sense of loss almost took over. Her nerve endings were sticking out all over and her early notes were full of how she knew Bill, how she felt, how she would miss him. These feelings weren't denied or set aside; they were put in perspective. A funeral tribute is not about the speaker; it's about the friend she remembers. Deb came through for Bill, for his family and for me. When I cautioned her to watch that her own stuff didn't get in the way of her job—the honouring of Bill—and to make the time to plan and rehearse, she understood my bluntness.

A tribute is a good way to remember a person; give yourself time to grieve and honour your own feelings. Then get to work. As a speaker you have the best and the worst of jobs. Whatever happens, do not dwell on the progress of your own surprise and grief and trouble making up your speech. The last time I heard someone do this, I knew more about him than I did about the person being remembered.

PATTERN

1. Honour the person. Your speech is a way of paying tribute to someone you liked and will miss. It is a chance to say how much that person meant to you.

2. Make a plan—and tie your speech to something solid. How do you see your friend in your mind? Did he or she have a hobby or a job that you can base your memories on? Do you have one outstanding picture that can form the base of your talk? Make a plan to help yourself get through the speech and give it a framework.

3. Outline how you knew the person. Were you childhood friends, neighbours, associates at work? Did you share a common interest in working with a service group? Establish your connection for the person's family and friends who don't know you.

4. Share specific memories that bring your friend before you. Your job is to recall your friend, to give yourself and others glimpses, verbal snapshots of his or her special qualities. Choose one or two good memories: a joke shared, a ritual at work, the time you were lost in Paris and your friend decided to spend the night in the police station. It's all right to smile as you remember the good times; it's a way of keeping that person in your life.

5. Keep it short. Don't strain your emotional reserves. Present your memories, say that you will miss your friend and *finish*. That's often the hardest part.

6. Crying is all right. Putting memories into words that you say out loud is very different than thinking them. Practise out loud to prepare yourself. In order to make a good funeral speech, you should know when to anticipate the tightening of your throat that means tears are on the way. The words that trip you up are often surprising—practice is the only way to be ready. Find out if and when you cry and how long you take. Then you know you can get through it. Pause. Breathe. Tell yourself you're okay. People will wait. You may want to make a gesture to let the audience know you are all right and to prevent any well-meaning attempt to usher you away from the microphone.

THE TOAST

Toasts are ceremonial tributes given on special occasions; the most common are a formal toast to a head of state (including the Queen), an impromptu toast and a wedding toast. Making these speeches can be a pleasure if you remember to brainstorm, plan and practise.

It is essential to include the signal and the verbal cue.

PATTERNS

Toast to a Head of State. The Protocol Office of the Secretary of State provides a simple outline for a toast to the Queen or her representative. It is a good model for brief, formal salutes. The person proposing the toast raises his or her glass and says, "Ladies and gentlemen, will you rise and raise your glasses in a toast to the Queen: the Queen—la Reine."

An Informal Toast. Often, when you're present at a celebration or dinner, someone will say, "let's have a toast," and look directly at you. Occasionally, you may wish to take the initiative; if your friend has just been appointed to the board of directors of the World Wildlife Federation, a toast is in order.

1. Be Prepared. If you can form three-part plans as you stand in line for a concert, you are used to being ready. During the soup course of a celebration dinner, think of several thoughtful and complimentary things to say. Good speakers spend much of their time thinking—and they get faster at it. They also think of the cook; make your remarks brief, or speak after dinner. Never let a fine meal cool.

2. Relax. Take the opportunity to express appreciation or congratulations; focus on the person you are speaking about. Your friends look forward to your words, so enjoy yourself.

3. Breathe. This is an informal setting but you still need a well-modulated, confident voice. Breathe.

4. Make one or two sincere remarks. If your friend has just received her pilot's licence, compliment the sense of adventure and attention to detail that led to her success. Use stories you heard about the training flights to illustrate the challenges involved.

5. Give the signal. Raise your glass and address your friend directly: "Congratulations on your pilot's licence, Valerie. We wish you good weather and smooth landings: [the cue] To Valerie."

WEDDING SPEECHES

Speeches are the landmines of the wedding reception. Too often, the bride and groom wait until the day before the wedding to ask someone to MC the reception or make a toast. In the midst of the excitement and partying, there is little time to prepare. To compound their nervousness and lack of preparation, would-be speakers listen to friends who advise them to have a drink to "loosen up." What often results is a five-minute mumble of semi-humorous anecdotes, insults more suited to a roast than a toast, and remarks that show no regard for the families present. To make things worse, the verbal mayhem is often recorded on videotape—and humiliation lives on.

How can this happen? How can families spend thousands of dollars on a reception and not insist on speakers whose skills and thoughtfulness they trust? If you think I'm exaggerating, consider the following examples. The more I researched this topic, the more callous were the stories.

- A man proposing a toast to the bride and groom said that for them it was love at first sight. They hopped into bed the night they met and didn't emerge for two days. True perhaps, but not a good choice for a family gathering.

- In toasting the bride and groom the best man enthusiastically recalled meeting the groom's boss Ben and his talented wife Zora. Too bad Ben was there with his present wife Olivia.

- Another speaker joked, "It's nice you decided to make it legal, James. I was afraid she'd be a live-in for years." The bride's father did not look pleased; he was there with his common-law partner of eight years.

- The MC proposed a toast to the parents of the bride. Because the bride's name was Hope St. Jean, he assumed her parents were called Mr. and Mrs. St. Jean. The bride's parents, however, were Marie and Jack Boddam and they were irate. The MC had embarrassed and infuriated the people who were paying the bills.

Everyone deserves a happy wedding day with speakers who respect the occasion and say kind things. If you're asked to do a toast, follow these rules of common sense:

- Honour the families and their guests. Respect the values of the people present. They don't need shock treatment or X-rated gags. The reception is not a roast or a time to embarrass others.

- Be sensitive. This is a very emotional occasion for everyone. Prepare ahead of time and find out who will be present and what is considered appropriate. If you're in doubt about some of your material, leave it out.

- Leave past histories and family composition alone! This is the single most dangerous landmine. Do not assume anything about the relationships of the people present. Ask them how they want to be mentioned; check their names carefully and omit all references to former mates and past history.

- Don't elevate yourself at the expense of others. Too many people speak to get a few laughs for themselves rather than to please the wedding party.

- Bring up happy, positive memories. Tell stories that outline the lives of the bride and groom in a considerate way. It's fun for the families to recall highlights of their lives and interesting for guests who don't know the couple well.

- If you can't speak—don't!

TURNING LANDMINES INTO GOLDMINES

Choose an MC you trust to keep the speeches moving and share the microphone wisely. Couples who want things to move smoothly can work out the order of the reception and provide a program including the order of speakers on the same card as the menu. Too many people assume that things will unfold magically—remember there is no set order of who does what. Plan carefully and ask speakers you trust well in advance. No one expects to get a good photographer or florist the night before; don't assume you'll get a good speaker at the last minute.

Who does the speaking? A friend or relative who is a good speaker and an affable host. The groom's childhood friend might be a great best man but a terrible speaker; get someone else to be the MC. He or she should enjoy large groups and be able to control access to the microphone in a friendly way. Insist on a good speaker. What speeches are given? Traditionally there is a toast to the bride or the bride and groom, and a toast to the parents of the bride. In reality, you can have whatever speeches you want done by whomever you wish. But keep the time in mind. Hotel managers say that couples want the food cleared quickly and the music started but the speeches roll on forever.

More brides are making speeches; as one woman said, "People have come to honour our marriage and that's what I want to thank them for."

What are you supposed to say in a toast to the bride and groom? It is a speech to wish the bride and groom happiness and share stories that give a sense of the couple. Your job as a speaker is to plan carefully, rehearse thoroughly and party later.

PATTERN

1. Make a plan. You need a three-part plan: introduction, body and conclusion. The theme is the happiness of the bride and groom in their lives together, their adventures, their family. During a reception you face competition from servers clearing dishes and a general hum of excitement. You need a strong plan to enable guests to follow your remarks easily.

2. Frame your speech. What sort of grabber will make a strong framework for your speech? Can you use the words of a favourite song, a special day the couple celebrates, a shared joke? If you start with such a reference, your conclusion is already set. Refer again to the song, the special day, the way they met and your speech will have unity.

   One father proposed a toast by noting that the wedding day was also the anniversary of the birth of Martin Luther King Jr. He went on to wish his daughter and son-in-law the qualities that King embodied: courage, vision and love.

3. Research. If you are a friend of the couple you will have a good source of anecdotes. If not, you have to research. Ask them for ideas; telephone family members, friends, business associates. Share the making of the speech and be sure to collect stories about both individuals. A good toast is well balanced.

4. Consider the wishes of the bride and groom. Talk to them about the speech, ask what they wish to have included, if there is anything to omit. Go over the names of family members and make notes. If one or both of them have children, how will they be mentioned? In a toast I heard recently, the speaker included the wishes of the children for their father and new mother.

   In the example of a toast to the parents of the bride, the speaker, Kim Mitchell, followed the wishes of the bride to toast all her parents. She refers to the four people by their first names instead of outlining who is married to whom. A toast is no time for a flow chart.

5. Use gentle humour. Try the stories out on your own family. Are they kind?

6. Practise. Your friends deserve the best. Make notes, revise your speech, experiment. If you work hard on a presentation for work, work equally hard to honour and delight your friends. Weddings are busy times; give yourself at least a few days to concentrate on the toast before the pre-nuptial festivities begin. The count-down given below may help. And be prepared with an extra set of notes. I once lost mine in the excitement of getting to the church on time.

7. Refer to the bride and groom by their names. Give them equal billing and refer to each in his or her own right. Avoid references like "We wish Sebastian and his wife much happiness." They'll both be happier if you talk about "Sebastian and Megan." Make eye contact with the bride and groom and let them know you are honoured to play this part in the ceremonies.

8. Give the signal. When you have given your friends the best gift possible, a good toast, give the verbal cues that everyone needs: Please join with me in a toast to the bride and groom. [raise your glass]: To the bride and groom—Megan and Sebastian.

9. Enjoy yourself *after* you are finished. Eat, rest and drink after the job is done.

A TOAST TO THE PARENTS OF THE BRIDE

by Kimberly Mitchell

> *Change is inevitable and with change comes growth. Over the past 13 years I've watched Lisa go from an "I'll try anything once" child to a serious, thoughtful woman. I don't think Lisa could have grown this much if it hadn't been for her family, especially her parents. They nurtured her as a child, watched her flourish with their love and care, and even helped her when she didn't know she needed help. Occasionally she was helped when she least wanted it. Like the time her father knew she had it for the boy behind the meat counter, and he decided to do his rendition of Quasimodo behind the shopping cart—just to get his attention. But most of all they have given her their support. No matter what she has done, no matter what life has thrown her way, they have always been behind her, and she, in turn, has always been behind them.*

Lisa really is one lucky person—she has an extended parent plan. She has four different people guiding her, four people sharing their love for her, and four different sets of ideas which have enabled Lisa to broaden her outlook on life. I'd like to make a toast to Lisa's parents and all the ways that they have helped her—to Marie-Ange, Raymond, Dawn and Patrick, Lisa's parents.

12-DAY COUNTDOWN FOR A GOOD WEDDING SPEECH

Day 1:
- Get the assignment. Ask the bride and groom if you will be speaking.

Days 2 & 3:
- Brainstorm and plan. Get a theme. Talk to friends.

Days 4 & 5:
- Talk to bride and groom. Design speech. Work on intro and main points.

Days 6, 7, 8:
- Talk to bridal party for stories. Check family names.

Days 9, 10, 11:
- Make notes. Practise.

Day 12:
- One last practice out loud. Good luck.

THEMES THAT WORK

Need help to get rolling? Here's a list of possible themes; they may trigger an idea for your toast. Most of them focus on everyday songs or objects. People relate to common items; while they may nod in agreement at classical quotations, they smile in surprise and delight when you mention something they recognize.

- The bride is like the flowers in the bouquet she carries: the enduring beauty of the rose; the loyalty of forget-me-nots, the mystery of the gardenia and the luck of the shamrock.

- The couple are like classic cars: he's got the universal appeal of the Volkswagen Beetle and she's got the joy of the rag-top convertible.

- Married life is like a fishing trip which they both enjoy: they have the equipment, the bait and the boat. And like all good trips, the true fun does not lie in the catch but in the experience.

- Marriage is like the song that goes "all my life's a circle"; as the moon rolls through the night sky, they will know the circles of joy, hard times, birth, romance and age. And the circle always comes back to their love.

- In Lithuania the couple is served a symbolic meal: wine for joy, salt for tears and bread for work. A good marriage has all three.

- This couple met while tree planting and wood is central to their lives—for heat and security; for happy campfires with friends; for magic and romance dreaming in the firelight.

- A gift to them of a set of keys: health, happiness and humour. And if a key is ever lost, they can find it again. The "key point" is a wonderful time together.

- The grandmother of the bride toasted a couple and compared marriage to the log cabin at the lake where they spend their summers. It has strength and a solid foundation, large clear windows through which they watch as the seasons pass and weather the storms together. In the water of the lake they see the reflection of themselves and remember how they fit. And the large, strong pines around the cabin shelter and protect their world, absorb the sound of healthy arguments and have sturdy limbs on which to hang a swing.

    The bride returned the compliment and said that when she was a little girl, she used to look at the night sky and wish on a star. Then she thanked everyone who had come to her wedding and said she was truly lucky because they were her stars, the people who had helped make her dreams come true.

Sample Outline of a Toast to the Bride and Groom

Alex Cardinal was asked to give the toast to the bride and groom at the marriage of his friends Farouk and Emily. These are the notes for his speech; he used the song "Amazing Grace" as the basis for his remarks.

Intro
- greetings to the bridal party, families and friends
- favourite song of the bride is "Amazing Grace"

- one line is "I once was lost but now I'm found/was blind but now I see."
- Emily and Farouk also have visions of what their love can bring them separately and together as a couple

Thesis
- we wish them a vision of happiness
  - in their careers
  - in the family they hope for
  - in shared adventures

Body
- careers: Emily is a child care and youth worker
  - caring, strong, perceptive woman
  - story of Brett and Duc
- Farouk is a technician in printing firm
  - artistic, competitive
  - remembers coming to Canada after escaping his own country by truck and boat
- family: family means love, support, freedom
  - Emily's life with her grandparents
  - Farouk's trouble at school and support at home
  - their plans for a new family with love for everyone
- shared adventures: love of travel, auctions, commitment to each other and freedom to grow

Conclusion
- We wish them happiness and joy. We hope that the love they share will help them build a future of possibility and caring, and know the hard times they have had will make them kinder people.
- I think of amazing grace as the love Farouk and Emily have for each other.
  They are not lost—they have found themselves and each other.
  They are not blind—they see love and a future together.
  We wish them amazing grace, amazing love and a life of health and joy.

Cue
Friends and family, I ask you to rise and join me in a toast to the bride and groom.—To Emily and Farouk, the bride and groom.

THE AFTER-DINNER SPEECH

After you have been initiated into the world of public speaking, someone will call and ask you to provide "the entertainment" at a luncheon meeting or banquet. Generally, you are expected to speak rather than tap dance. I love being an after-dinner speaker; the ambience is good and the audience friendly.

An after-dinner speech provides the intellectual dessert to the meal. It may be informative or persuasive, but its distinguishing feature is your awareness of the audience and your desire to please or stimulate them. Your audience analysis will help determine a topic that is appropriate without being heavy. Wildlife biologists working for the National Park System do not need more data on mosquito control. However, they may relate to your analysis of the most pesky species of all: the tourist.

PATTERN

Many topics you are familiar with will make good after-dinner speeches.

1. Tailor your speech to your audience. This may be the tenth time you've spoken on sailing around the world with your cat but you had better tie it in to the interests of the present group or you'll sink. Nobody likes generic speeches; they sound the same in any city and they're disappointing. Repeat performances are also boring for speakers; you'll lose your edge.

    Research the group and work on an upbeat approach. What do solo sailors and your audience of nurses have in common? Too much work to do in too little time? Bedpans in the night? Life or death emergencies? Find good parallels and you've earned your chocolate mousse.

2. After-dinner does not mean out-to-lunch. The intellectual skills of the audience should be respected. Have some thoughtfulness or challenge in your speech. Humour is welcome if it works for the topic and the occasion, but a string of unrelated jokes falls flat.

3. Have a challenging but not baffling topic. Analogies and anecdotes are more suited to this occasion than complicated proofs. A clear plan will enable your listeners to follow you easily.

4. Fit in with the occasion and enjoy yourself. Commenting on the occasion, interacting with audience members and referring favour-

ably to other speakers' remarks are all appropriate. Be friendly and reward the group's taste in speakers (you) by giving your best.

5. Prepare first—eat later. As the other guests dig into their kiwi cheesecake, you're getting your thoughts assembled, checking that your notes are handy and starting your breathing and relaxation exercises. At the same time, you're talking to the people at your table to find out more about the audience. Tune in to the mood of the event.

TURN THE GLASSES OVER AND OTHER DETAILS

What can trip you up when you speak? Here are a few pointers from seasoned speakers. Their advice may save your speech and your pride.

- Do not drink before you speak. Loosening up is a sure prelude to messing up. Good speakers eat lightly and drink not at all. Feast after your work is done.

- Consult the checklist "On Arrival" in Chapter 9. Take time to fix your hair and check your zipper before you join the group.

- Avoid overused phrases. Some words have become so trivialized by overuse that they are almost meaningless. Phrases guaranteed to annoy include "I know where you're coming from," "world class," "state of the art," "the bottom line," "in point of fact" and "have a nice day."

- How much is enough? Audiences want enough but not too much. Remember, the human mind can only absorb what the human seat can endure.

- Keep cool—keep focused. What happens when the person introducing you gets all the information wrong and rambles on? Take the advice Linda Tillery gives her gospel groups: "When a soloist starts to piss all over a piece, don't get distracted. Have inner composure."

GENTLE OF HEART: MORE ON WORDS

Is a boy living with his father considered a family? How do you differentiate between the mother who gave you birth and the mother who raised you? Are old people always retired? How do you introduce Danielle March, the wife of your client, Keith March?

These questions should give one message: our lives and social patterns are changing. You should be aware of lifestyles other than your own and respect those who live them. As a speaker, your language should reflect and value the lives of the people listening to you. Families don't depend on certain numbers or players; birth mothers, stepmothers and adoptive mothers are all important in our lives; senior citizens lead full lives, often working at paid or volunteer jobs; and Danielle and Keith March (alphabetical listing) are at the head table.

Words are very powerful things, and, under pressure, phrases we absorbed in our past often fall out of our mouths. When you speak in public, a hasty, unthinking remark can hurt or alienate members of your audience. You have an ethical responsibility to avoid spreading narrow-mindedness, even unintentionally.

How can you become more aware of others' lives? Listen. Think. Thoughtfulness and common sense are what you need. Consider the following scenarios.

- A government official outlines a new policy regarding breakfast programs in the schools. A friend tells her later that she used the phrase "We cannot gyp our students of the energy they need to learn." She is chagrined to have used a word that denigrates the gypsy race.

- Anna and Robert Sanchez object strongly to the person who says they come from a broken home.

- Liz Markovich, mother of Simon and Raffi, spends time replying to Renata, an engineer, who remarked, "Oh, you don't work."

- The MC for a company party keeps referring to "husbands and wives" and "spouses." There are other people present who wish his vocabulary acknowledged their partners.

- The chairperson of the fund-raising campaign for a youth centre in a large city has used the phrase "christian name" four times in the last half hour.

- Lin Wah leaves the meeting in a hurry. During coffee break, one of the advisory council asked him how he was adjusting to Canada. Lin Wah was born in Vancouver.

Linda Tillery and Heather Bishop are electrifying performers. As MCs, their humour, their warmth, their spirit bring the audience together. I've seen them both work 8,000 to 10,000 people, introducing upwards of five acts in an evening. They work hard for both the performers and the audience, and they create unity.

LINDA TILLERY

Linda Tillery is a Bay Area musician who performs regularly with a blues band, a jazz-vocal sextet, an a cappella group and her own band. She's a generous performer and MC.

SB: You use the phrase "sing musically" often. Do we also speak musically?

LT: *Yes we do. We speak slowly or quickly, loudly or softly, we add emphasis, use exclamations, and even use facial expressions to get our point across.*

SB: The question I hear you ask is "do you know the form?" What does knowing a form have to do with the ability to sing or speak well?

LT: *The standard song form for most popular music—country, gospel, rhythm and blues—is AABA: verse, verse, chorus, verse. And if you know the form or outline, you can move through the song without fear.*

SB: You speak of sharing culture through music. What does that mean?

LT: *When I sing or direct a choir, I share my African American heritage. In gospel music we express ourselves with dancing, clapping, shouting, moving around the stage, using the dominant seventh and minor third for harmonic coloration. That's culture, not religion. It's really African culture.*

SB: Is it important to you to share culture?

LT: *Yes, if it's received respectfully.*

SB: What makes a good speaker?

LT: *When you speak about something, you need to have a working knowledge of the subject. You need to have a great understanding of the material, to be thorough.*

SB: You are superb with large groups of people. I've seen you MC for 8,000 people and you are so alive, you work with them so well. Do you enjoy it?

LT: *Yes I do. There is power in numbers and also safety. And it took me a long time to realize the secret that less is more. You have to be really strong inside yourself to know that less is stronger. If you overload your audience, they can't absorb it. Think about how you are going to communicate to your audience so that you are not boring and you raise their level of understanding.*

INTERVIEW

HEATHER BISHOP

Heather Bishop is from Woodmore, Manitoba. Her powerful voice and love of life fill the stage when she performs. She has many recordings for children and adults to her credit. Her combination of wry humour and great honesty make her a popular MC.

SB: When an MC introduces a speaker or a musician, what does she or he do for the audience?

HB: *It's a big job. She really has to bring the event to what's happening for you. She needs to get the information out and keep you interested and focused, or help you focus on the next speaker. A good MC is an act in themselves.*

SB: What do good MCs do for a performer?

HB: *Focus the audience so they're settled down and ready for me. If they speak about me from the heart, it'll be great. A woman once gave me one of the best introductions I ever had; she said "By giving us herself, she gives us ourselves."*

There are usually one or two business things: rules of the hall, no smoking, upcoming events. They should mention a new album I have and if it's an audience I don't know well, the fact that I have many albums. If I'm signing albums, the audience needs to know when and where. That's my livelihood—I need it. Beyond that, speak from your heart.

SB: Are MCs supposed to know your work? Are they supposed to do their homework?

HB: *I wish they would and I think they should. When I'm an MC, I go through all the program notes and read up on the performers. It's easier if I know their work and can talk about how their stuff makes me feel. I talk to them and find out what's happening with them and if there's anything special they want me to say.*

At least learn how to pronounce someone's name. Nothing makes you feel more disconnected than somebody who can't say your name. Find out! Talk to the person. I ask people to listen to me say their name back to them 10 times until I have it in a way they're comfortable with.

SB: To introduce your music I have heard you speak honestly of many things, often very troubling subjects. How do you prepare to talk to your audience?

HB: *To use my gift as it's meant to be used, I need to ground myself. I need to connect. I make a circle with whomever I'm on stage with and I pray. My personal prayer is for wisdom, that I'm open and centred enough that my gift will come through me. I pray that*

*when I speak I will touch people's hearts and find the right words
to open doors for people.*

*The songs I have down perfectly; they're nailed down so I
can be free to let the words come. I keep my feet on the earth and
let my spirit travel. Honour your gifts and honour yourself. Let
the truth come through you. There's nothing more powerful than
truth.*

SB: Were you always so open on stage?

HB: *It took me years to come to a place of honouring and loving
myself. Then I could begin to share myself. At a very young age I
recognized that the people who touched me were those people
who spoke the truth. At 12 or 13 I discovered Nina Simone.
There I was, a young white teenager listening to an African
American woman and learning, learning, learning. The same·
with Buffy Sainte-Marie. The truth resonates with you. I wanted
to be someone who got up there and told the truth.*

*So when I decided I wanted to be a musician, it was clear to
me that I could not go on the stage and not be out as a lesbian.
Naturally, I thought I could never be a musician. How could I
speak openly and still have a career? So I began. I had spent
years struggling for all kinds of political issues: racism, sexism,
environmental and union issues. I was not going to go up on
stage and not speak the truth about my own struggle.*

*When you only put your voice to other people's oppression
and not your own, the truth is not resonating through you and
you're not in touch with your own power. There is nothing more
beautiful than watching someone centred in their own power.*

SB: How do you prepare for workshops?

HB: *I use a paper with seven or eight words or phrases on it to remind
me of important stuff. It's like a set list when I sing—every song
is in the place it's in for a reason. There is a flow that has to do
with laughing and crying and healing. And so I have to take
responsibility for the emotions I create in people. Always leave
your audience in a great place of empowerment and strength.*

SB: What do you think makes women speak out?

HB: *A combination of being inspired by seeing someone else do it and
something in your life happening that is the last straw—a chemical dump in your neighbourhood, the rape of your daughter.*

Something happens in your life that makes you say, "That's it! I can no longer be silenced. I have to speak up."

SB: What do people have to know to speak well?

HB: *The advice I give people is train yourself. It's not enough to have good ideas, not enough to have an okay voice and friends who think you're great. You have a responsibility to work your craft. If you are a speaker, take yourself seriously. Pick out the speakers you most admire. Read their stuff, watch them speak, learn how they do it. If you have a chance to talk to them, take advantage of that opportunity. Secondly, take every chance you find to learn. Go to workshops, discussions. Never stop training yourself in your craft. Never think that you know it all because you never will. Your gift is like a little candlelight and you need to learn from others so you can make it become a flame.*

SB: You said women speak out because it is the last straw. Do you think you will live to see people speak as the first straw?

HB: *I hope so and I feel like I'm almost seeing it. The last straw is happening for women at a much younger age so it's occurring as a first straw. I've seen young women of 18 or 19 doing what it took me 30 or 35 years to do and they are speaking out about it already. It's becoming the first straw. Sometimes you think these young women take so much for granted, they'll lose it all if they don't work. Then along comes a young woman who blows you away. We've opened doors and the process will continue—more and more doors will open.*

CHAPTER

8

THINKING ON YOUR FEET:

IMPROMPTU SPEAKING

I try to get excited and to get others excited. Most people are afraid of dying during their speech. And most people are afraid to let emotion enter into it. So they read a script—I mean they shouldn't have chairs, they should have beds for the audience.

— **David Nichol**

▲▲▲▲▲▲▲▲▲▲▲▲

You arrive at a reception for your regional humane society and one of the directors spots you hovering at the refreshments. Knowing you have five cats and a keen interest in banning the testing of products on animals, he asks if you would fill in for a speaker who can't make it. "Just a few minutes," he says. "Talk about anything on testing—I'm sure we'll find it interesting."

How do you react? "I don't—I forget nine-tenths of the English language" was the response of one person I coached. He is an artist, a potter whose work has been displayed around the world. His creativity didn't help him in all situations, however; when he consulted me several years ago, a request to speak turned his feet to clay.

Consider the impromptu the main window—it gives access to a variety of speaking opportunities. This chapter will help you become adept at thinking and speaking on your feet. As you improve your reaction time, you'll anticipate taking an active part in business and community meetings.

WINGING IT: THE IMPROMPTU SPEECH

Impromptu speeches are a challenge. Like unexpected overtime, they demand all your skills and nerve. You can handle an impromptu if you remember that it's like any other speech; it requires a thesis, a clear design and a strong finish. You just have to think faster. Consider the following techniques; they've been tested many times by people who have earned their wings.

1. Be prepared. This old motto works well for speakers. Predict when you may be asked to speak. If you are well known in your community, have recently received an award, or are friends with a desperate convenor, you may be called on. Get an attitude—a speaker's ear for the perfect story: news items, conversations in elevators, talk shows, radio interviews, children's questions. When you read magazines, make a mental note of interesting items. This doesn't have to be complex; you may have just heard a documentary on being more successful after the age of 45. How about a speech on what success means to you, or why you're looking forward to 45 (or 55, or 65)? Next time you're waiting for the meal to be served at a conference, plan what you would say if you were given five minutes.

2. Make use of your time. You will probably have a few hours or at least a few minutes to gather your thoughts. Don't panic! Instead, follow the procedure you would for any speech.

- Think of your subject. Choose one that's important to you and right for your audience.

- Establish your thesis. Pause and find out what you think. Determine one clear main idea. Be specific.

- Think of one or two supporting statements and examples.

3. Work out a brief outline. This is a speech—it needs a grabber, a thesis, points to prove that thesis and a strong conclusion. Once again, keep it simple. For the grabber, use something you've observed lately. Tell a story to set the mood and introduce your

topic. Did your daughter's car get sideswiped yesterday? That leads into speeches on the importance of friends, insurance, reflexes and chiropractors. I used that very example to start a speech on how I still rely on my mother to comfort me as I, in turn, reassure others. Mothers console us across miles, across time.

One good plan for an impromptu is past, present and future. What is the history of the group you are addressing? How have they worked together in the past? What present challenges do they face? What are their future resources? This outline can apply to many situations. Madame Jehane Benoît, a superb chef and prolific author, offered good advice to cooks and speakers alike: "I feel a recipe is only a theme which an intelligent cook can play each time with a variation."

Think of specific examples or details to support your main statements; no one expects you to have exact statistics but some concrete data will help.

4. Jot down your notes. Take time to write down a few words to keep you on track. Then use those notes and—

5. Breathe and enjoy yourself. Nervousness always gets you in the throat. *Breathe.* A good deep breath will clear your head and make you sound confident. At the same time, look as though you are enjoying yourself. Even in an impromptu situation the audience needs to know that you like talking to them. Express your pleasure: "I'm surprised but happy to be able to share this time with you—I've always valued this organization." Then get on with the speech.

6. Stick to the plan. Use your plan to speak with confidence and conviction. Don't ramble. Inexperienced speakers get so nervous, they forget to coach themselves and ramble in an attempt to fill time. Instead, channel your nervousness into planning your speech. Say what you want to say and save the filler for your memoirs.

7. Be brief. You're not expected to know everything so unless you were hoping for the chance and have a speech in your pocket, make your main points and stop.

8. Finish strong and sit down. An obvious point, you say. Watch nervous speakers—they never know if they've said enough. So they dither and ramble and mutter, repeat themselves, add unrelated points, stretch out their talk until you want to yell "enough."

Once you've covered your main point, told stories to illustrate it and made a strong final statement, you're finished. Sit down.

9. Have speeches and quotations in reserve. Take a lesson from David Nichol, an old hand at speaking. He has an "impromptu" that he alters for different occasions. Treat sections of your speeches as building blocks and use them to design a fresh talk for each group. It helps to keep a few quotations on hand. I'm not good at memorizing but have several short quotations that I've used many times, altering a word or two to suit the group. Here they are: the first one is often attributed to Bobby Kennedy, proof that he too had a good stockpile of versatile quotes.

> *"You see things, and you say 'Why?' But I dream things that never were, and I say, 'Why not?'"*
> **—George Bernard Shaw**

> *"Free your mind and the rest will follow."*
> **—k.d. lang**

> *"Every writer needs a built-in, foolproof, crap detector."*
> **—Ernest Hemingway**

> *"She got ninety-nine rows uh jaw teeth and git her good and mad, she'll wade through solid rock up to her hip pockets."*
> **—Zora Neale Hurston**

CRISIS CONTROL

A real impromptu is a surprise. It is not a speech that you decided to forget about. Never plan to speak impromptu. And never bore your audience with endless apologies about how surprised or unprepared you are.

FIVE-MINUTE WORKOUT

Spend a few minutes reading or listening to the news. Select several topics that interest you and plan a three-minute speech on one of them. Give yourself 10 minutes to plan and then try it out loud. How well does it hold together? How confident do you sound?

THE GOOD NEWS ON IMPROMPTUS

You do get better! The potter with feet of clay called me recently and told me that he enjoys speaking much more. He tries to think of an idea that starts with art and relates to a wider audience. He also said he's much faster on impromptus. When we first worked together, he considered an impromptu to be a request made the night before or morning of an event. Now, he's calm when they greet him at the door with, "We were hoping that you would say...."

A FEW WORDS

If you are often asked to bring greetings or make a few brief remarks before the guest speaker begins, think of a way to make your few minutes interesting for you *and* the audience. An easy way is to see what significant event happened on the day you are speaking. Did Sharon Wood scale Everest? Is it the anniversary of Harriet Tubman's birth? What about James Naismith—do you know when he invented basketball? How does that relate to the group? Choose a quotation from a book you're reading and challenge the group to apply it to their organization. In other words, don't fill time—use it. A quotation or example you give may be as interesting to the audience as the speech that follows. Every speaking opportunity counts.

THE NEW WAY: ENLARGING THE CIRCLE

My friend Elaine Wabi loves to tease me when we're on the road as speaking partners. She maintains that adults make her nervous— she'd rather be talking to school children about caribou hair tufting or antler carving, traditional native handiwork. The last time we went to make an equity presentation on fair treatment of visible and invisible minorities, she said to me, "I'll just sit in the car. If any of those folks want to share something with me, send them on over." Once she's in the room, she tells stories—long tales that make a point and an indelible impression. Elaine's talks require the participation of the audience; in this type of story-telling the listener's job is to find the lesson. As she says, "We may not find it necessary to finish a story. Native people expect others to know what we are talking about."

It's not hard to imagine her feelings as she remembers sitting in her grade nine science class when her teacher made the remark that Indians would drink anything, even Aqua Velva aftershave. Elaine, who had not told her classmates she was native, found herself speaking out: "I looked at him and told him I'd appreciate it if he'd take it back, maybe he shouldn't say things like that. This teacher was a big man, about 300 pounds, and he looked over at me. The whole class was silent and he said, 'Well, some Indians drink that,' and I said, 'Could you take that back too please.' My friend sitting beside me was pretty pale at this point and she was going, 'You can't say that to the teacher.' And I sat there and said, 'I'm sorry, you can't say those things.' So he said, 'Well, I know one Indian person who did that.' I said, 'Well, you can say that.' The whole class was dead silent. And then we went about our work and nobody said anything. After that, I was treated differently at school."

Elaine's stories and her way of telling them captivate audiences. In the old way of speaking, her soft voice, her measured timing, even her jokes would not have been considered appropriate. It's time, however, to widen the circle of who speaks and how we speak. I use the word thesis for convenience but it is only one of many words for idea or main point. Stories have a point and their own way of evolving. It is up to us as speakers and listeners to value different approaches. The point of speaking also varies. Vietnamese students I taught had a philosophical base to their work; when one man did a demonstration of how to make carrot juice, his focus was not on the accuracy of the process, but the importance of carrots. He wanted us to value carrots and the nutrition they provide. He said to us, "Knowing there are carrots should make you happy."

We can also widen the circle by making room for others. As children, we would call to each other, "Back up. Let everybody in." That's what members of a privileged group can do—back up, move over. As people who are already asked to speak, we can suggest the names of others to organizers and we can offer to share our time, to make joint presentations.

It's also important to know when not to speak; you're not an expert on everything. When I'm asked to talk on minority groups, I do my own stuff, but to make known the needs of the deaf community or the disabled community, I invite speakers from those groups to come with me. There are many fine speakers in this world; let's widen the circle and have all voices heard.

PANELS

Panels are a lively and effective way of examining an issue from different perspectives. The information given and the interaction among the panelists vary according to the occasion and the philosophy of the participants. Let's start with a straightforward panel on youth services in your community. When you are asked to participate it's important to determine your role. Is your job to

- give background on the topic?
- rev up the audience for other speakers?
- present one particular aspect?
- ease tension?
- put the topic in a perspective that is acceptable to the audience?
- present a different or opposing point of view?

In other words, if I'm part of a panel discussion on opening a group home for girls in my neighborhood, my function may be to assess the role such a facility would play in our community. Others will outline the need for the group home, the way it operates, the benefits, community involvement, etc.

Identify your function by discussing the program with the coordinator, telephoning other participants to discuss their viewpoints and using your common sense.

As part of your preparation, you should also make sure of how questions will be handled. Will the moderator assign the questions? Will panelists volunteer to answer? Will the audience direct questions to one or more panelists?

And now we come to the politics of the situation. Is the moderator unbiased? You find this out by contacting the moderator in advance and assessing her or his position. This is very important. You should ascertain that different points of view are allotted fair amounts of time and have equally good slots on the agenda. This is also the time when you discuss physical arrangements: floor mikes on the periphery of the audience so that speakers can look at the community as well as the panelists, adequate lighting so that everyone is visible, and a fair way of handling remarks.

Experienced panelists arrive early enough to meet the organizers and other participants, check the equipment and get the mood of the audience. During the discussion, be attentive to other speakers and to audience reaction. Your own credibility is often judged by how you treat others.

All this assumes you've been asked to be on the panel. What happens if no one representing your point of view has been asked? This happened last year in our community: as part of the referendum debate on whether or not the constitution of Canada should be changed, a townhall panel debate was arranged. Anglophones, francophones, the native community, the "yes" side and the "no" side all had representatives. All were men. When a women's group asked if women's interests were being presented, the answer was one of puzzlement; of course, women's concerns were being addressed— all these men would do it.

It is naive to believe that all groups concerned will be given a chance to talk; in the old way of speaking, only power groups were considered likely sources of speakers; it's time to work to be more inclusive. And members of minority groups must request time, insist on representation and be prepared for the old excuse—"There are no women (natives, people of colour) willing to do it." One response is to find a representative or speak yourself.

PRESENTATIONS

When you speak to a group in order to outline a policy, product or program, you must be ready to present a lot of information in an interesting way. Your success is measured by how well your audience understands and responds. Presentations can be tedious both because of the amount of material covered and because we think they are boring by definition. For this type of speech, as for any other, keep in mind the basics: make it interesting, make it organized, make it from the heart. Go for broke—make it entertaining.

Pinpoint what your audience needs to know. Supply a hand-out with basic information and focus your energy on explaining, convincing, answering questions—whatever you identify as your main function.

USE A VARIETY OF MATERIAL

Entertain at the same time you inform. If your material is detailed and perhaps a bit dry, vary the media you use. Overheads are good

—unless you use 35 in a row. Switch from overheads to slides to flipcharts to inject variety.

WORK WITH A PARTNER

Two education experts had to give an overview of how changing school curriculum affected the amount of time spent on language studies in the secondary system. Most of their findings relied on dozens of tables of statistics. Working as a team, they took turns guiding the audience through a lot of material. One speaker tended to be precise and analytical; the other was more the raconteur, giving examples of how students were affected. Together they appealed to all facets of the audience.

BE CANNY ABOUT TIME

Canny means shrewd or thrifty. If you've got 15 minutes on the program and a world of information to cover, choose your focus wisely. Don't overprepare and then rush to cram what should be an hour speech into a fraction of the time. Speak to the points you consider essential in that situation. Give the highlights and invite questions for later.

TALK TO PEOPLE—DON'T READ TO THEM

There is nothing more futile or alienating than watching someone read a report. There are human beings in front of you—talk to them. Your job is to explain a plan or convince them; the way to do that is to talk to them as you would in your own office, expressing your opinions and backing them up with good reasons. Be human; people are tired of being treated like inanimate data processors. If you prepare a report, always consider the need to present it verbally and think of an interesting way to do it.

RADIO AND TELEVISION INTERVIEWS

One of my friends joined a protest to stop the construction of a logging road through old growth forest. At one point, she chained herself to a huge pine to stop the loggers. A television interviewer asked if she was ready to die to save a tree. My friend was indignant. "He didn't even ask why I was there—I wanted time to give background on the situation." It was hard to explain to her that being chained to a tree with police officers all around is not exactly background time. The reporter wanted a newsbite, not a summary.

This is the challenge of interviews: how does our purpose jibe with the interviewer's needs? How can we get our message out there and feel confident in the process? Here's a sampler of suggestions from people on both sides of the microphone. They can be summed up in four phrases that apply to all impromptu speeches:

- be yourself
- think of the audience
- practise
- breathe!

BE YOURSELF

Talk to an interviewer as you would talk to your neighbour—try for a conversational tone; take your time and explain things. If we get excited or anxious about a radio or television interview, we can lose sight of the reason we're speaking and focus more on sounding impressive or correct. Last week I heard an otherwise direct and affable person say to an interviewer, "I hope my peers will continue to lend their support and help me move forward to a second term as their representative." He wanted to say he hoped his colleagues would vote for him; he had work he wanted to continue. In trying to sound sage, he turned conversational remarks into formal dialogue; instead of sounding sincere and open, he came across as stilted.

Sound as though you enjoy being interviewed; it makes the interview go smoothly and helps the image you project. In the first minute or so, explain clearly why you are speaking; it's important that you sound as committed as you really are. If people don't believe what you're saying, they won't listen to you.

How many of us spend hours wondering what to wear when we're asked to be part of a television talkshow? Pick an outfit you like and feel comfortable wearing; ask your friends if you look confident in your clothes. How you feel is the single most important thing; don't choose things that bind or bunch up around your neck.

Part of being yourself is being able to express yourself naturally; many television studios now have couches for their guests. And some of the couches swallow you. There you are, stuffed into the corner of a person-eating sofa, unable to lean forward or use your hands. Take time to find a seat or a position that frees you to use your full person to speak. If you need a back support, ask for one before the interview starts.

THINK OF THE AUDIENCE

How much does the audience know about the subject? I've found that interviewers want either a general discussion or a firm position. Quite often when I arrive, the interviewer needs a briefing on what the topic is—despite the fact that I've already submitted it. As one broadcaster said, "I should have more questions ready but it's hectic here. I just want a general overview of the subject and we'll get to the meaty part later. My listeners need to know the person first. They want basics—not a lot of background."

If you're speaking on a hot topic such as contract debates or civil disobedience, be ready for the hot-seat questions. And use them. I was once interviewed about a strike vote underway at the college where I worked. I was all set to talk about class sizes, hours of instruction, cut-backs and the quality of education. The question that crackled in my ear was, "Now, do you think you're overworked?" Mumbling desperately, I eventually got across the idea that I was teaching too many students for them to be learning enough to meet basic standards. Now, I'm more confident. Quite often the interviewer, or in the case of larger stations the researcher, tells me what turns the conversation might take and I ask why they want the interview on that day—what other issues are involved.

When I get a tough question, I answer directly. And I wait for the right moment to make my own point and to give the examples to support it. If necessary, I can bring the interview back to the reason I'm there: "You're right, this is urgent and that's what made me go to the municipal council in the first place...."

Stories will make any issue come alive. Interviewers and audiences delight in them. That's a question I'm always asked: have you got some good examples to give? Be ready, think of your audience and speak to them, give them anecdotes they'll remember. Just before you go into a radio or television studio, think of all the individuals who will be listening to you; picture your neighbours, the people you do volunteer work with. Those are your audience, speak to them as individuals, meet them in their circles of concern and bring them closer to yours.

PRACTISE

An interview is a speaking opportunity: organize, rehearse, relax.

ORGANIZE

- Research the program you're going to appear on; tune in to get a feel for the tone and atmosphere. Is it a morning show for people who work at home? Is it political? Does it have a morning second-cup-of-coffee feeling for lengthy interviews or is there more of a 60-miles-an-hour-on-the-freeway urgency about it? Does the interviewer ask penetrating questions? Does she give the guest enough time to answer? Are the questions well balanced and fair? Be prepared for what you're going to face. Learn the interviewer's name and use it naturally, without overusing it.

- Ask the contact person about the format of the interview. How long will it be? Do they want local examples? Is there a tie-in with other issues?

- Be sure of your one main point and your supporting ideas. Try the one-sentence shower test described in Chapter 2. The interviewer's job is to provide the introduction and conclusion.

- It is easier for the interviewer and the audience if you number your reasons. "Well, Joe, I think my dog Annie should be the next mayor. She's got the three essential qualifications: she's smart; she photographs well; and she loves catered receptions." Then elaborate.

- Use notes—a few key words or phrases. When the pressure builds, notes help, and if the interview goes on longer than you expected, a list of examples will help you avoid blanking out. Notes are easy for radio interviews—and I've made a mental list of three points for television interviews.

REHEARSE

- Rehearse at home. Have a friend ask you questions in keeping with the format and feeling of the program you will be on. Become familiar with using different questions as a basis for explaining your point of view.

- Be sure of the basics: who? what? where? when? why? how much?

- Rehearse your first line. If you are being interviewed by telephone, you are contacted several minutes in advance and asked to hold. You may or may not be able to hear the show live. Quite often, the waiting makes me nervous. I relax, breathe and wait for the interviewer to greet me. Several times during this period, I go over my first line. "Good morning, Sheila. No, black fly season is not over yet." Then, in response to her first real question, I give my most direct statement. Why practise such a simple thing as hello? To get the throat muscles relaxed, to get my voice warm and confident.

- Practise telling the stories out loud to get a feel for the way they sound. Stories don't come out as effortlessly as you want unless you have gone over them several times.

- Rehearse lines to keep the interview on track. You know a lot about your subject; that's why you were asked on the show. To the station, you are just one of many interviews. So when the interviewer asks something that is not relevant or seems to be filling time, say "Yes, that's a possibility, and there are several more aspects to consider. For example…." Don't wait for an invitation; in most cases, you have only three to five minutes, and they speed by.

RELAX

- Sound like yourself.

- Co-operate with the interviewer if possible. Get to the station early enough to meet him or her and come prepared with a short (four to six lines) biography; it saves both of you work. Prepare a brief statement of your main points for the interviewer.

- Acclimatize yourself to the activity of a television station.

Concentrate on speaking to the interviewer and ignore the bustle around you.

- Centre yourself. In extreme cases—you are either put on the spot or no one remembers who you are and they've lost your press kit—focus on why you are speaking. Things will work out.

- Talk to people—don't sound like you are reading assembly instructions. If you listen carefully to radio shows, you'll be able to hear when others read their remarks; it sounds like an address. The vocabulary and cadences are not as natural as normal speech. You'll also be able to watch television novices following the teleprompter; their look of concentration gives them away. Be yourself.

- Work with interviewers as much as possible. Don't:
  — give yes or no answers repeatedly. Take the questions and work with them. Explain your answers and give examples.
  — knock the media on air.
  — say "no comment."
  — be tempted to speak about things beyond your area of knowledge.
  — lie.
  — let other people put words in your mouth. If necessary say, "No, that picture isn't quite accurate. Let me tell you what really happened."
  — ignore time signals. The hand placed on your arm, the question that requires a summary—those are your signals to wrap it up.
  — hog the spotlight. Give others credit if you are part of a group.

- Take care of yourself. If you're on a phone-in show, crank calls can slip in and you can be subjected to a harangue. Stand up for yourself and look to the host for help. When you speak about anything that rocks the status quo, take a friend for support. If your telephone number is in the book, monitor calls carefully. I once spoke to a researcher about an upcoming interview on words we carry around with us that wound others; we discussed sexist stereotyping, systemic racism and homophobic taunts. When I finished, she said, "Are you sure you want to give your name on the air?" Some people assume that anyone who presents an idea publicly is therefore open to target practice.

BREATHE

A deep breath is the best thing in the world; it calms you and helps your throat muscles relax. Before you speak, breathe in-2-3-4, out-2-3-4. If you think you have to rush to get through everything, do the opposite. Stop, breathe and slow down. You may say fewer words but your audience will hear more. No one listens to a speaker who rushes from nervousness. That one good breath can clear everything in your head and make you feel and sound solid.

I asked a radio announcer with a few years of experience what he had learned about sounding good on air. His answer surprised me: "Speak clearly. If you want to sound good on radio, check your enunciation. I'm a farm boy and I never used to finish my words; I never used any endings so words like 'going' and 'taking' always came out 'goin' and 'takin'.' It doesn't work on radio; finish your words."

BE PROUD

You'll always hear or see glitches you wish you could erase. Never mind. You did your best to present information or a point of view; the very fact it made it on air is important. Learn from your experience and remember to feel good about the time you took to speak.

DAVID A. NICHOL

David Nichol is a trusted personality in thousands of Canadian households. His "Insider's Report" is one of the most widely distributed food publications in the world. Nichol's ability to speak sincerely to strangers has made him one of our country's most famous marketing executives. During this interview, Nichol developed his own system of public speaking: the Gordie Howe Approach.

SB: Why do you make speeches?

DN: *Because I care. You know, Gordie Howe, in all his years playing hockey, before every game, he had a ritual. Just before he went onto the ice, he used to go into the washroom and throw up....*

When you speak, you have a tremendous obligation to your audience—these people are giving you their time and you have to entertain or educate them. Most people just try to fill time, fill up their 20 minutes. Instead, they should take a lesson from Gordie Howe. They should care so much, it hurts.

SB: How important is it that people in business speak well?

DN: *A large part of business is selling; selling means convincing people. You can't convince people except through communication; therefore, people with good communication skills, written or oral, have an enormous advantage.*

SB: How do people convince you about a product or a concept?

DN: *If it's a product, seeing the product. Having their arguments well marshalled. Being able to communicate on an emotional level.*

SB: Is it important to be able to speak in business on an emotional level?

DN: *Absolutely! Everything is emotion. You need a good balance between logic and emotion.*

SB: Why do people believe you and your personal advertising techniques?

DN: *I care, and I care about what people think of what I say. That concern comes through.*

SB: Do you enjoy talking to groups?

DN: *You know, I hate public speaking, I just absolutely detest it. Public speaking is a form of examination. You go up in front of 2 or 2,000 people and bare your soul in terms of capabilities. And people can tell if a speaker is a phony, if they care, if they believe in the subject, if they respect the audience, and if they're a vital human being or part of the army of living dead. Now if people can figure that out about you, especially if you have an established public image, that is a very high-risk situation.*

I know the emotional price I'm going to pay every time I speak. I know the emotional energy I'm going to use and I could be using it to create the best Dutch Butter Cookie in the world. And yet there are certain audiences that it's important to persuade, and so I use that energy to do it.

SB: Do you get scared?

DN: *People should be nervous; if you're not scared to death before you give that speech, chances are it's going to be a bomb.*
     Don't be afraid of the fear. Use it to your advantage.

SB: How do you use the nervousness positively and avoid making a fool of yourself?

DN: *Fighting it through the first time. For me, that's Blenheim High School, Heart of the Golden Acres, down near Chatham, Ontario, 2,500 people, a public speaking contest—"My trip to Mammoth Cave." That is the first speech I gave—stalactites, stalagmites—in front of 2,000 kids who know you're a jerk anyway. After that, they lock you in a room and give you a title for an impromptu speech and 15 minutes to prepare. Then it's back in front of 2,000 kids for "It Happened on My Christmas Vacation."*
     And you go all around the small towns doing the speeches and you get used to it. Getting up is not so hard to do, especially if you're Irish like I am and have a touch of the old malarkey. All of that fear gets the adrenalin going and you use that adrenalin. You say to yourself, "let's just go and get 'em." You get tired and bored of being scared to death.

SB: When is a speech really exciting?

DN: *When you get all of that energy going and you get up and speak without notes.*

SB: Do you know what you're going to say?

DN: *Sure, it's all written down in point form. I like the security blanket of those little cards. But when you get off to a good start, when you're enthusiastic, you can forget about the notes and let the good times roll. When the spirit hits you, when you've spent a lot of time planning and you're totally prepared, then you don't need the notes.*
     Too often, speakers, including me, go to the security blanket when it's not necessary.

SB: How do you speak to your employees and management teams?

DN: *Same way. I try to get excited, and to get others excited. Most people are afraid of dying during their speech. And most people are afraid to let emotion enter into it. So they hang onto that script, they read it—I mean, they shouldn't have chairs, they should have beds for the audience.*

SB: What speech of yours do you like?

DN: *I am most proud of the introduction to the Ursaki Award speech when I talk about my theory of the filter in the minds of human beings. I knew what I wanted to say but it was all extemporaneous. If I could give a whole speech like that, I'd be happy.*

SB: What makes a business meeting good?

DN: *Whether anything comes out of it. And that's usually a function of being organized in terms of knowing what you want to accomplish and having a plan to get there.*

SB: If you had all the beginning speakers of the world assembled in your office, what would you tell them? What is the most important part of speaking well?

DN: *Emotion—use it. Don't be afraid of it. If you're not nervous, your speech isn't going to be good.*

DANCING TO THE SUN:
LAST WORDS OF ADVICE

I just say I am going to be able to do it. Usually, if I think I can do it, I am able to.
— **Erin Volkert, age nine, talking about her first speech**

▲▲▲▲▲▲▲▲▲▲▲▲

My hope is that thousands of people will find some help in this book and rise up with courage and conviction. I want to hear everyone's voice and share in the joy of encouraging each other. And some people need a little more time, some extra help. It's like dancing; as eager as I am to join in the salsa or line-dance, I can never quite remember the steps. While everyone else heads to the dance floor, I'm the one asking questions of the endlessly patient instructor.

Here are questions about speaking I've heard many times in my workshops, usually during coffee break or on the way to lunch. I hope that some of them will give you the private coaching you need. After the questions are checklists, a collection of helpful reminders I put together with a group of good speakers and fine listeners.

Will you write my speech?

No, I can't do that because it wouldn't be your speech, you

wouldn't feel it. And you'd have to read it! Don't be misled by public figures who read their speeches; theirs is the old top-down style, to give information, to make an impression. The new way is to connect, to have a conversation. You make conversation, you don't write it.

Take the information you have and organize it clearly—then find a framework to hang it on. That's where I can help. At the end of this section are half a dozen simple, interesting approaches.

Can I change the topic I was asked to speak on?

Yes you can, and sometimes you should. Don't speak on a topic that isn't in your heart or your experience; instead change the topic to match something that is honestly yours. For instance, I can't speak on the value of volunteerism—but I can talk on what I've given and what I've gained as a volunteer. Experienced speakers stick to what they know.

How long should the grabber and introduction be?

It depends on your topic. A general rule is 15-20 percent for the introduction, 70 percent for the body and 10 percent for the conclusion. However, if your topic is a tough one—wage freezes, date rape, fishing rights for native peoples—you may have to work longer on the introduction in order to bring your listeners into your circle of concern.

How important is correct grammar?

Good grammar makes for a smoother speech and faster comprehension. Some people put a lot of emphasis on grammar—I had a man call me last week after I did a radio interview to tell me I had used the same cliché twice. But grammar isn't everything, especially in speaking—unless it is so sloppy that it interferes with your audience's ability to listen.

Ask a friend to listen to you, to check any glaring errors. When you listen to speakers you admire, evaluate what makes them so good. How accurate is their grammar? I pay special attention to endings—put "ing"s on words that need them.

What do I say to people who are introducing me?

They need help. Prepare a sheet with a brief outline of your professional background, some personal details to give a human dimension to the remarks and some sort of a grabber. Be sure to include any books or articles you have written and some indication of your expertise. Work hard on your biography—it's in your own interest. If the person introducing you hasn't read this book, they may read directly from your sheet.

What can you use as a grabber? If you're a bird watcher, toymaker or volunteer at a food bank, put it down. It gives you a human touch.

Be sure to find the person making the introduction and ask to review his or her remarks; a bad lead-in can be very hard to overcome.

It takes me so long to make up a speech. Am I doing something wrong?

Do you remember learning any new skill? When I first started using a computer, booting the program took most of my morning. And trying to use the mouse—how long did it first take you to get the cursor to go where you wanted? That's the way with speaking—it takes time and practice.

You have to think of your own concerns, your audience, sort out what you want to say and need to say, throw stuff out, find a great framework and grabber, get it together. I let it simmer inside me for days or weeks.

What hangs speeches up?

Many things—not thinking of your audience; not taking the time to make things interesting as well as accurate; retreating inside yourself and talking to yourself instead of to other people; reading your material; not making conversation but sounding like an instruction manual instead of a human being. All this comes from nervousness. And there are three principles that stand out.

- Practise! People often tell me their wooden delivery is due to fear—and that's the end of it. I don't deny the severity of nervousness—I've had to lie down before a speech to ease the knots in my stomach. But nervousness is a phase, not a terminal condition. Practise! Get a good coach. Speaking well is partly a gift and partly a skill that can be developed. Think of it like swimming—you don't expect to be good without hours of practice.

- Don't rush important material. Kate Scott, a lawyer in a northern community, gets nervous and blushes when she speaks in court. She says, "Sometimes when I get nervous, I shorten it too much—I try to skip from thing to thing. I know in my head what I mean but I get so nervous, I don't explain each point thoroughly and no one else understands."

Respect your own ideas and take time to explain things clearly. People who look uninterested may simply be concentrating.

- Mental hygiene. Joan Mason talks about cleaning up your mind before you speak. "If something is screwing your mind up in your life, you may flash back to it in public. Mental hygiene is necessary to a focused speech." She advocates working things out at home or taking time to clear your mind and your inner self before you speak.

  Clean up first is also her advice for dealing with hostile audiences. Address the troublesome issue first, put it in the open and deal with it. After that, the audience may be able to focus on the rest of your talk.

Why don't more people ask for help with their speeches?

There's a deep-rooted misconception that if you can talk you can make a speech. Some people don't realize they are poor speakers and therefore don't know they need help. For others it's embarrassing, like saying they can't do something simple like get a glass of water. And they underestimate the power of a good speech.

I feel so isolated when I stand up to speak. What can I do?

Wrap yourself with reassurance. Look at people who show interest in their eyes. If possible, I try to stand on the same level as the audience and position myself close to the people in the first rows. If there is a centre aisle, I stand in it with people on either side. It makes me feel protected, less isolated and more a part of the group. Look forward to speaking to those people. Stand and breathe and look as if you can do it—you'll feel more confident.

Do I have to use overheads?

No. They are useful if you need to present statistics or a diagram. But they are not a required part of every business presentation. And unless you are unsure of the literacy level of your audience, do not read the overheads to the audience.

When shouldn't I speak?

Don't shoot yourself in the foot. Last week I saw a group of 600 waiting for the key-note speaker; everyone was geared up for a speech on humour and things were running late. At that point, the new co-ordinator for community groups was introduced and she spoke for 15 minutes on the mandate for outreach. For variety she used overheads that showed statistical tables. Of course the print was too small to be read by anyone past the first three rows. Don't do it to yourself; don't set up resistance.

What frustrates you the most about speakers?

Three lines:

- "I know you can't see this but…"

- The person who reads, "Good evening. My name is… and it's a pleasure to join you."

- "Oh yes, I practise; I try to read it over a couple of times."

Should I take a speaking course and be videotaped?

A video can be helpful for experienced speakers who want to refine their style. As a way of learning to speak, it doesn't work well. It concentrates on you the speaker, how you come across, *your* eye contact and mannerisms, how well *you're* doing. What's your focus as a speaker? Your aim is to connect with the audience; what do they think? What's their body language saying? How are they connecting with you?

Videotaping that is concerned only with how good you are misses the point. It puts the emphasis on image rather than connection and communication. Save the videotape until you are more experienced. If you want feedback, ask your friends or colleagues.

What if my hands tremble?

Trembling hands are only a problem if your audience is so aware of your anxiety that they can't concentrate. Use the magician's trick—divert their attention. Have a helper to change overhead transparencies or manage a flipchart and use heavy cards for your notes. They don't flutter when you turn them.

How do you look so relaxed? It seems as if you're talking to us instead of making a speech.

I work at it. At home I go through my material and get the information and examples in order. I find a story or an everyday occurrence to use as a framework, one that I understand and like. If the examples are good, ideas start sparking. Then I listen to myself. If I seem to be lecturing, I stop and try to imagine I'm talking to people in my livingroom. That's how I find the words and the tone. When I actually make the speech I look at the audience and try to connect. It's not easy; if I'm nervous, I have to make myself focus.

The rest of the stuff—checking room set-ups, microphones, etc.—it's plain work, attention to detail.

I have to make a speech tomorrow. How can I make it interesting?

Depending on your topic, one of these might work. Audiences enjoy relating plans and theories to everyday objects. Even better, they remember what you say.

- Seed catalogues: The spring ritual of choosing, dreaming, selecting leads to planting, hard work and crops.

- Spicing your work: Using techniques that combine the sweet and the savoury to get a good product.

- Loons: This prehistoric bird is like many of us; it has an eerie call, knows when to duck and manages to survive.

- Fishing: Successful people are like good anglers. They are patient, know what bait to use, have the right equipment and keep a good tension on the line. They know when to reel in and when to let go. On top of that, they share the catch.

- Parades: The view is different depending on your position —on the float or on the sidelines.

- Inukshuks: Lifelike figures of rock erected by the Inuit in the Arctic. They serve as directional markers on treeless horizons to guide those who follow. They remind us of our dependence on one another. What Inukshuks do we erect in our daily business and personal lives?

- Packing the knapsack of success: For a hike you need a compass to keep on track; a first aid kit for emergencies; an apple for health; wool socks for the times you get cold feet; and a warm sweater for comfort. How do these things translate to the skills and values you will need for a successful personal journey?

BE PREPARED: USING THE CHECKLISTS

When you sign up for a wilderness adventure, hiking in Costa Rican rainforests or paddling the Nahanni River, you receive a package of trip information. Most valuable are the checklists. By referring to these lists, you can quickly determine if you have done sufficient preparation and have all the equipment necessary for each facet of the trip: personal belongings, first aid and repair kits, nature books and charts, kitchen gear.

Use these checklists in the same way. Start with the main menu and then consult the ones you need. A quick glance will remind you of essential items. The trick is to remember the lists!

CHECKLISTS: MAIN MENU

Use these lists to remind you of various aspects of your preparation. Then consult the ones most appropriate to your situation.

1. Equipment to Take With You

2. What to Ask Your Contact Person

3. Questions to Ask About Your Audience

4. Matching the Format to the Audience and Occasion

5. Purpose of Your Speech

6. Is Your Speech in Shape?

7. What to Check for in a Rehearsal

8. On Arrival

9. Are You Prepared?

10. Taking Care of Speakers

11. When You Are Part of a Panel

12. Using Audio-Visual Back-Up

13. Using Tapes

14. Using Visual Back-Up

15. Saving Face When You Make Mistakes

16. Speech Breakdowns

17. Handling Unexpected Media Coverage or Interview Requests

18. Evaluation

1. Equipment to Take With You

Keep all material for your speech in carry-on luggage.

1. speech notes

2. extra set of notes

3. pen and paper

4. music or book for relaxation

5. tapes/slides/film

6. handouts: reports, outlines, booklets

7. watch

8. short biography for person introducing you and/or media

9. extra glasses/lens cleaning solution

10. identification and health care numbers

11. medication

12. props

13. A-V equipment and spare parts, extension cord

14. clothes pegs or spring clips to fasten notes to lectern in breezy conditions

15. timetable

16. address of meeting and map

17. name and telephone number of speaking location

18. name and number of contact person and back-up contact

19. business cards

20. press release

21. umbrella

22. tissues or handkerchief

23. comfortable shoes

24. change of clothes in case of accident or spill

25. cash for personal expenses

2. WHAT TO ASK YOUR CONTACT PERSON

1. TIME, DATE, PLACE

2. What is the purpose of the meeting/conference?

3. Exact directions to the meeting place, even if you are being met.

4. Name and phone number of local contact and back-up contact.

5. Telephone number of hotel to leave at home.

6. Time limit.

7. Names and topics of other speakers.

8. The occasion.

9. Dress guidelines.

10. Will the proceedings be taped? Does it matter?

11. Questions about your audience: see Checklist 3.

12. What kind of room will you speak in? What kind of sound system is there?

13. Who takes care of your equipment needs?

14. Have you told the contact person your time of arrival, special dietary needs and how to recognize you?

15. How will your expenses be covered? When will you be paid?

16. Where is the most convenient place to park?

3. QUESTIONS TO ASK ABOUT YOUR AUDIENCE

1. Why you? Why did they choose you as a speaker?

2. What is the group or organization?

3. What is the occasion?

4. What does the audience know about the subject?

5. Are they interested/uncertain/hostile?

6. Has anybody ever talked to them about the subject before?

7. How much background is necessary?

8. Are there internal politics to be aware of?

9. Will there be a question period?

10. Do they know the level of expertise you bring to the subject?

11. What sort of local colour would be useful?

12. Is there a possibility of a negative response to prepare for?

13. Is there anything special about the date, place or group?

14. Basic Information: size of group/age range/gender/occupational background/racial composition/traditional or alternative family groups/level of education/disposable income/concerns/interests and hobbies/languages spoken.

4. MATCHING THE FORMAT TO THE AUDIENCE AND OCCASION

1. How much time have you been given?

2. Are you the only speaker?

3. How much does the audience already know about your subject?

4. What is their attention span?

5. What time of day and where in the program are you speaking?

6. Would a speech followed by a question-and-answer period be better for a knowledgeable group?

7. How long a question period does the group need?

8. Are you prepared to be put on the spot?

9. Would your speech be strengthened by A-V back-up or by a joint presentation?

5. PURPOSE OF YOUR SPEECH

agitation? information?
demonstration? inspiration?
education? interrogation?
entertainment? persuasion?
evaluation?

1. Is it to advocate a position?

2. Is it to change your listeners' minds?

3. Is it to be liked?

4. Is it to reinforce a belief?

5. Is it to explain or demonstrate?

6. Is it to advance your own position? (pass the interview, get elected, etc.)

7. Is it to speak your mind on something you consider important?

6. IS YOUR SPEECH IN SHAPE?

1. Does your speech sound like you?

2. Do you like it?

3. Do you believe in what you are saying?

4. Are you having a conversation with the audience?

5. Is there a thesis and three main points?

6. Is the grabber effective?

7. Is there a strong finish?

8. Do you need all of the speech?

9. Do you need to supply a title for the program? Is there a good line or example to appeal to the audience?

10. Are there ethical, logical and emotional appeals?

11. Are the transitions from one point to another smooth?

12. Is the speech suitable for
    • the audience?

- the time allotted?
- the occasion?

13. Is your language inclusive? Have you avoided words that are racist, sexist or homophobic?

14. Have you practised with your notes?

15. Does your test audience like and understand your examples?

16. Have you timed your speech? Not for you the phrase: "I know I'm running overtime, but I just have six more points."

17. Can you state your thesis in one sentence?

18. More on language. Have a friend check your speech for phrases that slip out unthinkingly:
    - Have you avoided racist/sexist stereotyping?
    - Do you use non-sexist words for occupations?
    - Check the obvious landmines, using words like "black," "white," "queer," "retarded," in stereotypical ways.
    - Racism is often a result of omitting anyone who is not of the dominant race. Does your speech mirror the experience of a cross-section of our society?
    - Do you honour a person's origin? Do you make an effort to pronounce names correctly?
    - Do your words acknowledge and value a diversity of lifestyles and family units?

7. What to Check for in a Rehearsal

1. How do you sound? Reading over your notes is not the same as a rehearsal; set up a lectern and practise out loud.

2. Practise with the notes you will use.

3. Listen to yourself:
    - do you sound confident?
    - are you rambling?
    - is your material interesting?
    - are you having a conversation with the audience?

4. Do your words sound natural?

5. Is your eye contact effective?

6. Recruit a practice audience. Which of your main points or examples do they enjoy and/or remember?

7. Do they find your speech logical and complete?

8. Do you handle props and visuals easily?

9. Get rid of clunkers—overly complicated examples, awkward or affected language, boring and unnecessary statistics.

8. ON ARRIVAL

1. Check in with the organizers; they'll be relieved you've arrived.

2. Put belongings in a secure place.

3. Private time: before things speed up take time to check notes, adjust clothes, attend to personal details.

4. Check the room with one of the co-ordinators:
   Is the seating and placement of chairs appropriate?
   Is the lighting adequate?
   Is there a watch or clock to monitor time?
   Is there a lectern that facilitates full communication?
   Is there water handy?
   Is the microphone working? Test it. Locate the on/off switch.
   Is the technician present? Explain your needs and test equipment. ("May I see the first three slides, please.")
   Are paper and pen handy if you expect written questions from the floor?
   Do the floor mikes promote a feeling of community and discussion?

5. Mingle with other speakers and panelists; compare notes.

6. Talk to audience members and get a feeling for the group.

7. Introduce yourself to the moderator and the person introducing you. Have they got your name right? Ask about details of the intro.

8. Make sure your notes are ready.

9. Psych yourself up. These people want to hear what you have to say.

9. ARE YOU PREPARED?

What if...

1. the electricity goes off?

2. a fire bell rings while you are speaking?

3. the room is set up in a different way than you requested?

4. double the number of people show up?

5. you lose your notes?

6. the translator or signer is late?

7. you can't find the room?

8. the speaker ahead of you rambles on and on?

9. there's a storm and you're an hour late starting?

10. you can't go at the last minute?

11. other panel members don't show up?

12. the microphone doesn't work

13. your speech isn't geared to the audience?

14. someone heckles you?

15. you spill food on your clothing?

16. the media shows up unexpectedly to cover the event and do an interview?

10. TAKING CARE OF SPEAKERS

If you are co-ordinating arrangements for a speaker, focus on making the event rewarding for both the audience and the speaker.

1. Provide full information about the audience and the occasion. Send the speaker a reminder two weeks before the event.

2. Determine speaker's needs (room set-up, A-V) in advance. Check requirements regarding accommodation.

3. Ask for a biography in advance and make sure the person introducing the speaker actually sees it ahead of time.

4. Set a fair and realistic agenda. Don't let the business meeting

ramble and ask a speaker to cut short his presentation.

5. Offer to meet the speaker. If she gets to the hotel on her own, make sure she is pre-registered and leave the number of her liaison person.

6. Assign a liaison person to show the speaker around and introduce him to others. Don't drop your guest after he's spoken; the liaison stays with the speaker for the whole event and makes sure he is included.

7. Show the speaker the room where she will be speaking and introduce her to the A-V technician. Help her test the microphone and check acoustics. If there are visual aids, assist her in putting them up.

8. Pay all expenses such as hotel room and meals and provide a form for travel costs. Have the fee ready.

9. Send the speaker copies of any press reports of the event.

11. When You Are Part of a Panel

Before You Leave

1. What is the purpose of the panel presentation?

2. Why have you been asked to participate?

3. What position have you been asked to represent:
   - supplier of background information?
   - proponent of a particular stand?
   - representative of an interest or professional group?
   - community member?

4. Talk to the moderator. Is she or he unbiased? The moderator's attitude may be reflected in the treatment of each speaker, the assigning of questions and the limiting of discussion.

5. Are different points of view allocated fair amounts of time?

6. Do they have equally good slots on the agenda?

7. What is the format:
   - individual presentations followed by questions?
   - one speaker followed by questions to or from a panel?
   - presentations only?

- questions only?

8. How will questions be handled:
   - moderator assigns questions?
   - questioner directs remarks to panelist(s)?
   - panelists volunteer responses?

When You Arrive

1. Talk to other panelists. Is there adequate variation in presentations?

2. Do you have enough information and experience to change your approach if there is too much overlap?

3. Listen carefully to other presenters. You may be able to make direct links with their remarks or find significant points of difference.

4. Give direct eye contact to each speaker: the audience will notice if you read, look around or appear bored.

5. Your body language is important during the *entire* program. You are speaking, verbally or non-verbally, all the time you are present.

12. Using Audio-Visual Back-Up

Before You Leave

1. Does your A-V material support your speech?

2. Is it big enough, simple enough, colourful enough?

3. Do maps and charts show enough detail?

4. Do the graphs have a minimum of lines?

5. Does the material speak to the mind and/or the emotions?

6. Have you rehearsed with it?

7. Does your test audience understand the A-V immediately?

8. If you are using slides, have you edited them? Use only as many as you need to make your point.

9. Are slides in order and numbered? Is your name on them?

10. Do you have all support material in your hand when you leave

home? If you are flying, make sure it is in your carry-on luggage.

11. If you are supplying equipment, take spare bulbs and extension cords.

When You Arrive

1. Is there a technician? Introduce yourself—this person is important to you.

2. Explain your needs clearly; can you supply a script with cues?

3. Test the microphone and other equipment *with* the technician.

4. If you are doing your own work, find the electrical outlets.

5. Position the screen.

6. Test the controls.

7. Do you need someone to dim the lights? Do they know the cues?

8. Do the flipcharts flip?

9. Are there plenty of markers?

10. Is the overhead projector positioned and focused? Are your transparencies in order and easy to handle?

Always make time for sound and equipment checks.

13. USING TAPES

1. Does the sound fill the room comfortably?

2. Do you have all the tapes on hand?

3. Test the tapes with the equipment you will be using.

4. Is the tape ready to go without any fiddling?

5. Do you or your assistant know how to work the controls?

6. If you have to fast forward, have you noted the exact numbers on the tape counter?

7. Have you rehearsed?

8. Is there back-up equipment on site?

14. Using Visual Back-Up

1. Have you rehearsed with the visuals and the equipment?

2. If you are using an illuminated pointer, can you handle it well and evenly?

3. Test the equipment well ahead of time. It's your speech— insure it.

4. Have you got the right tape? Are slides in order? Make sure they're not reversed.

5. Adjust focus and volume level in advance.

6. Know how to remove a slide that sticks.

7. Rehearse with your assistant; they should know cues (significant phrases) and approximate time for A-V. Note if lights have to be turned on and off.

8. Locate light switches in advance. If electrical panels have banks of switches, find the ones you need and label them.

9. Extension cords should be taped down so people don't trip on them.

10. Check sight lines by sitting in the audience and looking at the screen and speaker's position.

11. Turn off the projector at the end so that people aren't blinded by a dazzling white screen.

12. After using the equipment, leave it alone until the presentation is complete.

13. Thank the technician before you leave.

14. Always be prepared to do your speech without the back-up material. If a mechanical breakdown occurs, don't tinker with the machinery until your audience is frustrated. Apologize and go ahead without it.

15. Saving Face When You Make Mistakes

1. Admit the mistake. "You are right. I made a mistake; I'll check this point and get back to you."

2. Don't over-apologize. People can accept a mistake; they get impatient when you refer to it frequently.

3. Move on. "Aside from this error, the point is still valid," or "Now, we'll look at the major focus of my presentation."

16. SPEECH BREAKDOWNS

Questions You Can't Answer

1. Repeat the question into the mike so the audience can hear it. Use your discretion regarding which questions to repeat.

2. Admit you don't know the answer.

3. Promise to get back with the information.

Hecklers

1. If the comment is valid, repeat it to the audience and deal with it.

2. If the remark is rude or inappropriate, ignore it.

3. If the speaker is too disruptive to ignore, offer to speak to him or her later.

4. Do not play platform chicken and invite the heckler up to speak.

5. Remain cool. "Look, why not allow me to finish. I was asked to speak here."

6. If you anticipate hecklers, think up a few responses in advance. "You're my very first heckler, could you come back when I've got more experience." (Thanks to Rita Rudner.)

7. Don't be heavy-handed. If you are ruder or more sarcastic than the heckler, you'll seem frightened. You may even lose audience support. Remain patient.

Crying

1. Crying is one of many emotional reactions to situations that move you. It's normal.

2. Know where in your speech you will cry—find this out in rehearsal—and anticipate it.

3. If you know you will cry, try to estimate how long it will last; you have the reassurance that you will stop.

4. If the tears come unexpectedly, pause and give yourself time. Then continue.

5. When you start to cry, make a gesture to let the audience know you're all right, and when you are finished, carry on. Do not apologize.

6. You may have to fend off kindly attempts to remove you from the stage. If you know you might cry, you can explain this to other platform members in advance.

7. Never sniff into an open mike.

Running Late

1. *You* won't run overtime because you will have practised your speech.

2. If problems arise because the speakers before you are running late, what can you do?

   a. Assess the situation. Are you presenting an opposing point of view and need all the time you were originally allotted? Or are you presenting a complementary position? Can you allow a colleague to elaborate?

   b. Pass a note to the moderator outlining how long your speech is. Suggest that she or he make the decision to go overtime or give the present speaker a time signal.

3. If the moderator does not take action, and if the previous speakers go overtime, you may still need to give your full presentation. Explain to the audience that the schedule is running late, but you trust they want to have the full story and you need their feedback. Assume you are dealing with reasonable people.

17. Handling Unexpected Media Coverage or Interview Requests

1. Be courteous. The reporter is doing a job and will get news of your speech to a wider audience.

2. Do not be unnerved (or overly flattered) by an insistent reporter.

3. Keep to the checklist "On Arrival."

4. Ask how long the interview will take. Take care of your business first.

5. Be sure to leave yourself five minutes between the interview and your speech. If you will be too rushed, offer to do it afterwards.

6. Be prepared. Have a brief biography to give to the reporter and a few good stories to illustrate your main point. Stories are the heart of media reports.

7. If the proceedings have attracted a lot of media coverage, don't be anxious. Concentrate on your speech and the audience.

18. EVALUATION

1. Did you say what you wanted to?

2. Did you like your speech and the way you sounded?

3. How did you feel at the end of your presentation?

4. Was there a good feeling in the room?

5. What was the feedback from others—audience members and organizers?

6. What did the audience response or questions tell you?

7. What will you change the next time?

8. What will you keep the next time?

SOURCES

p. 1   "Rise Up, Rise Up..." from "Rise Up," recorded by The Parachute Club. Lyrics: L. Fernie; additional lyrics: L. Segato. Music: L. Conger, L. Segato, S. Webster, B. Bryans. ©1983.

p. 10   "While both sexes fear public speaking..." from Faludi, Susan, "Speak for Yourself," in the feature column "HERS," *New York Times Magazine,* January 26, 1992, p. 11.

p. 58   "I went to the bathroom..." from Schaef, Anne Wilson, *Meditations for Women Who Do Too Much* (San Francisco: Harper San Francisco/Hazelden, 1990).

p. 63   "Gathering random facts..." from Overbury, Stephen, *Finding Canadian Facts Fast* (Toronto: Methuen, 1985) p. xii.

        "There are at least three things..." *Ibid.* p. 85.

p. 64   "There is no such thing as..." from Suzuki, David, *Metamorphosis* (Toronto: Stoddart, 1987) p. 5.

p. 95   "It does not follow..." from Brunk, Conrad G., "Professionalism and Responsibility in the Techno-logical Society," in Deborah Poff and Wilfrid Waluchow, eds., *Business Ethics in Canada* (Scarborough: Prentice Hall Canada, Inc., 1987) p. 66.

p. 155 "The dreaded evening of the Smithsonian speech..." from Faludi, Susan, *op. cit.*

p. 168 "Day by day I found courage..." from Reagon, Bernice Johnson, "Sweet Honey: A Cappella Activists," *Ms.* Magazine, volume III, number 5, Lang Communications Inc., p. 29.

INDEX

(Numbers in bold face refer to featured interviews and speeches.)